The
Least
You
Should
Know
About
English

FORM B

The Least You Should Know About English

Basic Writing Skills

TERESA FERSTER GLAZIER

Western Illinois University

HOLT, RINEHART AND WINSTON

New York   Chicago   San Francisco   Atlanta
Dallas   Montreal   Toronto

Form B of *The Least You Should Know About English* is essentially the same as Form A except that it has different sentences and writing assignments. Therefore the two forms may be used in alternate semesters. A few additions have been made to Form B: more entries in "Words Often Confused," two chapters on verb forms, some paragraphs for practice, some extra review exercises, and two extra essays.

Library of Congress Cataloging in Publication Data

Glazier, Teresa Ferster.
  The least you should know about English.
  1. English language—Composition and exercises.
I. Title.
PE1413.G57   1979   808'.042   78–13935
ISBN: 0–03–044586–8

To the Instructor

This book is for students who have resisted the rules of English composition for twelve years and who may profit from a simplified approach. The main features of the book are these:

1. It's truly basic. Only the indisputable essentials of spelling, grammar, sentence structure, and punctuation are included because research has shown that teaching too much of these things is not the way to help students learn to write.
2. It stresses writing. Although at first glance it may appear to be merely a workbook, writing is emphasized. Besides doing the exercises, the students are asked to write their own sentences to exemplify the rules. And the small but important section beginning on page 182 presents simple writing assignments progressing from free writing and personal writing to persuasive writing with a thesis, summary writing, and finally the letter of application. Ideally, some writing is done in preparation for each class period—original sentences, a complete thesis statement, a rough draft, a final draft, or a revision. Students learn to write by writing.
3. It uses little terminology. A conjunction is merely a connecting word, gerunds and present participles are *ing* words, a parenthetical constituent is an interrupter. Students work with words they know rather than learn a vocabulary they'll never use again.
4. It has one hundred practice sentences for most rules, as well as some practice paragraphs.
5. It provides perforated answer sheets at the back of the book so that the students can correct their own work, thus teaching themselves as they go.
6. It takes modern usage into account. Accepted forms (as reported by Robert G. Pooley in *The Teaching of English Usage*) such as *It is me* and *Everybody . . . they* are recognized.
7. It provides for the instructor a packet of ditto master tests *ready to run*, covering each section of the book. These tests are free upon adoption of the text and may be obtained through the local Holt representative or by writing to the English Editor, Holt, Rinehart and Winston, 383 Madison Avenue, New York, N.Y. 10017.

Along with the ditto master tests, a daily test is valuable. A single sentence (such as *They're going there with their son* for the "Words Often Confused" chapter) dictated at the beginning of each class hour and corrected on the spot will provide an incentive for doing each day's exercises.

Students who have heretofore been overwhelmed and discouraged by the complexities of English should, through mastering simple rules and through writing and rewriting simple compositions, gain enough competence and confidence to cope with a regular composition course.

T.F.G.

Macomb, Illinois
November 1978

Acknowledgments

Many people have had a hand in writing this book. Most important, Kenneth Glazier, Jr., Christopher Glazier, and Gretchen Glazier Boyer have written exercises and revised early drafts. To Robert Jacobs, former head of the English Department at Western, I owe the opportunity and incentive to write the book, and to Dwain Preston I am grateful for unfailing support. My colleagues Teresa Edwards, Carol Johnson, Rick Osborn, Tina Perdue, Randy Smith, Bob Sweazy, Duane Taylor, and Rick Van Etten, and my former colleagues at the College of San Mateo, Betty Pex, Louise Hazelton, and Ruth Teel, have all made helpful suggestions. I am grateful also to the reviewers of Form A: Michele Barale, University of Chicago; Bernard A. Bearer, Trenton State College; W. Michael Clippinger, Indiana Vocational Tech; Charles Cobb, Los Angeles Pierce College; Dixie Goswami, University of Tennessee, Knoxville; Lynn Klamkin, DePauw University; James K. Murphy, West Georgia College; Sharon Pearson, Eastern Illinois University; Philip A. Sbaratta, North Shore Community College; Blanche Skurnick, City College of the City University of New York; David Skwire, Cuyahoga Community College; and Roy Underwood, Livingston University. The people at Holt—particularly Lester A. Sheinis, editor par excellence—have always been supportive. And finally, the book would never have been finished without the willing and skillful help of Helen France, who has typed innumerable revisions.

Contents

The
Least
You
Should
Know
About
English

What Is the Least You Should Know?

What **Is** the Least You Should Know?

Most English workbooks try to teach you as much as they can. This one will teach you the least it can—and still help you get by in college English courses. You won't have to bother with predicate nouns and subordinating conjunctions and participial phrases and demonstrative pronouns and all those terms you have been hearing about for years. You can get along without them if you will learn thoroughly a few basic rules. You *do* have to know how to spell common words; you *do* have to recognize subjects and verbs to avoid writing fragments and run-together sentences; you *do* have to know a few rules of punctuation—but rules will be kept to a minimum.

Unless you know these few rules, though, you will have difficulty communicating in writing. Take this sentence for example:

Let's eat grandfather before we go.

We assume the writer is not a cannibal but that he merely failed to capitalize and put commas around the name of a person spoken to. If he had written

Let's eat, Grandfather, before we go.

then no one would misunderstand. Or take this sentence:

The instructor flunked Mac and Chris and Ken passed.

Did Chris flunk or pass? There's no way of knowing unless the writer puts a comma either after *Mac* or after *Chris*. If he writes

The instructor flunked Mac and Chris, and Ken passed.

we know Chris flunked, but if he writes

The instructor flunked Mac, and Chris and Ken passed.

then we know Chris passed. What you will learn in this course is simply a few rules to help make your writing so clear that no one will misunderstand it.

The English you will learn to write in this course is called Standard English, and it may be slightly different from the English spoken in your community. All over the country, various dialects of English are spoken. In northern New England, for example, people leave the *r* off certain words and put an *r* on others. Former President Kennedy used to say *dollah* for *dollar*, *idear* for *idea*, and *Cubar* for *Cuba*. In black communities many people leave the *s* off some verbs and put an *s* on others, saying *he walk* and *they walks* instead of *he walks* and *they walk*.

But no matter what English dialect people *speak*, they all must write the same dialect—Standard English. You can say, "Whacha doin? Cmon," and everybody will understand, but you can't write that way. If you want your readers to understand what you write without having to decipher it like a foreign language, you will have to write the way English-speaking people all over the world write—in Standard English. Being able to write Standard English is essential in college, and it probably will be an asset in your career.

Learning to write is like learning math. You can get along in life without algebra and geometry, but you can't get along very well without simple addition and subtraction. So it is with writing. You can get along without many of the complicated rules, but you can't get along without a few simple ones. Most of us would rather buckle down and memorize the addition and subtraction tables than count on our fingers and toes the rest of our lives. Likewise it makes sense to learn a few rules of writing now rather than to muddle along never knowing how to write properly.

It is important that you learn every rule as you come to it because many rules depend on the ones before. For example, unless you learn to pick out subjects and verbs, you will have trouble with run-together sentences, with fragments, with subject-verb agreement, and with punctuation. The rules in this workbook are brief and clear, and it should not be difficult to master all of them . . . **if you want to.** But you do have to want to!

Here is the way to master **the least you should know:**

1. Do the first exercise (ten sentences). Then tear out the perforated answer sheet at the back of the book and correct your answers. If you miss even one answer, study the explanatory page again to find out why.
2. Do the second exercise and correct it. If you miss a single answer, go back once more and study the explanatory page. You must have missed something. Be tough on yourself. Don't just think, "Maybe I'll hit it right next time." Go back and master the rules, and *then* try the next exercise. It is important to correct each group of ten

sentences before going on. That way you will discover your mistakes while you still have sentences to practice on.

3. You may be tempted to quit when you get several exercises perfect, but don't do it. Make yourself finish every single exercise. It's not enough to *understand* a rule; you have to practice it. Just as understanding passing and shooting in basketball won't help unless you actually get out there onto the court and play, so understanding a rule about writing isn't going to help unless you practice using it until it becomes automatic. That's why hundreds of practice sentences have been put in this book.

But rules and exercises are not the most important part of this book. The most important part begins on page 182—when you begin to write. The writing assignments, grouped together for convenience, are to be used along with the exercises. Writing is the fun part of English. We all have ideas we'd like to express, and the writing assignments will help you get started.

Mastering these essentials will take time. Generally, college students are expected to spend two hours outside of class for each hour in class. You may need more. Undoubtedly, the more time you spend, the more your writing will improve.

At the end of a semester, when one class was asked how the course could be improved, the almost unanimous recommendation was, "Tell the students the first day that the course isn't a breeze. The stuff looks simple, but it's not. You have to work. If you slide through the first weeks, you're sunk. But if you do all the exercises, you'll learn a lot."

Spelling

1 Spelling

Anyone can learn to spell. You can get rid of most of your spelling errors by the time you finish this book **if you want to.** Simply follow the five suggestions given in this section.

SUGGESTION I. On page 285 at the back of this book write correctly every misspelled word in the papers handed back to you. Review them every day until you have them memorized. That will take care of most of your errors. As a starter for your list, write these two expressions that you possibly misspell:

all right

a lot

Take a good look at them, copy them onto page 285, and from now on remember that each of them is two words.

SUGGESTION II. Learn to break words into their parts. These words are made up of two shorter words:

over run	overrun	room mate	roommate
over rate	overrate	with hold	withhold

And learn to spell such prefixes as *dis, inter, mis,* and *un.* Then when you add a word to the prefix, the spelling will be correct:

dis appear	disappear	mis spell	misspell
dis appoint	disappoint	mis step	misstep
dis approve	disapprove	un natural	unnatural
dis satisfied	dissatisfied	un necessary	unnecessary
dis service	disservice	un nerve	unnerve
inter racial	interracial	un noticed	unnoticed
inter related	interrelated		

SUGGESTION III. Learn the following words that are often confused:

WORDS OFTEN CONFUSED

a, an

Use *an* before a word that begins with a vowel sound (*a, e, i, o,* and *u* when it is sounded *uh*).

an orange, an essay, an heir (silent *h*), an honest man (silent *h*), an umbrella, an umpire, an uncle, an ulcer (all the *u*'s sound like *uh*)

Use *a* before a word that begins with a consonant sound (all the sounds except the vowels) plus *u* or *eu* when it sounds like *yu*.

a pencil, a hotel, a history book, a university, a uniform, a union, a unit (all the *u*'s sound like *yu*), a European trip (*Eu* sounds like *yu*).

accept, except

Accept is a verb. (Verbs are explained on p. 38.) Use *except* when it's not a verb.

I *accept* your invitation

Everyone came *except* him.

advice, advise

Advise is a verb. Use *advice* when it's not a verb. Pronounce these words correctly, remembering that the *s* sounds like *z*, and you won't confuse them.

I *advise* you to go.

I don't need any *advice*.

affect, effect

Affect is a verb. Use *effect* when it's not a verb. If *a, an,* or *the* is in front of the word, then you know it isn't a verb, and you'll use *effect*.

The lack of rain *affected* the crops.

The lack of rain had an *effect* on the crops.

The lack of rain had a bad *effect* on the crops.

all ready, already

If you can leave out the *all* and the sentence still makes sense, then *all ready* is the form to use.

I'm all ready to go. (*I'm ready to go* makes sense.)

Dinner is *all ready*. (*Dinner is ready* makes sense.)

If you can't leave out the *all* and still have the sentence make sense, then use *already* (the one with the *all* left in it).

I'm already late. (*I'm ready late* doesn't make sense.)

are, or, our

Are is a verb. *Or* is used between two possibilities, as tea *or* coffee. *Our* shows we possess something.

We *are* studying English.

Take it *or* leave it.

Our class meets at eight.

brake, break

> *Brake* means "to slow or stop motion." It's also the name of the device that slows or stops motion. *Break* means "to shatter."
>
> You *brake* the speed of a car.
> You slam on your *brakes*.
> You *break* a dish or an engagement or a track record.

choose, chose

> I will *choose* a partner right now.
> I *chose* a partner yesterday.

clothes, cloths

> Her *clothes* were attractive.
> We used soft *cloths* to polish the car.

coarse, course

> *Coarse* describes texture, as *coarse* cloth. *Course* is used for all other meanings. Remember this sentence: Of *course you* are taking this *course*. Find the three *u*'s in that sentence and then remember that those words are always spelled with *u*.
>
> Her suit was made of *coarse* material.
> Of *course* I enjoyed that *course*.

complement, compliment

> A *complement* completes something. *Compliment* means "praise." Remember "*I* like compliments," and you will remember to use the *i* spelling.
>
> A 30-degree angle is the *complement* of a 60-degree angle.
> She gave him a *compliment*.

conscience, conscious

> The extra *n* in *conscience* should remind you of NO, which is what your conscience often says to you. The other word *conscious* simply means "aware."
>
> My *conscience* bothers me because I ignored him.
> I was not *conscious* that it was raining.

desert, dessert

> *Dessert* is the sweet one, the one you like two helpings of. So give it two helpings of *s*. The other one, *desert*, is used for all other meanings.
>
> We had apple pie for *dessert*.
> Don't *desert* me.
> The camel moved slowly across the *desert*.

does, dose

> *Does* is a verb. A *dose* is an amount of medicine.
> He *does* his work well.
> She *doesn't* care about cars.
> He took a *dose* of medicine.

forth, fourth

Fourth with four in it is a number. Otherwise use *forth*. Note that while *fourth* has *four* in it, *forty* does not. Remember the word *forty-fourth*.
This is our *fourth* game.
That was our forty-*fourth* point.
She walked back and *forth*.

have, of

Have is a verb. When you say *could have*, the *have* sounds like *of*, but it must not be written that way. *Of* is a preposition (see p. 44).
I should *have* finished my work sooner.
Then I could *have* gone home.
I often think *of* him.

it's, its

It's always means "it is" or "it has" (see p. 25). *Its* is a possessive (see p. 31).
It's too late now.
It's been a long time.
The committee gave *its* report.

knew, new

Knew has to do with knowledge (both start with *k*). *New* means "not old."
I *knew* that I wanted a *new* job.

know, no

Know has to do with knowledge (both start with *k*). *No* means "not any."
I *know* she has *no* money left.

EXERCISES

Underline the correct word. Don't guess! Refer to the explanatory pages if necessary. When you have done ten sentences, tear out the perforated answer sheet on page 205 and correct your answers. Correct each ten sentences before going on so that you will catch your mistakes before attempting the next exercise.

After you have finished this section and the following one, you will be given a printed test. Your goal should be to learn these words so well that you will be able to do that test perfectly.

□EXERCISE 1

1. I should (have of) registered for this (coarse course) earlier.
2. I hope it will have (a an) (affect effect) on my writing.
3. That's the (forth fourth) (complement compliment) I've received on my work.

4. I (advice advise) you to (accept except) their offer, (are or) you may lose the job.
5. We (knew new) she had given us (a an) honest answer.
6. Those (coarse course) polishing (clothes cloths) may scratch the finish of your car.
7. I'd (advice advise) you not to (brake break) the speed limit on this road.
8. (Are Our) plans include a trip through the Mojave (Desert Dessert).
9. I've become (conscience conscious) of my weight and am refusing (desert dessert).
10. (It's Its) all completely (knew new) to me.

□EXERCISE 2

1. I (know no) I should have followed his (advice advise).
2. The (coarse course) I (choose chose) yesterday may (affect effect) my whole life.
3. She was (all ready already) to go (accept except) for buying her ticket.
4. A (complement compliment) always has a good (affect effect) on anyone.
5. My dog chewed (it's its) (knew new) leash to pieces.
6. We (are our) planning a rap session for the (forth fourth) Tuesday in March.
7. I (all ready already) have too much work to do.
8. I (choose chose) a Big Mac yesterday, but today I'm going to (choose chose) cherry pie.
9. I should (have of) taken my (clothes cloths) to the cleaner yesterday.
10. I (knew new) I couldn't (brake break) my car quick enough to avoid a collision.

□EXERCISE 3

1. We should (have of) known that (are our) luck wouldn't hold.
2. My (conscience conscious) bothered me after I (knew new) the whole story.
3. He had to (choose chose) among the three girls who had invited him.
4. Wrestling is (a an) individual sport; basketball is (a an) team sport.
5. (Are Our) (knew new) house is (all ready already) to move into.
6. (Its It's) location is (a an) asset because (it's its) near a lake.
7. I like to walk back and (forth fourth) along the beach.
8. No one was (conscience conscious) of his shabby (clothes cloths).
9. I'm going to (brake break) my rule and have some (desert dessert).
10. It (does dose) make a difference whose (coarse course) you take.

□EXERCISE 4

1. I decided to (accept except) her invitation.
2. Of (coarse course) I was pleased with her (complement compliment).
3. (It's Its) always nice to be appreciated.

4. Having appropriate (clothes cloths) certainly (does dose) give one self confidence.
5. By January 2 I usually (brake break) my New Year's resolution.
6. (It's Its) time the cat had (it's its) kittens.
7. The drought had a bad (affect effect) on the corn crop, but it didn't (affect effect) the hay crop at all.
8. His (conscience conscious) should have told him not to (desert dessert) her when she was ill.
9. We're planning (a an) European tour for (are our) (forth fourth) anniversary.
10. A (does dose) of that medicine would (have of) finished me.

□EXERCISE 5

1. Since I got my sewing machine, I've bought no (knew new) (clothes cloths).
2. This is an important (coarse course) for (a an) engineering department to offer.
3. Of (coarse course) the lunch should (have of) been ready.
4. That woman (doesn't dosen't) (know no) her own mind.
5. I'm (conscience conscious) of what she wants me to do, but I'm not going to follow her (advice advise).
6. I (know no) (are our) plan is sound.
7. I should (have of) chosen track, but I (choose chose) swimming instead.
8. The (forth fourth) time I won through sheer luck.
9. All those (complements compliments) had a good (affect effect) on Mike.
10. You can't (choose chose) what happens to you, but you can (choose chose) how you react.

□EXERCISE 6

1. The strikers walked back and (forth fourth) in front of the factory.
2. I had (know no) time for relaxing.
3. His opinion (doesn't dosen't) (affect effect) me at all.
4. I've (all ready already) written a (forth fourth) draft of my paper.
5. Now (it's its) finished (accept except) for the final typing.
6. She (choose chose) to (brake break) the rules and must suffer the consequences.
7. I should (have of) prepared the (desert dessert) ahead of time.
8. I (knew new) he'd (choose chose) her for his partner.
9. I got into my old (clothes cloths) and found some (coarse course) (clothes cloths) for cleaning the basement.
10. I should (have of) remembered that (it's its) a holiday.

□EXERCISE 7

1. I wasn't (conscience conscious) that she was planning to (advice advise) the group.
2. I slammed on the (brakes breaks), but it was (all ready already) too late.
3. The collision (coarse course) was set, and there was (know no) way out.
4. I've decided to take fewer (clothes cloths) on my trip.
5. The smog had a bad (affect effect) on the pine trees in the mountains.
6. I didn't like his (advice advise), but I should (have of) been willing to (accept except) it.
7. He (choose chose) to cross the (desert dessert) by camel rather than by car.
8. (It's Its) time for a new ball game.
9. A (does dose) of his own medicine might have a good (affect effect).
10. I (knew new) I shouldn't (brake break) the speed limit.

□EXERCISE 8

1. I wasn't (conscience conscious) of what the (affect effect) would be.
2. I didn't (choose chose) her; she (choose chose) me.
3. They had (all ready already) put (forth fourth) great effort.
4. We took (are our) car in for (it's its) tune-up.
5. The rule (doesn't dosen't) (affect effect) anyone (accept except) our supervisor.
6. My (conscience conscious) (doesn't dosen't) bother me because I didn't (brake break) any rule.
7. This (coarse course) is making me (conscience conscious) of my spelling.
8. The bear walked back and (forth fourth) in (it's its) cage.
9. (It's Its) time for (desert dessert).
10. Everyone (choose chose) to go home (accept except) me.

□EXERCISE 9

1. It (does dose) seem that he's giving her a bit too much (advice advise).
2. (A An) uniform plan is (all ready already) in operation.
3. Of (coarse course) all I wanted was (a an) honest opinion.
4. (It's Its) about time for us to have (are our) house painted.
5. We would (have of) had it done last year if we had had the money.
6. I (knew new) I should (have of) studied more for that test.
7. The bike was missing (it's its) handlebar.
8. (It's Its) not wise to cross the (desert dessert) in the daytime.
9. I (know no) this is at least the (forth fourth) time he has dented a fender of his car.
10. He claims his parking (brake break) didn't hold.

☐**EXERCISE 10**

1. (It's Its) (all ready already) too late to register to vote.
2. Do you (advice advise) me to (accept except) their offer?
3. It won't (affect effect) you, will it?
4. Last spring I (choose chose) wild colors for my (knew new) (clothes cloths).
5. He (doesn't dosen't) like to offer (advice advise).
6. I should (have of) given her a (complement compliment) on her tennis.
7. I was never before so (conscience conscious) of how old my car is.
8. (Coarse Course) grains and fiber (are our) good for (are our) health.
9. Even fancy (deserts desserts) can be made of (coarse course) grains.
10. (It's Its) not easy to (choose chose) a career.

WRITING YOUR OWN SENTENCES

Writing your own sentences is the best way to master the words you have been studying. On a separate sheet write five sentences using some of the words you have had trouble with.

WRITING ASSIGNMENT

Turn to page 182 for your first writing assignment.

WORDS OFTEN CONFUSED (continued)

Here are more words that are often confused. Study them carefully, with their examples, before attempting the exercises. When you have mastered all 36 of the word groups in these two sections, you will have taken care of many of your spelling problems.

lead, led

> The verb *lead* is pronounced lēēd.
> I will *lead* the parade today.
> I *led* the parade yesterday.

loose, lose

> *Loose* means "not tight." Note how l o o s e that word is. It has plenty of room for two *o*'s. The other one, *lose*, has room for only one *o*. Use it for all other meanings.
> My shoestring is *loose*.
> They are going to *lose* that game.
> Don't *lose* your cool.

moral, morale

Moral has to do with right and wrong. *Morale* means "group spirit." Pronounce them correctly, and you won't confuse them—móral, morále.

It was a *moral* question.

The *morale* of the team was excellent.

passed, past

Passed is a verb. Use *past* when it's not a verb.

He *passed* the house.

He walked *past* the house (it's the same as *He walked by the house*, so you know it isn't a verb).

He is living in the *past*.

He was going on his *past* reputation.

peace, piece

Remember "piece of pie." The one meaning "a *piece* of something" always begins with *pie*. The other one, *peace*, is the opposite of war.

I gave him a *piece* of my mind.

They signed the *peace* treaty.

personal, personnel

Pronounce these two correctly, and you won't confuse them—pérsonal, personnél.

He had a *personal* interest in the election.

He was in charge of *personnel* in the factory.

principal, principle

Principal means "main." Both words have *a* in them:

principal

main

The *principal* of the school spoke. (main teacher)

The *principal* difficulty is time. (main difficulty)

He lost both *principal* and interest. (main amount of money)

A *principle* is a "rule." Both words end in *le*:

principle

rule

He lived by his *principles*. (rules)

I object to the *principle* of the thing. (rule)

quiet, quite

Pronounce these two correctly, and you won't misspell them. *Quiet* is pronounced *qui et*.

Be *quiet*.

The book is *quite* interesting.

than, then

Than compares two things. Then tells when (*then* and *when* sound alike and both have *e* in them).

I'd rather have this *than* that.

Then he started home.

their, there,
they're

Their is a possessive (see p. 31). *There* points out something and is spelled like *here*. Remember "here and there." *They're* always means "they are" (see p. 25).

 Their house is painted pink.
 There is where I left it.
 There were clouds in the sky.
 They're planning to come.

threw, through

Threw means "to throw something" in past time. If you don't mean "to throw something," use *through*.

 He *threw* the ball. I *threw* away my chance.
 I walked *through* the door.
 He *threw* the ball *through* the window.

to, too, two

Two is a number. Too means "more than enough" or "also." Use *to* for all other meanings.

 I have *two* brothers.
 The lesson was *too* difficult and *too* long. (more than enough)
 I found it difficult *too*. (also)
 It was *too* much for *two* people *to* eat.

weather, whether

Weather refers to atmospheric conditions. *Whether* means "if".

 Whether I'll go depends on the *weather*.

were, where

Were is a verb. *Where* has *here* in it, and both *where* and *here* refer to a place.

 Were you the winner?
 Where is he? Here he is.
 Where are you? Here I am.

who's, whose

Who's always means "who is" or "who has" (see p. 25). *Whose* is a possessive (see p. 31).

 Who's there?
 Who's been using my tennis racket?
 Whose book is this?

woman, women

Remember that the word is just *man* or *men* with *wo* in front of it.

 wo man . . . woman . . . one woman
 wo men . . . women . . . two women

you're, your

> *You're* always means "you are" (see p. 25). *Your* is a
> possessive (see p. 31).
>   *You're* very welcome.
>   *Your* toast is ready.

EXERCISES

Underline the correct word. When you have finished ten sentences, tear out the answer sheet on page 207 and correct your answers. WATCH OUT! Don't do more than ten sentences at a time, or you won't be teaching yourself as you go.

□EXERCISE 1

1. He's (to too) lazy to study, and his (conscience conscious) (doesn't dosen't) even bother him.
2. (Their There They're) probably (all ready already) at the theater.
3. Her style is (to too two) formal for me.
4. I didn't (loose lose) the card; I (threw through) it away.
5. I have to see the (personal personnel) director about the job.
6. My (principal principle) reason for wanting that job is that (it's its) closer to home (than then) my present job.
7. That's (were where) I met the people who (were where) so helpful.
8. I'm (quiet quite) sure this book will appeal to (you're your) interests.
9. I don't know (weather whether) that's a (moral morale) solution.
10. (Their There They're) record indicates that (their there they're) dependable.

□EXERCISE 2

1. (It's Its) more fun to have a wedding reception at home (than then) at a hotel.
2. I think I (passed past) the main entrance.
3. I think I drove (passed past) the main entrance.
4. She was always (their there) for me to turn to.
5. He (threw through) the ball (threw through) the picture window.
6. That (woman women) is going to (lead led) the demonstration for (woman's women's) rights.
7. My dad says that students in his day spent more time on (their there they're) studies (than then) students do today.
8. I don't (know no) the (principal principle) reason for his decision.
9. (Who's Whose) responsible for (you're your) success?
10. (Peace Piece) and (quiet quite) were all she asked for.

□EXERCISE 3

1. They may (loose lose) their (peace piece) of land if they don't watch out.
2. Samuel Johnson wrote that the chains of habit are (to too) weak to be felt till they are (to too) strong (to too) be broken.
3. The (woman women) were (quiet quite) sure (their there) proposal would win.
4. (Who's Whose) proposal finally won?
5. (Their There They're) going to make (to too two) trips, aren't they?
6. (You're Your) absolutely right that (their there they're) is (know no) chance of winning.
7. She (threw through) her arms around him for a moment; (than then) she ran.
8. (Who's Whose) going out in this (weather whether)?
9. The (moral morale) of the marchers was high because they were marching for a (principal principle).
10. (Loose Lose) papers were blowing all over (are our) lawn.

□EXERCISE 4

1. (You're Your) (personal personnel) opinion is important to me.
2. (Who's Whose) car was it, and (were where) did you see it?
3. (You're Your) (quiet quite) sure, are you?
4. She (lead led) the (peace piece) rally.
5. I don't (know no) (weather whether) he's older (than then) Jamie or not.
6. I stayed up until (to too two) in the morning reading that book on economic (principals principles).
7. (It's Its) been (to too) (quiet quite) this evening to suit me.
8. My (principal principle) objection to the law is (it's its) (loose lose) wording.
9. It will have (to too) many interpretations.
10. Such laws have not been effective in the (passed past).

□EXERCISE 5

1. (It's Its) (to too) early to (know no) the results of the election.
2. (Are Our) candidate may (loose lose) because of the poor turnout.
3. We've had (quiet quite) bad (weather whether) all week.
4. My (principal principle) objection to that cloth is that it's (coarse course).
5. She's exactly the (woman women) I'm looking for.
6. The (moral morale) of the (personal personnel) in that company is high.
7. The employees all take a (personal personnel) interest in their jobs.
8. (Their There They're) all happy in (their there they're) work.

9. (Their There) loyalty is greater (than then) that of employees in other companies.
10. I (threw through) the magazine away when I was (threw through) reading it.

□EXERCISE 6

1. (Who's Whose) interested in going (their there)?
2. She asked (weather whether) (you're your) sure (you're your) fiancé will come to the party.
3. The (principal principle) river of the United States is the Mississippi.
4. We drove (passed past) their house.
5. We (passed past) their house (quiet quite) late last night.
6. A (woman women) stopped me (to too) ask directions.
7. His (principal principle) concern was in keeping the children (quiet quite).
8. Were you (were where) the action was?
9. (Who's Whose) side (were where) you on?
10. This week's (weather whether) is better (than then) last week's.

□EXERCISE 7

1. I wonder (who's whose) car that is.
2. (You're Your) lucky if (you're your) car will start in this (weather whether).
3. The (knew new) ruling will (affect effect) everyone (accept except) Sharon.
4. Don't stay out (to too two) long.
5. She (all ready already) has more (clothes cloths) (than then) she needs.
6. I gave him a (peace piece) of my mind even though he didn't ask for my (advice advise).
7. I don't (know no) (weather whether) he can overcome all those difficulties.
8. Please give this your (personal personnel) attention.
9. The club (woman women) were finally (threw through) with (their there) meeting.
10. She tried to find someone to (lead led) the drive for the United Fund.

□EXERCISE 8

1. When (you're your) finished writing (you're your) paper, I'll type it.
2. (Were Where) did you hide that last (peace piece) of cake?
3. (You're Your) car has lost (it's its) shine.
4. I parked the car; (then than) I walked up to (their there) door.
5. That goes against my (moral morale) (principals principles).
6. My shoe was so (loose lose) that it made a blister.

7. The (principal principle) reason the team lost was (it's its) lack of good (moral morale).
8. We (knew new) we would (loose lose) (are our) final game.
9. She (lead led) her class in math, but she didn't (lead led) in chemistry.
10. She walked back and (forth fourth) in her kitchen for a while; (than then) she went out.

□EXERCISE 9

1. The (woman women) in charge of decorations was not sure (weather whether) she would have enough help.
2. She went (threw through) the membership list and (choose chose) some members to phone.
3. (Were Where) are all the (woman women) who offered to help?
4. I need (peace piece) and (quiet quite) when I write a paper.
5. I (threw through) away my rough draft; (than then) I turned in my final copy.
6. (Their There They're) is (know no) need to worry now.
7. I met a (woman women) from the town (were where) I used to live.
8. I always (passed past) her house on the way to school.
9. I (choose chose) my own (coarse course) of action that winter.
10. He (lead led) the choir (accept except) during the summer months.

□EXERCISE 10

1. I (know no) there's (know no) truth to the rumor; (it's its) pure hearsay.
2. (You're Your) (quiet quite) stunning in those (clothes cloths).
3. This (weather whether) is (to too) cold for me.
4. I know his (principals principles) won't let him (accept except) a bribe.
5. I (threw through) away all my notes after I (passed past) the (coarse course).
6. (Were Where) (were where) you when I needed you?
7. That's the (forth fourth) traffic ticket he's had.
8. Thanks for the (complement compliment); (you're your) much (to too) kind.
9. (Who's Whose) going to (choose chose) the color scheme?
10. (It's Its) not going to (brake break) me to take you to the movies.

WRITING YOUR OWN SENTENCES
On a separate sheet write five sentences using the words you have had the most difficulty with.

WRITING ASSIGNMENT
Turn to page 183 for your second writing assignment.

SUGGESTION IV. Learn one spelling rule. Most spelling rules have so many exceptions that they are not much help, but here is one that has almost no exceptions and is really worth learning.

RULE FOR DOUBLING A FINAL CONSONANT

Double a final consonant when adding an ending beginning with a vowel (such as <u>ing</u>, <u>ed</u>, <u>er</u>) if the word

   1. ends in a single consonant,
   2. preceded by a single vowel (the vowels are <u>a, e, i, o, u</u>),
   3. and the accent is on the last syllable.

We'll try the rule on a few words to which we'll add *ing*, *ed*, or *er*.

begin   1. It ends in a single consonant—*n*,
      2. preceded by a single vowel—*i*,
      3. and the accent is on the last syllable—*begín*.
      Therefore we double the final consonant and write *beginning*, *beginner*.

stop   1. It ends in a single consonant—*p*,
      2. preceded by a single vowel—*o*,
      3. and the accent is on the last syllable (there is only one).
      Therefore we double the final consonant and write *stopping*, *stopped*, *stopper*.

benefit   1. It ends in a single consonant—*t*,
      2. preceded by a single vowel—*i*,
      3. but the accent is not on the last syllable; it is on the first—*bénefit*.
      Therefore we do not double the final consonant. We write *benefiting*, *benefited*.

sleep   1. It ends in a single consonant—*p*,
      2. but it is not preceded by a single vowel; there are two *e*'s.
      Therefore we do not double the final consonant. We write *sleeping*, *sleeper*.

kick   1. It does not end in a single consonant. There are two—*c* and *k*.
      Therefore we do not double the final consonant. We write *kicking*, *kicked*.

Note that *qu* is really a consonant because *q* is never written without *u*. (Look in your dictionary and see.) Think of it as *kw*. In words like *equip* and *quit*, the *qu* acts as a consonant. Therefore *quit* does end in a single consonant preceded by a single vowel, and the final consonant is doubled—*quitting*.

You'll be wise to skip the rest of this explanation. It concerns exceptions that you'll never have trouble with, and they may simply confuse you.

They are included here merely to make the rule complete. So *skip on to the exercises.*

1. Consider *w* or *y* at the end of a word a vowel. *Row, sew, sow, toy* all end in vowels, and the rule does not apply.
2. Consider *x* at the end of a word as two consonants *ks. Box, flex, fix* all end in double consonants, and the rule does not apply.
3. One common word *bus* may be written either *bussing* or *busing.* The latter is more common.

EXERCISES

Add **ing** to these words. Correct each group of ten by using the perforated answer sheet in the back of the book before going on.

□EXERCISE 1

1. put *ting*
2. control *ling*
3. admit *ting*
4. mop *ping*
5. plan *ning*
6. hop *ping*
7. jump *ing*
8. knit *ting*
9. mark *ing*
10. creep *ing*

□EXERCISE 2

1. return *ing*
2. swim *ming*
3. sing *ing*
4. benefit *ing*
5. loaf *ing*
6. nail *ing*
7. omit *ting*
8. occur *ing*
9. shop *ping*
10. interrupt *ing*

□EXERCISE 3

1. begin *ing*
2. spell *ing*
3. prefer *ing*
4. fish *ing*
5. hunt *ing*
6. excel *ling*
7. wrap *ping*
8. stop *ping*
9. wed *ding*
10. scream *ing*

□EXERCISE 4

1. feel *ing*
2. motor *ing*
3. turn *ing*
4. add
5. subtract
6. stream *ing*
7. expel *ling*
8. miss *ing*
9. get *ting*
10. stress *ing*

□EXERCISE 5

1. forget *ting*
2. misspell *ing*
3. fit *ting*
4. plant *ing*
5. pin *ning*

6. trust *ing*
7. sip *ping*
8. flop *ping*
9. reap *ing*
10. cart *ing*

□EXERCISE 6

1. attend *ing*
2. compel *ling*
3. nap *ping*
4. curl *ing*
5. amount *ing*

6. obtain *ing*
7. dream *ing*
8. crawl *ing*
9. crop *ping*
10. descend *ing*

□EXERCISE 7

1. permit *ting*
2. despair *ing*
3. eat *ing.*
4. develop *ing*
5. quit *ting*

6. exceed *ing*
7. finish *ing*
8. hit *ting*
9. flinch *ing*
10. refer *ring*

□EXERCISE 8

1. regard *ing*
2. equip *ping*
3. kick *ing*
4. sit *ting*
5. knock *ing*

6. sleep *ing*
7. skip *ping*
8. leap *ing*
9. ship *ping*
10. mention *ing*

□EXERCISE 9

1. stir *ring*
2. mend *ing*
3. shriek *ing*
4. murmur *ing*
5. view *ing*

6. meet *ing*
7. speak *ing*
8. succeed *ing*
9. pretend *ing*
10. defer *ring*

□EXERCISE 10

1. pull *ing*
2. predict *ing*
3. redeem *ing*
4. patrol *ling*
5. slant *ing*

6. steam *ing*
9. tip *ping*
7. rip *ping*
8. spend *ing*
10. trip *ping*

SUGGESTION V. Have someone dictate this list of commonly misspelled words and mark the ones you miss. Then memorize the correct spellings, working on ten at a time.

Be sure to pronounce the following words correctly so that you won't misspell them: *athlete, athletics, environment, government, probably, sophomore, studying.* Also try to think up memory devices to help you remember correct spellings. For example, you *labor* in a *laboratory,* and the *r* separates the two a's in *separate.*

SPELLING LIST

1. absence	36. discussed	71. intelligence
2. actually	37. disease	72. interest
3. all right	38. divide	73. interfere
4. amateur	39. dying	74. involved
5. among	40. eighth	75. knowledge
6. apology	41. eligible	76. laboratory
7. appreciate	42. eliminate	77. length
8. argument	43. embarrassed	78. library
9. athlete	44. encouragement	79. likely
10. athletics	45. environment	80. lying
11. awkward	46. especially	81. marriage
12. becoming	47. etc.	82. mathematics
13. beginning	48. exaggerate	83. meant
14. belief	49. excellent	84. medicine
15. benefit	50. exercise	85. necessary
16. bicycle	51. existence	86. neither
17. buried	52. experience	87. ninety
18. business	53. explanation	88. ninth
19. certain	54. extremely	89. occasionally
20. college	55. familiar	90. opinion
21. coming	56. February	91. opportunity
22. committee	57. finally	92. parallel
23. competition	58. foreign	93. particular
24. consider	59. forty-fourth	94. physically
25. criticism	60. government	95. planned
26. deceive	61. grammar	96. pleasant
27. decision	62. grateful	97. possessive
28. definite	63. guarantee	98. possible
29. definitely	64. guard	99. practical
30. definition	65. guidance	100. preferred
31. dependent	66. height	101. prejudice
32. development	67. hoping	102. privilege
33. difference	68. humorous	103. probably
34. dining	69. immediately	104. professor
35. discipline	70. independent	105. prove

106. psychology
107. punctuation
108. pursue
109. receipt
110. receive
111. recommend
112. reference
113. relieve
114. religious
115. rhythm
116. ridiculous
117. sacrifice
118. safety
119. scene
120. schedule

121. secretary
122. seize
123. senior
124. sense
125. separate
126. severely
127. shining
128. significant
129. similar
130. sincerely
131. sophomore
132. speech
133. straight
134. studying
135. succeed

136. success
137. surprise
138. thoroughly
139. though
140. tragedy
141. tried
142. truly
143. unfortunately
144. until
145. unusual
146. using
147. usually
148. Wednesday
149. writing
150. written

CONTRACTIONS

Two words condensed into one are called a contraction.

is not	isn't
you have	you've

The letter or letters that are left out are replaced with an apostrophe. For example, if the two words *do not* are condensed into one, an apostrophe is put where the *o* is left out.

do not	don't

Note how the apostrophe goes in the exact place where the letter or letters are left out in these contractions:

I am	I'm
you are	you're
he is	he's
we are	we're
they are	they're
there is	there's
it is	it's
it has	it's
he has	he's
they have	they've
I shall	I'll
she will	she'll
I would	I'd
they would	they'd
are not	aren't
cannot	can't
do not	don't
have not	haven't
should not	shouldn't
let us	let's
who is	who's
who has	who's
where is	where's

One contraction does not follow this rule:

will not	won't

In all other contractions that you are likely to use, the apostrophe goes exactly where the letters have been left out.

Note especially *it's, they're who's, and you're*. Use them whenever you mean two words. See page 31 for the possessive forms—*its, their, whose,* and *your.*

EXERCISES

Put an apostrophe where a letter or letters have been left out. In the first sentence, for example, you will put an apostrophe in **Everyone's** and in **where's**. Tear out the perforated answer sheet at the back of the book, and correct each group of ten sentences before going on.

□EXERCISE 1

1. Everyone's having a great time, but where's Don?
2. We're studying contractions, and I'm finally getting the hang of them.
3. Who's going to the symphony with me?
4. I'm almost finished with my work, and I'll go if you'll wait for me.
5. He either couldn't or wouldn't agree to their proposal.
6. Having the right to do it doesn't mean it's right to do it.
7. If they're not coming, I hope they'll at least phone.
8. You're going to help with the campaign, aren't you?
9. If you'll do the dishes, I'll cook the dinner.
10. I don't mind cooking, but I've always hated doing dishes.

□EXERCISE 2

1. She'll have finished typing her term paper before I've written my first sentence.
2. If we're not going to reach the cabin by sunset, let's camp here.
3. Won't we be late if we don't start immediately?
4. He's missed so many classes that he can't expect to pass the course.
5. Whose car is she driving?
6. I wonder why he hasn't mentioned this before.
7. I haven't eaten since morning, but I'm not hungry.
8. I've had very little luck growing avocado plants from seeds.
9. Can't you find their number, or isn't it in the phone book?
10. Doesn't she take the bus to work?

□EXERCISE 3

1. I haven't even enough change to feed the parking meter.
2. Where's my umbrella?
3. Who's been using it?
4. I'd appreciate it if they'd bring it back.
5. It's been a year since I've seen him.
6. He's been out of the country for six months, but he's back now.
7. There's to be a party for him tonight, and we're going.
8. Aren't you coming, or haven't you been invited?
9. We've all been looking forward to it.
10. I'm sure there'll be a big crowd.

□EXERCISE 4

1. I'm not sure you're correct in your conclusion.
2. There's more to it than that.
3. It's a complicated problem and can't be solved easily.
4. I've been reading a book on astronomy, and I've learned a lot.
5. I didn't know that a quasar is a celestial object from four to ten billion light-years distant.
6. It's impossible to imagine such a distance, isn't it?
7. Can't you type, or don't you have a typewriter?
8. We've quit using some old grammatical forms that have gone out of date.
9. Why bother about them when they're no longer essential?
10. It's no use to fight a battle that's going to be lost in the end anyway.

□EXERCISE 5

1. It's more important to concentrate on rules that are essential.
2. I'm beginning to feel sure of a number of them that I've been working on.
3. There's nothing like practice to make the use of a rule automatic.
4. I wish I'd learned some of these rules long ago.
5. If you've something of value to say, it's important to know how to say it.
6. It's not always easy, but it's possible.
7. Don't run; you'll slip on the ice.
8. We've had icy streets ever since we've been back from our trip.
9. It's no fun to walk in this weather; I'm staying inside.
10. We've decided to go skiing if it snows this weekend.

□EXERCISE 6

1. It's necessary to have a dictionary if you're going to improve your vocabulary.
2. If you'll learn some word roots, you'll find your vocabulary growing.
3. Don't try to look up every new word.
4. It's better to look up only those words you're vaguely familiar with.
5. Look up words you've wondered about.
6. They're the ones you'll learn most readily.
7. If you'll keep a list of new words, that will help.
8. It's important also to use the new words you've learned.
9. Use a word three times, and it's yours.
10. It's true that a good vocabulary and academic success usually go together.

□EXERCISE 7

1. It's important to read good writing if you're going to write well.
2. If you'll read more, you'll find your writing will improve.

3. You'll not only increase your vocabulary, but you'll notice how ideas are presented.
4. You'll see how a magazine article develops a thesis statement.
5. It's good to watch for sentence variety too.
6. We've decided to go to Hawaii for our vacation.
7. I've never been there, and there's no place I'd rather go.
8. We haven't made reservations; we'll just take a chance on finding a place to stay.
9. It's not too difficult, I hear, in the off-season.
10. I've been reading Hawaiian history, and I'm all ready for the trip.

□EXERCISE 8

1. It's easy to do the exercises if you're sure of the rules.
2. I'm sure now of contractions.
3. There's nothing to it if you remember to put the apostrophe where a letter or letters have been left out.
4. Now I'm sure of the difference between **its** and **it's**.
5. He's been to Florida, but he hasn't been to New York.
6. She's sorry she won't get to go to the play.
7. I'm following a study schedule now, and I'm better satisfied with myself.
8. He hasn't started writing his job applications; he'll have to hurry.
9. There isn't much color in the woods now except for the bittersweet.
10. They'd like to come, but they're tied up for the weekend.

□EXERCISE 9

1. Where's the person who's supposed to make the punch?
2. And who's in charge of the buffet? It's not been prepared.
3. Where's the committee? Who's responsible?
4. She's always making something; if it isn't clothes, it's macrame plant hangers.
5. It's good his family is understanding; he's in need of support.
6. It's true that the government is planning a new space program.
7. They've included women and minority candidates this time as astronauts.
8. Isn't it about time?
9. I'm really working at my writing now, and it's improving.
10. I'm keeping a vocabulary list too, and I've learned some new words.

□EXERCISE 10

1. We're busy redecorating our house and haven't time for much else.
2. We've given the living room a first coat of paint, and now it's ready for the second.

3. I've never done any painting before, and I'm enjoying it.
4. It's satisfying to see the house look its best for a change.
5. Besides, we've saved a lot of money.
6. We've not decided what we're going to do next.
7. He's been away for a long time, hasn't he?
8. Isn't it amazing how he's learned so much from his new job?
9. I've no idea what he's going to do when he returns.
10. Nobody's given me any information.

WRITING YOUR OWN SENTENCES

Doing exercises helps one learn a rule, but even more helpful is using the rule in writing sentences. On a separate sheet write five sentences using contractions, especially any you have had trouble with.

WRITING ASSIGNMENT

From now on you will be expected to continue with the writing assignments (which begin on page 182) along with doing the exercises.

POSSESSIVES

The trick in writing possessives is to ask yourself the question, "Who does it belong to?" (Modern usage has made *who* acceptable when it comes first in a sentence, but if you want to sound like an old-fashioned English teacher, you can say, "*Whom* does it belong to?" or even "*To whom* does it belong?") If the answer to your question does not end in *s*, then add an apostrophe and *s*. If it does end in *s*, simply add an apostrophe.

one boys bike	Who does it belong to?	boy	Add '*s*	the boy's bike
two boys bikes	Who do they belong to?	boys	Add '	the boys' bikes
the mans hat	Who does it belong to?	man	Add '*s*	the man's hat
the mens hats	Who do they belong to?	men	Add '*s*	the men's hats
childrens game	Who does it belong to?	children	Add '*s*	children's game
one girls coat	Who does it belong to?	girl	Add '*s*	girl's coat
two girls coats	Who do they belong to?	girls	Add '	girls' coats

This trick will always work, but you must remember to ask the question each time. If you just look at the word, you may think the name of the owner ends in an *s* when it really doesn't.

Cover the right-hand column and see if you can write the following possessives correctly. Ask the question each time.

the womans dress	woman's
the womens ideas	women's
Jacks apartment	Jack's
James apartment	James'
the Smiths house	the Smiths'
Mr. Smiths house	Mr. Smith's

(Sometime you may see a variation of this rule. *James' book* may be written *James's book*. That is correct too, but the best way is to stick to the simple rule given above. You can't be wrong if you follow it.)

In such expressions as *a day's work* or *Saturday's game*, you may ask how the work can belong to the day or the game can belong to Saturday. Those are simply possessive forms that have been in our language for a long time. And when you think about it, the work really does belong to the day (not the night), and the game does belong to Saturday (not Friday).

A word of warning! Don't assume that because a word ends in *s* it is necessarily a possessive. Make sure the word actually possesses something before you put in an apostrophe.

Possessive pronouns are already possessive and don't need anything added to them.

my, mine	its
your, yours	our, ours
his	their, theirs
her, hers	whose

Note particularly *its, their, whose,* and *your.* They do not take apostrophes (see p. 25 for the contractions, the forms that stand for two words and take apostrophes). As a review, put a sheet of paper over the right-hand column below, and write the correct forms (contractions or possessives) on it. Then check your answers. If you miss any, go back and review the instructions on contractions and possessives.

(It) raining. It's _____ It's
(You) car needs washing. Your _____ Your
(Who) to blame? Who's _____ Who's
(They) planning to come. They're _____ They're
The cat drank (it) milk. its _____ its
(Who) been sitting here? Who's _____ Who's
The wind lost (it) force. its _____ its
(Who) going with me? Who's _____ Who's
My book has lost (it) cover. its _____ its
(It) all I can do. It's _____ It's
(You) right. You're _____ You're
(They) garden has many trees. Their Their
(It) sunny today. It's _____ It's
(Who) car shall we take? Whose _____ Whose
The club lost (it) leader. its _____ its
(Who) umbrella is that? Whose _____ Whose
(You) too late now. You're _____ You're
I have lost (they) address. their _____ their
Do you have (you) ticket? your _____ your
(They) always late. They're _____ They're

EXERCISES

Put the apostrophe in each possessive. WATCH OUT! **First**, make sure the word really possesses something; not every word that ends in **s** is a possessive. **Second**, remember that possessive pronouns don't take an apostrophe. **Third**, don't be confused because the word seems to end in **s**. You can't tell whether it really does end in **s** until you ask the question "Who does it belong to?" In the first sentence, for example, "Who did the car belong to?" "Aileen." Therefore you will write **Aileen's.**

□EXERCISE 1

1. Aileen's car is parked nearer the exit than ours.
2. It looks more like a girl's coat than a boy's.
3. This morning's forecast was for snow.
4. Is that van yours or Jim's?
5. Which car is older, yours or ours?
6. Choirs from all over the city competed.
7. Andy's motorbike was standing in the driveway.
8. I spent more than a week's wages on that one-day trip.
9. We watched the bird building its nest with twigs and bits of string.
10. Jeff's chief diversion is sailing a small boat.

□EXERCISE 2

1. We stopped at the Browns' cottage for the night.
2. James keeps his hair cut short.
3. James' hair is cut short.
4. Norman's dad is the foreman at the plant.
5. It's not mine; it must be yours.
6. Janet's watch had stopped, and she missed Wednesday's class.
7. I looked at women's watches but didn't find any I liked.
8. There was a sale on men's shoes but none on boys' shoes.
9. The audience was impressed with the coach's announcement.
10. The bear stood on its hind legs and waited for food to be thrown to it.

□EXERCISE 3

1. Cathy's talent in dancing helped her get a scholarship.
2. He had every day's work planned in detail.
3. Susan's hobby is collecting shells.
4. She was eager for her youngest son's arrival.
5. That bracelet isn't hers; I think it's Lisa's.
6. He wouldn't listen to anybody's advice.
7. The Women's Club had its annual bazaar on Saturday.

8. The note invited him to the mayor's reception.
9. Each day's work gave her a sense of satisfaction.
10. I was tired after the morning's workout.

□EXERCISE 4

1. The table had lost one of its legs.
2. I was surprised at Michael's decision.
3. Pat's desk is always tidy, but Trudy's is a mess.
4. We all met in the twins' room and then went over to Bonnie's.
5. The puppy was being nuzzled by its mother.
6. My dad's car is smaller than my grandfather's.
7. We went to see Roy's performance at the Little Theater.
8. The child's delight was obvious.
9. Philip's mind was made up; he had made his decision.
10. I was impressed with the salesman's presentation.

□EXERCISE 5

1. The pioneer's daring and courage helped develop the frontier.
2. The father's ambition for his son was boundless.
3. His car is always in top shape, but hers frequently needs repair.
4. She accidentally took someone else's coat instead of her own.
5. Ray's moped is faster than Scott's.
6. The students' diplomas were handed out by the president.
7. The children's shoes were soaked from the rain.
8. The instructor read everybody's paper aloud.
9. One person's paper had good details; another person's was amusing.
10. Charles Dickens' novels have stood the test of time.

□EXERCISE 6

1. Most of Margaret's free time is spent in skiing.
2. That store sells only women's and girls' clothing.
3. My mother's hobby is making miniature gardens.
4. Whose car is that in the driveway?
5. It's probably either Ralph's or Allen's.
6. I'm not asking for anyone's permission.
7. Do you sell women's ski jackets?
8. We're going to stay at my brother-in-law's cottage.
9. The ladies enjoyed the lecturer's wit.
10. The dog ran immediately to its master.

☐EXERCISE 7

1. Beth's social life is interfering with her studying.
2. The president's speech was inspiring.
3. Ivan's ability in juggling is quite a social asset.
4. We watched Saturday's game on TV.
5. Last night's reception was a great success, and we're looking forward to today's meeting.
6. Dad's garden occupies most of his weekends.
7. I borrowed my uncle's car for the afternoon.
8. I don't intend to do someone else's job.
9. My sister's fiancé is here for the weekend.
10. The world's longest river is the Nile.

☐EXERCISE 8

1. Janice's watch is always slow while Charles' watch is always fast.
2. He wasn't listening to his dad's words.
3. The robin left its nest in my apple tree when its young flew away.
4. The banks of the Missouri River frequently cave in.
5. Mr. Jones' office is on the top floor.
6. Mr. Jones is in his office from 9:00 to 4:00.
7. I like Carl Sandburg's poetry.
8. Honolulu's skyline is as impressive as those of mainland cities.
9. The family were all pleased about Judy's new job.
10. We didn't know what to do with Richard's old car.

☐EXERCISE 9

1. This is mine, and that's yours.
2. My typewriter should have its ribbon changed.
3. Paul's Stingray was a graduation gift from his parents.
4. Someone's wallet was lying on the steps.
5. He did each day's work to the best of his ability.
6. Tchaikovsky's Fourth Symphony is my favorite.
7. Its theme keeps running through my head.
8. The president's decision differed from that of the dean.
9. The invitation was to the Hardings' reception.
10. What is Cindy's phone number?

☐EXERCISE 10

1. Our house is smaller than theirs.
2. He can't get a scholarship because his parents' income is high.
3. Today's problems are different from those in my dad's day.

4. Roger gave a slide talk at the club's annual meeting.
5. Roger's picture was in the paper last night; Guy's was in last week.
6. He performed magic tricks for the children's party.
7. The child's tricycle was in the middle of the Carpenters' driveway.
8. It wasn't anybody's fault.
9. I've been following my instructor's advice and doing all the exercises.
10. Derrick's confidence was boosted by getting an A on that paper.

WRITING YOUR OWN SENTENCES

On a separate sheet write five sentences using possessives.

Review of Contractions and Possessives

Put in the necessary apostrophes. Try to get these exercises perfect. Don't excuse an error by saying, "Oh, that was just a careless mistake." A mistake is a mistake. Be tough on yourself!

□ EXERCISE 1

1. I'd like to get another person's point of view.
2. They're getting on each other's nerves.
3. He's decided to follow the doctor's advice.
4. He didn't want to meet Gail's parents.
5. Teams from all over the country entered the meet.
6. Hasn't she agreed to work in the president's office?
7. He's been working in a men's and boy's wear store all summer.
8. I'm not interested in joining a women's club.
9. The women's and girls' showers are close to the lake, but the men's and boys' showers are farther away.
10. We're invited to the Smiths' cottage, but we can't go.

□ EXERCISE 2

1. Herbert used Mr. Jones' camera to photograph yesterday's game.
2. Shouldn't you leave a bit of ice cream for Francis' sister?
3. My car has lost its shine, and I've got to wax it.
4. Who's been invited to their barbecue?
5. Won't there be a big crowd?
6. There'll be everyone they've ever known.
7. It's true that there's no way to learn to write except by writing.
8. Often I can't understand a rule, but then the exercises make it clear.
9. I couldn't make possessives before; now they're easy.
10. I'm also learning some words I've always misspelled.

□EXERCISE 3

1. There'll be more snow tonight, I'm afraid.
2. Loren's car doesn't have snow tires, and he's going to need them.
3. He'd better buy some, or he'll be in trouble on those hills.
4. I thought I'd go home often, but I haven't had time.
5. We made use of Gwen's record player and Diane's records.
6. Jennifer's majoring in piano, and Becky's majoring in voice.
7. Isn't she going to follow her tutor's advice?
8. We're planning to go to Robin's cottage tomorrow.
9. I'm sure we're going to have fun.
10. Isn't it too bad she's missing Jean's wedding?

□EXERCISE 4

1. The Browns' garden looks as if a gardener cared for it.
2. It's the result of Mr. Brown's hours of work.
3. I can see Mrs. Brown's hand in it too of course.
4. It's getting windy; I'm going to shut the doors.
5. The men's and women's lockers are on different floors.
6. I'm invited to lunch at Ruth's.
7. One's decisions in college may have a long-lasting effect.
8. I'm not sure you're making the right choice of color for that room.
9. Its small size really demands a light color, don't you think?
10. It's not a light room to begin with because it hasn't many windows.

In this student paper add the necessary apostrophes to the contractions and possessives.

□EXERCISE 5

There's a little lake with steep rocky sides and crystal clear water that you can see down into forever. Some say it's bottomless, but everyone agrees it's deep.

There's one spot where a big tree grows over the lake, and someone's tied a rope to one of its branches to swing on. It's a great sensation, I discovered, to swing out over the water and then let go. I think everyone gets an urge to yell as loud as possible to enhance his awkward dive. It's a great feeling to cast off from the high rocks holding onto the rope as it swings out over the water. Just before the farthest point of the rope's travel is the best place to let go and drop into the water. Those with initiative try flips and twists as they dive, but however it's done, it's a great sensation. Some say it's for kids, but I hope I never grow too old to have fun at it.

2

Sentence
Structure and

2   Sentence Structure and Agreement

The most common errors in freshman writing are fragments and run-together sentences. Here are some fragments:

Having given the best years of his life to his farm
Although we had food enough for only one day
The most that I possibly could do
Even though I tried very hard

They don't make complete statements. They leave the reader wanting something more.

Here are some run-together sentences:

We missed Nancy she is always the life of the party.
We had a wonderful time everyone was in a great mood.
I worked hard I should have got a better grade.
It was raining the pavement was slippery.

Unlike fragments, they make complete statements, but the trouble is they make *two* complete statements which should not be run together into one sentence. The reader has to go back to see where he should have paused.

Both fragments and run-together sentences bother the reader. Not until you can get rid of them will your writing be clear and easy to read. Unfortunately there is no quick, easy way to learn to avoid them. You have to learn a little about sentence structure—mainly how to find the subject and the verb in a sentence so that you can tell whether it really is a sentence.

FINDING SUBJECTS AND VERBS

When you write a sentence, you write about *something* or *someone*. That *is* the subject. Then you write what the subject *does* or *is*. That is the verb.

Birds fly

The word *Birds* is the something you are writing about. It's the subject, and we'll underline it once. *Fly* tells what the subject *does*. It's the verb, and we'll underline it twice.

Since the verb often tells what the subject does, it is easier to spot than the subject. First spot the verb in a sentence and then ask *Who* or *What*. For example, if the verb is *fly*, ask *who* or *what* flies. The answer will be the subject. Study the following sentences until you understand how to find subjects and verbs.

Birds fly north in the spring. (Who or what flies? Birds fly.)

Migrating birds fly north in the spring and south in the fall. (Who or what flies? Birds fly).

John drove his car. (Who or what drove? John drove.)

Last week John drove his car to the coast. (Who or what drove? John drove.)

After finishing classes John drove his car to his home on the coast.

(Who or what drove? John drove.)

The following verbs don't show what the subject *does*. They show what the subject *is* or *was*.

Nick is my brother. (Who or what is? Nick is.)

That boy in the blue jeans and red shirt is my younger brother. (Who or what is? Boy is.)

That boy standing by the car with the tan top is my brother. (Who or what is? Boy is.)

Melanie seems happy these days. (Who or what seems? Melanie seems.)

The movie was interesting. (Who or what was? Movie was.)

Sometimes the subject comes after the verb.

In the stands were five thousand spectators. (Who or what were? Spectators were.)

Where is the fire? (Who or what is? Fire is.)

There was a large crowd at the party. (Who or what was? Crowd was.)

There were not nearly enough plates for everybody. (Who or what were? Plates were.)

Here was positive evidence. (Who or what was? Evidence was.)

Note that *there* and *here* (as in the last three sentences) are never subjects. They simply point out something.

In commands the subject often is not expressed. It is *you* (understood).

Open the door! (You open the door.)

Eat your spinach! (You eat your spinach.)

EXERCISES

Underline the subject once and the verb twice. Find the verb first, and then ask **who** or **what**. When you have done ten sentences, tear out the perforated answer sheet at the back of the book and correct your answers. Be sure to correct **each group of ten** before you go on so that you will learn from your mistakes.

□EXERCISE 1

1. The rains came early that spring.
2. I planted two small palms in my planter.
3. That trip was the best experience of my life.
4. Diet is important for health.
5. That big shady tree was a refuge during all my childhood.
6. Franz Schubert earned less than a thousand dollars in his entire lifetime.
7. Change is the only certainty.
8. Clear writing depends on some rules.
9. Stop! (You)
10. The Mounties always get their man.

□EXERCISE 2

1. There was a pretty little spruce by the gate.
2. He traveled by bus from the Atlantic to the Pacific.
3. The Time Machine by H. G. Wells is a classic science fiction novel.
4. She has great confidence in her daughter.
5. There lay my lost briefcase.
6. Say it simply. (You)
7. Mr. Stepp understands his students' problems.
8. Mr. Puette is also a concerned instructor.
9. We had fifty inches of snow that winter.
10. Road conditions usually improve at the county line.

□EXERCISE 3

1. There in the rain stood our pony.
2. The cheetah is the fastest of all land animals.

3. Beyond the dunes I saw the lake.
4. I watched the white froths of foam on the slate and silver water.
5. Sign here. (You)
6. Captain Cook brought back many artifacts from his journeys.
7. They are now prized possessions in museums all over the world.
8. The double coconut palm bears the largest and heaviest seed of any plant.
9. A single nut weighs up to 50 pounds.
10. The fruit requires ten years to ripen.

□EXERCISE 4

1 Children pick up anxieties and fears from their parents.
2. Anxiety is usually fear of oneself.
3. Self-confidence dispels anxiety.
4. Fasten your seat belts. (You)
5. He's a neophyte to Washington politics.
6. What is a neophyte?
7. A neophyte is a beginner.
8. There were fifteen cheerleaders for the opposing team.
9. Keep off the lawn. (You)
10. There is still a chance.

□EXERCISE 5

1. Write on one side of the page only. (You)
2. The harp echoed in the empty auditorium.
3. The rock group turned up the volume.
4. The man in the blue shirt is the lead trumpet.
5. The Sirens of Titan is a science fiction novel by Kurt Vonnegut, Jr.
6. The abandoned mine shaft was at the top of the hill.
7. In the woods was a tree house.
8. There was a white pine in the field ahead of us.
9. Here was the end of the trail.
10. John Mason Brown called writing "delightful agony."

□EXERCISE 6

1. She drove across the continent by herself.
2. He was my favorite high school teacher.
3. He influenced me greatly.
4. During my freshman year he encouraged me in sports.
5. During spring vacation I visited the Dunes State Park in Indiana.
6. I wrote steadily for three hours.

7. At the end of that time I had a pretty good paper.
8. I enjoyed the experience.
9. The class liked the paper too.
10. I like compositions better than exercises.

□EXERCISE 7

1. My vocabulary is not as large as my father's.
2. He always kept word lists.
3. He used new words frequently.
4. He sat in front of our big dictionary for hours at a time.
5. I admired his persistence.
6. He was a self-educated man.
7. We watched two weaving skaters and their little dog on the smooth lake.
8. Then we heard the clear call of a cardinal.
9. The cardinal's scarlet coat contrasted with the snow.
10. Rooftop solar panels are the ultimate as status symbols across the land.

□EXERCISE 8

1. My mother made wonderful angel food cakes.
2. She never iced them.
3. Out of the swirling snow appeared my little brother.
4. The drifts were as high as the windows.
5. We tunneled our way to the barn.
6. Turn off your light. (you)
7. Save electricity. (you)
8. That evening we went to a play at the Little Theater.
9. It was a drama by Ibsen.
10. I enjoyed every moment of it.

□EXERCISE 9

1. The Arctic tern travels 12,000 miles during its annual migration.
2. The Queen Elizabeth II is the largest passenger liner in service today.
3. Today I learned the meaning of the root loqu.
4. It means "to talk."
5. Thus a loquacious person talks a lot.
6. And the root sol means "alone."
7. Therefore a soliloquy is a "talking alone."
8. The chuckwagon races are the most exciting part of the Calgary Stampede.
9. It takes a driver and two outriders for each chuckwagon.
10. The participants compete year after year.

□EXERCISE 10

1. Our sun is five billion years old.
2. The invisible "black holes" in space were once huge stars.
3. A "black hole" is simply the remnant of a collapsed star.
4. The star's top-heavy gravity crushed it down to the size of a golf ball.
5. Then gravity crushed it further to "nothing."
6. Thus it "disappeared."
7. It became a "black hole."
8. Our universe has unthinkable numbers.
9. It is ten billion light-years to the farthest quasar.
10. There are 100 billion galaxies in the universe.

SUBJECTS NOT IN PREPOSITIONAL PHRASES

We are not going to name many grammatical forms in this book, and the only reason we are mentioning prepositional phrases is to get them out of the way. They are always a bother in analyzing sentences. For example, you might have difficulty finding the subject and verb in a long sentence like this:

> Under these circumstances one of the fellows drove to the North Woods during the first week of his vacation.

But if you cross out all the prepositional phrases like this:

> ~~Under these circumstances~~ one ~~of the fellows~~ drove ~~to the North Woods during the first week~~ of ~~his vacation~~.

then you have only two words left—the subject and the verb. And even in short sentences like the following, you might pick the wrong word as the subject if you did not cross out the prepositional phrases first.

> One of my friends lives in St. Petersburg.
> Most of the team went on the trip.

The subject is never in a prepositional phrase. Learn to spot prepositional phrases so that you can get them out of the way. It is much easier to see the structure of a sentence without them.

A prepositional phrase is simply a preposition and the name of something or someone. Read through this list of prepositional phrases so that you will be able to recognize one when you see it:

above the desk	**over** the desk
across the desk	**past** the desk
against the desk	**through** the desk
around the desk	**to** the desk
at the desk	**toward** the desk
behind the desk	**under** the desk
below the desk	**upon** the desk
beneath the desk	**with** the desk
beside the desk	**within** the desk
by the desk	**about** them
for the desk	**among** them
from the desk	**between** them
in the desk	**except** them
inside the desk	**of** them
into the desk	**without** them
like the desk	**after** vacation
near the desk	**before** vacation
on the desk	**during** vacation

since vacation
until vacation
along the street

beyond the street
down the street
up the street

EXERCISES

Cross out the prepositional phrases. Then underline the subject once and the verb twice. Correct each group of ten sentences before going on.

□EXERCISE 1

1. One of the most interesting places on our trip was the Japanese garden in the East West Center.
2. We followed a bamboo shaded path through the garden.
3. Clumps of ferns bordered the path.
4. Near the path flowed a little stream.
5. In small pools beside the stream were orange and black and white tropical fish.
6. Here and there were Japanese stone lanterns.
7. At the top of the garden was a small waterfall.
8. Stone slab steps beside the waterfall led to a Japanese teahouse.
9. An atmosphere of peace enveloped the garden.
10. Some of the best things in life are still free.

□EXERCISE 2

1. Behind our house is a row of tall poplar trees.
2. In the front are some blue spruces.
3. In the summer dozens of birds nest in our trees.
4. Among the noisiest are the blue jays.
5. In winter many birds visit our feeder for grain and seeds.
6. Of them all, the magpies are the most colorful.
7. From branch to branch hops a small gray squirrel.
8. From the deep woods I hear the call of a thrush.
9. One of my fondest memories is of a chat with my grandmother.
10. After all the years, I still remember her face.

□EXERCISE 3

1. On the walls of his room hang many travel posters.
2. In the summer and during shorter vacations he does a lot of traveling.
3. Both of us like antiques.
4. Most of our antiques are family heirlooms.
5. Three of my friends have scholarships this year.
6. Each of them works hard at his studies.
7. Most of the students are serious about this course.

8. A couple of them write excellent papers already.
9. Only one percent of the professional engineers in the nation are women.
10. All of the engineering schools, however, welcome women.

□EXERCISE 4

1. Most of the singers in the choir practice daily.
2. In May the majority of them go on the spring tour through the Midwest.
3. At the end of the tour they give a concert at home.
4. One of the most durable satisfactions in life is creative work.
5. Sometimes people with very little training are excellent counselors.
6. My counselor in high school helped me tremendously.
7. In my spare time I work on my spelling list.
8. In most of my papers I now catch my misspelled words.
9. Even my letters to my family now have fewer spelling errors.
10. At last I feel a sense of accomplishment.

□EXERCISE 5

1. One of her great characteristics is her sense of humor.
2. On one wall of his office was a striking painting of geometric patterns in shades of blue.
3. One of her brothers went into the field of electronics.
4. Most of the students on this campus prefer semesters to quarters.
5. One of the great problems today is the shortage of meaningful jobs for young people.
6. Ice on the road made travel hazardous.
7. Around the bases of the birch trees bare patches of ground appeared.
8. The sight of the old buildings along the river reminded him of the past.
9. A line of evergreen trees near the marina broke the wind.
10. In each forked tree branch were white webs of wet snow.

□EXERCISE 6

1. After three days in Tallahassee we left for home.
2. Neither of us wanted to leave.
3. In my new job I found congenial associates and challenging work.
4. Through the streets and into the woods the children ran.
5. All of them were on a holiday.
6. In the evenings she took courses toward her new career.
7. Most of her courses were interesting and informative.
8. In spite of many difficulties she passed with honors.
9. One of her professors gave her great praise for her research.
10. All of her family were proud of her.

□EXERCISE 7

1. One of my favorite stories is "The Secret Life of Walter Mitty."
2. Like Mitty, most of us at times live in daydreams.
3. Most of my friends have their own cars.
4. None of them have new cars though.
5. People in English-speaking countries speak different dialects.
6. All of them, however, write the same Standard English dialect.
7. Half of the population of Alaska lives in its largest city, Anchorage.
8. Through no effort of its own, Saudi Arabia sits on top of the greatest reservoir of liquid energy on earth.
9. Genetics is at the center of the stage in today's biology.
10. The noise in that restaurant was insufferable.

□EXERCISE 8

1. The average age of Neanderthal man was 29 years.
2. In a pencil dot there are more atoms than people on earth.
3. The brightest star in the sky is Sirius in the constellation Canis Major.
4. In his struggle for an education he had little time for recreation.
5. In his reading and studying he found pleasure enough.
6. After hours of waiting, I finally boarded the train.
7. On his wall hung pictures of his children and his grandchildren.
8. I prefer games of skill to games of chance.
9. Writing is a way of learning about yourself.
10. A thesis statement with its supporting reasons gives the plan for a paper.

□EXERCISE 9

1. The vibrating tones of the saxophone rose above the other sounds.
2. In the middle of the piece the cymbals crashed.
3. Slowly the sound of the chords died away.
4. Much of the friction of daily life results from tone of voice.
5. In the midst of all the confusion and frustration came a telephone call.
6. She juggled all of her various duties successfully.
7. One of her great qualities was her planning ability.
8. During the holidays bird lovers flock to woods and marshes and meadows for the National Audubon Society's annual Christmas bird count.
9. Most of the participants are experienced bird watchers.
10. The results of the bird count are important for conservation purposes.

□ **EXERCISE 10**

1. The linking of three spacecraft 200 miles above the earth was another first for the Russians.
2. The five Russian cosmonauts worked together for five days on various experiments.
3. The environmentalists worry about the destruction of natural resources.
4. The majority of people, though, give little thought to future generations.
5. One of the committee members voted against the measure.
6. Much of the foreign relief effort bogged down in red tape.
7. In the sixteenth century extraordinary changes affected the whole of Europe.
8. In a successful marriage each contributes something to the development of the other.
9. Behind much of the growing popularity of bicycling is an expanding network of motor-free trails.
10. Symbiosis is the living together of two different organisms in a mutually beneficial relationship.

WRITING ASSIGNMENT

As you do the writing assignments that begin on page 182, are you keeping a list of your misspelled words on page 285?

MORE ABOUT VERBS AND SUBJECTS

Sometimes the verb is more than one word. Here are a few of the many forms of the verb *drive*:

I drive	I will be driving	I may drive
I am driving	I will have been driving	I could drive
I have driven	I will have driven	I might drive
I have been driving	I am driven	I should drive
I drove	I was driven	I would drive
I was driving	I have been driven	I must drive
I had driven	I had been driven	I could have driven
I had been driving	I will be driven	I might have driven
I will drive	I can drive	I should have driven

Note that words like *not, ever, never, only, always, just, really, already* are not part of the verb even though they may be in the middle of the verb.

Keith had never driven to the cottage before.

I had always before driven to the cottage by myself.

She should just have driven around the block.

Two other forms—*driving* and *to drive*—look like verbs, but neither can ever be the verb of a sentence. No *ing* word alone can ever be the verb of a sentence; it must have a helping verb in front of it.

Larry driving home. (not a sentence because there is no proper verb)
Larry was driving home. (a sentence)

And no verb with *to* in front of it can ever be the verb of a sentence.

To drive down the river road. (not a sentence because there is no proper verb and no subject)
I like to drive down the river road. (a sentence)

These two forms *driving* and *to drive* may be used as subjects, or they may have other uses in the sentence.

Driving is fun.   To drive is fun.

But neither of them can ever be the verb of a sentence.

Not only may a verb be composed of more than one word. There may be more than one verb in a sentence:

Steve painted the house and planted trees in the yard.

Also there may be more than one subject.

Steve and Marie painted the house and planted trees in the yard.

EXERCISES

Underline the subject once and the verb twice. Be sure to include all parts of the verb. Also watch for more than one subject and more than one verb.

□EXERCISE 1

1. I should have learned about subjects and verbs in high school.
2. At least I am learning them now.
3. At the beginning of the year I could not concentrate.
4. Now I am improving.
5. I have been going to the library almost every evening.
6. I should have been studying more at the beginning of the semester.
7. I certainly should have started my term paper sooner.
8. Now I may not finish it in time.
9. I must not hand it in late.
10. Next time I definitely will start sooner.

□EXERCISE 2

1. The wind tore the needles from the white pine and scattered them around the yard.
2. The sleet and snow obliterated the view of the road.
3. I shoveled the walks but did not tackle the driveway.
4. A downy woodpecker was hammering away at a tree in search of insects.
5. Hugh went to the woods and cut a spruce for a Christmas tree.
6. He sawed off the lower branches and put the Christmas tree in the stand.
7. The children unpacked the decorations and put them on the tree.
8. The decorations had been used for three generations.
9. Some of the tinsel-framed pictures had been made 60 years before.
10. Everyone was in a good mood and had a good time.

□EXERCISE 3

1. The chief themes of rock music are romance and rebellion.
2. Rock records are made by recording rhythm section, string group, vocal group, and lead singer separately on different tracks.
3. Then all of the tracks are "mixed."
4. The result can be better than a concert production.
5. The record business has become the biggest part of the entertainment industry.
6. It now makes more money than either television or movies.
7. The 1,200 recording companies annually take in over $2.5 billion.
8. I have been wondering about your concert.
9. Will you be giving it next week?
10. Of course I am coming to hear it.

□EXERCISE 4

1. Americans must decide between more jobs or cleaner air and water.
2. The saying has always been "clean as driven snow."
3. Now the saying must be changed to "dirty as driven snow."
4. Car exhausts and factories are spewing poisonous lead into the air.
5. The poisonous lead is picked up by the snow.
6. In 1930 there were 77 million elms in U.S. cities and towns.
7. Then the Dutch elm disease struck and has spread to 41 states.
8. Now there are only 34 million elms.
9. The federal government is spending about $4 million a year to seek a cure for the disease.
10. Americans are becoming more aware of their natural as well as of their cultural heritage.

□EXERCISE 5

1. One distinction between man and the other primates is in the use of tools.
2. Nonhumans use tools only in rudimentary ways.
3. Tool use among nonhuman primates does not progress from one generation to another.
4. The human species stores up information about tools.
5. It is passed on from generation to generation.
6. Tool using by humans has progressed a long way.
7. For settling any quarrel, maturity is essential.
8. But only one of the two people needs to be mature in order to handle a situation.
9. In a disagreement there is just one question to ask.
10. That question is, "What's important here?"

□**EXERCISE 6**

1. America's love affair with bicycles is blossoming anew.
2. The spurt in popularity of two-wheelers is climbing, with the help of high gasoline prices.
3. The moped is also gaining in popularity.
4. The space program has selected six women, three black men, and one Japanese American man to train as astronauts.
5. One upcoming space project will be to get a better view of Saturn and its rings.
6. No spacecraft has yet flown by Saturn.
7. Can you find the constellation Pleiades in the night sky?
8. With no help from anyone, he is putting himself through college.
9. He has matured mentally as well as physically.
10. He should do well in his career.

□**EXERCISE 7**

1. He had worked at his job faithfully and deserved a promotion.
2. The Cougars and the Hornets played an extra inning.
3. His appreciation of comedy has never progressed beyond "The Three Stooges."
4. Sometimes she made dried flower arrangements and sometimes miniature Japanese gardens.
5. In my reading I have been learning a lot of miscellaneous facts.
6. A giraffe's tongue may be as long as one and a half feet.
7. Badgers can run backward as fast as forward.
8. Gulliver's Travels is considered one of the greatest satires in the English language.
9. It was written by Jonathan Swift.
10. In Gulliver's voyage to Lilliput we can see ourselves as small and ridiculous people.

□**EXERCISE 8**

1. An attempt is being made to stop crime as a career.
2. Many criminals commit crime after crime, year after year.
3. Now an attack on the problem has begun in 24 major cities.
4. The program has been funded so far by the Law Enforcement Assistance Administration.
5. Under this program it is taking only about 60 days in some cities between arrest and trial for the habitual criminal.
6. In 30 months the nationwide program has put away over 5,000 hardcore criminals for terms averaging more than 14 years each.
7. The program was partially responsible for a slight reduction in big-city crime in 1977.

8. Swift and sure justice has proved an effective deterrent to the habitual criminal.
9. Criminals fear most a speedy trial and the certainty of punishment.
10. State and local officials are planning to continue the program.

□EXERCISE 9

1. At least 205 Americans have won damage suits each worth a million dollars.
2. Excessive awards are forcing the cost of liability insurance up for everyone.
3. For faster, cheaper justice, more disputes should be settled out of court.
4. Legal procedures must also be streamlined.
5. After the snowstorm they walked into the woods to see the striking beauty of the trees.
6. They had never before seen trees with so many sparkling white ice crystals.
7. He broke an icicle off a tree and dropped it in the snow.
8. Farther on, the view of the frozen lake was blocked by buildings along the bank.
9. Have you read All the President's Men by Woodward and Bernstein?
10. Robert Redford and Dustin Hoffman gave memorable performances in the movie.

□EXERCISE 10

1. Anxiety is an all-over sensation and is felt in the body as well as in the mind.
2. Growing up and adapting to life are difficult processes even under the best of circumstances.
3. In this country many older people are going back to college and sometimes starting new careers.
4. Many choose a community college as a start and then transfer to a four-year institution.
5. These students are usually highly motivated and are successful in their courses.
6. Continuing education is becoming an important part of American life.
7. The shimmering lights and the shifting imagery of stained-glass windows have entranced people for sixteen centuries.
8. Yesterday some of us went to the Botanic Garden and saw a banyan tree.
9. From its branches long roots hang to the ground and eventually become trunks.
10. A single tree thus may have many trunks.

GETTING RID OF RUN-TOGETHER SENTENCES

Any group of words having a subject and verb is a clause. The clause may be independent (able to stand alone) or dependent (unable to stand alone). Every sentence you have worked with so far has been an independent clause because it has been able to stand alone. It has made a complete statement.

If two such independent clauses are written together with no punctuation, or merely a comma, they are called a run-together sentence. We noted some run-together sentences on page 38. Here are some more:

> The girls made the fire the boys cooked the steaks.
> The girls made the fire, the boys cooked the steaks.
> The book was interesting therefore I read it rapidly.
> The book was interesting, therefore I read it rapidly.

Such run-together sentences can be corrected in one of three ways:

1. Make the two independent clauses into two sentences.

> The girls made the fire. The boys cooked the steaks.
> The book was interesting. Therefore I read it rapidly.

2. Separate the two independent clauses with a semicolon. Note the connecting words (underlined) that may come between independent clauses.

> The girls made the fire; the boys cooked the steaks.
> The book was interesting; I read it rapidly.
> The book was interesting; therefore I read it rapidly.
> The book was interesting; consequently I read it rapidly.
> I worked overtime; thus I finished my project early.
> I was late; nevertheless I made the plane.
> I was too busy to go; also I wasn't really interested.
> I will enjoy the work; furthermore I need the money.
> I wrote a thesis statement; then I began my paper.

Other words that may come between independent clauses are *however, likewise, moreover, otherwise.* All of these connecting words require a semicolon in front of them.

But be sure that such words really do come between independent clauses. Sometimes they are merely interrupters (see p. 155) as in the following sentences:

> I decided, therefore, to paint the kitchen.
> It took me weeks, however, to get started.

3. **Connect the two independent clauses with a comma and one of the following connecting words: and, but, for, or, nor, yet, so.**

The girls made the fire, but the boys cooked the steaks.
The book was interesting, and I read it rapidly.
I must hurry, or I'll never finish.
I haven't seen that movie, nor do I want to.
He was not outgoing, yet I liked him.

THE THREE WAYS TO PUNCTUATE INDEPENDENT CLAUSES
The book was interesting. I read it rapidly.
The book was interesting; I read it rapidly.
The book was interesting, and I read it rapidly.

Learn these three ways, and you will avoid run-together sentences.

EXERCISES

In each independent clause underline the subject once and the verb twice. Be ready to tell why the sentence is punctuated as it is.

□EXERCISE 1

1. I have been learning some word roots; a knowledge of word roots helps to increase one's vocabulary.
2. I've just learned the meaning of the root mal; it means "bad."
3. A malignant disease is a bad disease, and malicious gossip is intentionally bad or harmful gossip.
4. Malinger is an interesting word; it means "to pretend to be in bad health to avoid work."
5. My small brother sometimes malingers to avoid mowing the lawn; I frequently malinger during the World Series.
6. I've also learned the meaning of the prefix a at the beginning of a word; it means "not."
7. Asymmetrical means "not symmetrical," and atypical means "not typical."
8. I'm tired of symmetrical flower arrangements; I am going to make an asymmetrical one.
9. Writing is hard work, but it's satisfying.
10. It's not much fun to write, but it's fun to have written.

□EXERCISE 2

1. I've started to study every night and at last am getting somewhere.
2. I am learning to concentrate, and I'm learning about sentences.
3. I don't need to know the names of all the parts of a sentence, but I do need to get a sentence sense. *will*
4. I must know subjects and verbs, or I won't understand clauses.
5. A knowledge of clauses is essential; otherwise I won't punctuate correctly.
6. I now recognize independent clauses; consequently I am avoiding run-together sentences.
7. I've worked hours on this paper; it's beginning to sound better.
8. I must not forget to proofread it; I may catch some errors.
9. First I will read it through carefully for spelling errors; next I will go through it again to catch run-together sentences.
10. Finally I will read it aloud slowly; such reading will catch any omitted words.

Most of the following sentences are run-together. In each independent clause underline the subject once and the verb twice. Then separate the two clauses with the correct punctuation—comma, semicolon, or period with a capital letter. Remember that the semicolon and the period with a capital letter are interchangeable. Thus your answer may differ from the one at the back of the book.

□EXERCISE 3

1. My high school adviser was close to me she was almost my best friend.
2. She was busy but she always made time for me.
3. Sometimes she would just sit and listen occasionally she would give advice.
4. At first I wasn't interested in her suggestion about a career then I changed my mind.
5. It is going to take time but eventually I should get a good position.
6. I hope to finish college in three more years then I'll apply for a job.
7. Some people can study with the stereo on I can't.
8. It isn't the easiest or best way to learn.
9. Each person does the best that he can under the circumstances but sometimes the circumstances are too difficult to overcome.
10. In education we need a balance between receiving and sending reading is receiving writing is sending.

□EXERCISE 4

1. Last week I applied for part-time work at the hospital. I went for an interview on Monday.
2. I was wearing my gray suit, it is cut better than my tan one.
3. I had typed my application, I wanted to make a good impression.
4. I had just half an hour to get to the appointment, and my car wouldn't start.
5. Luckily Jan had jumper cables and managed to start the car.
6. I got there on time. I got the job.
7. The first step toward success is to learn to work, work is more important than luck.
8. David Lloyd George said: "Don't be afraid to take a big step if one is indicated. You can't cross a chasm in two small jumps."
9. The Martian Chronicles by Ray Bradbury is a collection of science fiction stories, their theme is the colonization of Mars by mankind.
10. I, Robot by Issac Asimov is a collection of short stories about the history of robots, it sees them advancing from simple baby sitters and factory workers to the actual governing force of all mankind.

□EXERCISE 5

1. Boettcher Hall in Denver is the first "surround" music hall in the country, the orchestra is in the center of the hall with the audience seated all around it.
2. No seat in Boettcher Hall is farther than 85 feet from the stage, and most are within 65 feet of it.
3. Law schools, medical schools, and graduate schools all over the country are accepting a larger number of qualified minority students, attempts are being made to find, enroll, and support these students.
4. I've been trying to budget my time this semester, it's difficult.
5. My time budget hasn't worked very well so far, but I'm still trying.
6. Eventually the household computer may be as much a part of the house as the kitchen sink, it will program the washing machine, the sewing machine, and a robot vacuum cleaner.
7. Some of his statements are thought provoking, others are just provoking.
8. He is always ready to criticize, yet he himself cannot tolerate criticism.
9. These exercises aren't difficult, but they take time.
10. I'm doing them all, for I find them helpful in my writing.

□EXERCISE 6

1. Creating is always more satisfying than acquiring, making a table is more fun than buying one.

2. He made an elegant coffee table from an old door and two cardboard cartons, the center panel of the door and the cartons were enameled white and the rest of the door was enameled black.

3. You will have to remove the old finish on that cupboard, or the new finish will never be right.

4. Strip the cupboard of old wax and varnish, then apply a mixture of boiled linseed oil and turpentine and finally finish the piece with clear varnish.

5. The old sewing machine was her favorite antique, it had belonged to her mother.

6. She cleaned it with coal oil and polished it with lemon oil.

7. The sea lions at the zoo had been fed too many fish, they ignored those thrown by the visitors.

8. The blue whale is the largest animal ever to inhabit the earth, some specimens have weighed 131 tons.

9. A sable antelope at the zoo had a one-day-old baby, she prodded it with her knee to make it practice walking.

10. Always behave like a duck, keep calm and unruffled on the surface but paddle like the devil underneath.

□EXERCISE 7

1. A politician is worried about the next election, a statesman is worried about the next generation.

2. The biggest oil spill of all time occurred off the Brittany Coast in 1978, the French were outraged and started an investigation of the American-owned supertanker.

3. He thought he knew a lot about politics, but actually he knew little.

4. In 1977 nearly half of the world's armament sales were made by the U.S., the U.S. has the questionable honor of being the champion arms peddler of the world.

5. Costa Rica maintains almost no armed forces, that is one reason for its relatively high per capita income.

6. The public steals millions of dollars worth of food and clothes from stores, and the same public pays it back in higher prices.

7. The world's most valuable painting is the Mona Lisa in the Louvre, it was assessed for insurance purposes at $100,000,000.

8. Chairman Mao Tse-tung denounced China's greatest scholar and thinker, Confucius, Mao hated traditional learning and intellectuals.

9. Now Confucius is coming back into favor, China is trying to rebuild its ravaged educational system.

10. George Bernard Shaw wrote four novels in the first nine years of his writing career, none was accepted by a publisher.

□EXERCISE 8

1. Many Americans are choosing handlebars rather than steering wheels these days, Americans in 1973 bought more bikes than cars.
2. It's not just the children either, their parents are buying bikes too.
3. They have a dual concern of keeping fit and preserving the environment.
4. The six Outward Bound schools in the United States enroll close to 6,000 students a year, their philosophy makes use of stress and adversity to build character.
5. They use the wilderness to teach personal growth, the students gain confidence in and perspective on their own daily lives by facing adversity.
6. The six schools are open year-round, they offer a wide range of environments and climates to choose from.
7. His clothes were torn by the brambles, and his feet were blistered.
8. We went to Jasper Park last summer, and on our way we stopped and walked on a glacier.
9. Happiness comes from sharing experiences, it does not come from owning things.
10. Henry Ford said, "Old men are always advising young men to save money, that is bad advice, don't save every nickel, invest in yourself, I never saved a dollar until I was forty years old."

□EXERCISE 9

1. The once desolate Demilitarized Zone between North and South Korea is still not inhabited by man, but perhaps for that very reason it has become a haven for birds and animals.
2. The zone stretches for 151 miles between North and South Korea, it is 2.5 miles wide.
3. After the war the zone was a land of bomb craters and shell holes, but now nature has taken over.
4. Observation planes still patrol it, and the sights of innumerable guns sweep it constantly.
5. But abandoned fields have turned into marshes for waterfowl, and thickets provide a home for Asian river deer.
6. In the mountainous parts, lynx and tigers roam, pheasants wander across abandoned roads.
7. The zone is one of the few places in the world unharmed by pesticides and herbicides, thus wildlife can flourish.
8. The most spectacular inhabitant of the zone is the Manchurian crane, a striking white, black, and red bird with a wingspan of eight feet and with an elaborate mating ritual including wing flapping, bows, and leaps into the air.

9. Once there were hundreds of these cranes but now only a few flocks remain three of the flocks winter in the DMZ.

10. The crane is the symbol of the South Korean airline and also is something of a national symbol.

□EXERCISE 10

1. The first man to reach the North Pole alone was Naomi Uemura, he planted the Japanese flag on the pole on May 1, 1978.
2. Uemura was then at the top of the world everywhere that he looked was south.
3. His sledge had been pulled across the frozen Arctic by his 17 huskies it took 57 days to travel 477 miles.
4. Sometimes temperatures dropped as low as −68 degrees Fahrenheit and blizzards slowed him down.
5. He wore modern thermal underwear but the rest of his clothing was Eskimo gear.
6. One morning he was awakened by the barking of his dogs and he saw a giant white polar bear coming toward his tent.
7. Uemura was frightened and decided to play dead in his sleeping bag.
8. The bear destroyed the tent and ate the food supply then he poked the sleeping bag and turned it over.
9. Uemura lay still in the bag and finally the bear wandered off.
10. The next morning the bear returned and Uemura shot him at a range of 55 yards.

WRITING YOUR OWN SENTENCES

On a separate sheet write five sentences, each containing two independent clauses, and punctuate them correctly. Be sure to master this section before you go on; it will take care of many of your punctuation errors.

WRITING ASSIGNMENT

Continue with your writing assignments that begin on page 182. Are you listing all your misspelled words on page 285?

GETTING RID OF FRAGMENTS

There are two kinds of clauses—independent, which we have just finished studying, and dependent. A dependent clause has a subject and verb just like an independent clause, but it can't stand alone because it begins with a dependent word such as

after	that, so that
although, though	unless
as, as if	until
because	what, whatever
before	when, whenever
even though	where, wherever
how	whether
if, even if	which, whichever
in order that	while
since	who, whom
than	whose

Whenever a clause begins with one of the above dependent words (unless it is a question, which would never give you any trouble), it is dependent. If we take an independent clause such as

We finished the game.

and put one of the dependent words in front of it, it becomes dependent:

After we finished the game
Although we finished the game
As we finished the game
Before we finished the game
If we finished the game
Since we finished the game
That we finished the game
When we finished the game
While we finished the game

The clause can no longer stand alone. As you read it, you can hear that it doesn't really say anything. It does not make a complete statement. It leaves the reader expecting something more. **It is a fragment** and must not be punctuated as a sentence.

To correct such a fragment, simply add an independent clause:

After we finished the game, we went to the clubhouse.
While we finished the game, the others waited.
We gave up the court when we had finished the game.
We were happy that we had finished the game.

In other words **EVERY SENTENCE MUST HAVE AT LEAST ONE INDEPENDENT CLAUSE.**

Note in the examples above that when a dependent clause comes at the beginning of a sentence, it is followed by a comma. Often the comma prevents misreading, as in the following sentence:

When he entered, the room became quiet.

Without a comma after *entered*, the reader would read *When he entered the room* before realizing that that was not what the author meant. The comma makes the reading easy. Sometimes if the dependent clause is short and there is no danger of misreading, the comma is omitted, but it is easier and safer simply to follow the rule.

Six Sentences That Show How to Punctuate Clauses

I gave a party. Everybody came. I gave a party; everybody came.	(two independent clauses)
I gave a party; moreover everybody came.	(two independent clauses connected by *also, consequently, furthermore, however, likewise, moreover, nevertheless, otherwise, therefore, then, thus*)
I gave a party, and everybody came.	(two independent clauses connected by *and, but, for, or, nor yet, so*)
When I gave a party, everybody came.	(dependent clause at beginning of sentence)
Everybody came when I gave a party.	(dependent clause at end of sentence) The dependent words are *after, although, though, even though, as, as if, because, before, how, if, even if, in order that, since, than, that, so that, unless, until, what, whatever, when, whenever, where, wherever, whether, which, whichever, while, who, whom, whose.*

If you remember these six sentences and understand the rules for their punctuation, most of your punctuation problems will be taken care of. It is essential that you learn the words in the above chart. If your instructor reads some of the words, be ready to tell which ones come between independent clauses and which ones introduce dependent clauses.

EXERCISES

Write S if the clause is independent and therefore a sentence. Add the period after it. Write F if the clause is dependent and therefore a fragment not to be punctuated as a sentence. Then add an indpendent clause to make the fragment into a sentence. If the dependent clause comes first, put a comma after it. When you have finished ten sentences, tear out the answer sheet at the back of the book and correct your sentences before going on.

□EXERCISE 1

_F_ 1. Whenever you are ready to leave, *we'll go.*

_S_ 2. Fragments must not be punctuated as sentences,

_S_ 3. On the horizon the moon was just coming up,

_F_ 4. Because I tried harder and harder and finally succeeded, *I was pleased,*

_F_ 5. That she was a loving and trusting person *was her best trait.*

_F_ 6. If I would study more and spend more time writing my papers *my grades would improve*

_F_ 7. After I had studied for two hours without stopping *my head began to ache.*

_F_ 8. Although I had never been in Oakland before *I had heard much about it.*

_F_ 9. Wherever I went on those busy streets *I was careful to look for traffic.*

_F_ 10. There was always something of interest *to see at the old museum,*

□EXERCISE 2

_F_ 1. Where we had the most wonderful picnic last year *was on a tiny island*

_F_ 2. While she sat in the shade and drank lemonade *I mowed the lawn.*

_S_ 3. Don't try to stop me,

_F_ 4. Because I know she will understand *I will explain my problem to her.*

_F_ 5. After I came home and took a long shower *I felt revived.*

_F_ 6. Because most of my spelling problems are caused by writing too fast, *I am learning to write slower.*

_F_   7. As I become more and more sure of my sentences *my writing becomes easier*

_S_   8. I enjoy writing papers,

_F_   9. Before I took this course and learned a few rules *my writing was horrible*

_S_   10. The rules aren't really so difficult *once you understand them*

□EXERCISE 3

_F_   1. Even though he had taken her out once

_F_   2. Although I didn't know that he was resigning

_F_   3. When he had rested up after his long trek

_F_   4. Something that I had always wanted to do

_F_   5. When you try your hardest and then get a poor grade

_S_   6. Make out a study schedule,

_F_   7. Which is what I should have done long ago

_F_   8. While he just stood there and waited

_S_   9. Keep calm.

_F_   10. Although I could think of nothing to say

□EXERCISE 4

_S_   1. The snowplow was a welcome sight.

_F_   2. Since it had been snowing for two days

_S_   3. He asked her to go out for coffee.

_F_   4. Which she declined to do

_F_   5. When he placed his name on the ballot

_S_   6. He campaigned faithfully for weeks,

_S_   7. I never tired of talking to her,

_F_   8. Whenever I remembered those days in the North

_F_   9. If I had it to do over

_S_   10. I couldn't see very far ahead

Underline the subject once and the verb twice in both the independent and the dependent clauses. Then put a broken line under the dependent clause.

□EXERCISE 5

1. You have to practice until using the rules of writing becomes automatic.
2. If you use this book correctly, it will help you to write better.
3. The only difference between an independent and a dependent clause is that the dependent clause begins with a dependent word.
4. If you know the dependent words, you'll have no trouble.
5. If you don't know them, you may not punctuate your sentences correctly.
6. A comma is required when a dependent clause comes first in a sentence.
7. No comma is required when the dependent clause comes last.
8. When you have done a few sentences, the rule becomes easy.
9. It will help you when you are punctuating your papers.
10. When you punctuate correctly, your reader can read your writing with ease.

□EXERCISE 6

1. The trouble with most children's television programs is that they do everything for the child.
2. I believe that a child should have time for spontaneous play.
3. "Mr. Roger's Neighborhood" is a good program for children who get too much negative criticism.
4. His neighborhood is a special place where everyone is an important person.
5. Mr. Roger's central message is that each person is acceptable and unique.
6. This is a psychiatric theory that is good for adults too.
7. It's also a major tenet of the Judeo-Christian ethic.
8. I don't know what tenet means.
9. I've just looked it up in the dictionary and find that it means "belief."
10. I'm looking up more words than I used to.

Underline the dependent clauses in these sentences.

□EXERCISE 7

1. I now look up almost all the words that I don't know.

2. When I look them up immediately and learn them in their context, I am more likely to remember them.

3. In 1976 there were 800,000 junior college students who were 25 to 34 years of age and 490,000 who were over 35 years of age.

4. Many of these adult students go on to new careers which they are preparing themselves for.

5. It is impossible to describe the color red to someone who has always been blind.

6. I ordered chilled vichyssoise but had no idea what it would be.

7. They have reached the age when they take the elevator instead of the stairs.

8. Did our genetic inheritance come about through blind chance or as the result of some purposeful thrust that pervades the universe?

9. The chimp at the zoo clapped his hands when the onlookers clapped theirs.

10. When they stopped, he continued clapping.

□EXERCISE 8

1. Since I started to keep a journal, I've begun to enjoy writing.

2. I think that I'll write something in my journal every day now.

3. When I write my own sentences, I really learn the rules.

4. Anyone can learn to spell if he sets his mind to it.

5. When you write a paper, say what you think.

6. Do not worry about what you "ought to say."

7. You cannot write well unless you have conviction.

8. A diplomat is someone who remembers a lady's birthday but forgets her age.

9. You can make any situation tolerable if you work at it.

10. Our forefathers didn't need as much machinery to run a farm as we need to run a lawn.

□EXERCISE 9

1. Self-discipline is the only discipline that really matters.

2. Since he couldn't find love, he sought esteem.

3. That judge has been successful with juvenile cases because he cares.

4. As far as my family is concerned, they always back me.

5. When I wanted to get away, I'd climb up that little hill to my fort.

6. Even though it's now gone, that fort was the important spot of my childhood.

7. Some matter in the universe is so dense that one teaspoonful of it would weigh as much as 200 million elephants.

8. The light from one galaxy started to come to us 100 million years ago when dinosaurs were on earth, but it is reaching us only now.

9. When you love your work, the difference between work and play disappears.

10. When I have written a good paper, I feel satisfied.

□EXERCISE 10

1. On the windows were the curtains that had hung in her college room.

2. When she looked at them, she thought of those rewarding days.

3. As she reminisced, she hung some pictures.

4. She hung them exactly where she wanted them.

5. She was doing what she had always wanted to do.

6. The use of garbage as fuel is becoming an increasingly popular idea as we face a growing shortage of energy.

7. Some farmers are objecting to the mechanization of farm jobs even though mechanization makes farming more efficient.

8. They are complaining that too many jobs will be lost.

9. The mechanization, however, is usually of jobs that are difficult for people to do.

10. Mechanization may save an industry even though some jobs are lost.

WRITING YOUR OWN SENTENCES

Now that you are aware of independent and dependent clauses, you can vary the sentences you write. On a separate sheet write eight sentences, **each containing two independent clauses** connected by one of the following words. Be sure to use the correct punctuation—comma or semicolon.

consequently	and
but	thus
therefore	nevertheless
however	then

Now make up eight sentences, **each containing one independent and one dependent clause,** using the following dependent words. If you put the dependent clause first, put a comma after it.

although	unless
after	until
while	because
since	if

Finally, look through the papers that have been handed back to you, and write correctly any fragments or run-together sentences that have been marked.

MORE ABOUT FRAGMENTS

We have seen that a dependent clause alone is a fragment. Any group of words that does not have a subject and verb is also a fragment.

Paid no attention to his parents (no subject)
Joe thinking about all his problems (no adequate verb. Although *ing* words look like verbs, no *ing* word alone can ever be a verb of a sentence. It must have another verb in front of it.)
Speeding along the highway (no subject and no adequate verb)
The announcement that we had expected (no verb for the independent clause)

To change these fragments into sentences, we must give each a subject and an adequate verb:

He paid no attention to his parents. (We added a subject.)

Joe was thinking about all his problems. (We put a verb in front of the *ing* word to make an adequate verb.)

Speeding along the highway, he had an accident. (We added an independent clause.)
The announcement that we had expected finally came. (We added a verb for the independent clause.)

Sometimes you can tack a fragment onto the independent clause before or after it; other times it is better to make it into a new sentence.

Are fragments ever permissible? Increasingly fragments are being used in advertising and in other kinds of writing. On pages 73–74 you will find some advertisements that use fragments. The fragments are used to give a dramatic pause between ideas or to emphasize each individual part of the sentence. But always they are used by writers who know what they are doing. They are used intentionally, never in error. Until you are an experienced writer, stick with complete sentences. Especially in college writing, fragments should not be used.

EXERCISES

Write S (sentence) or F (fragment). Put a period after each sentence, and make each fragment into a complete sentence. Don't skip any of these. Be tough on yourself. By making every one of these fragments into a sentence, you'll learn to avoid fragments in your own writing.

□EXERCISE 1

_F_ 1. Thinking we had missed the turn several miles back and not wanting to turn around, *we kept on going.*

_F_ 2. Leaving me standing there holding the bag, *my mother went to unlock the door.*

_F_ 3. Not just guys my own age but younger and older people too. *Seventeen people were going on the trip,*

_S_ 4. He wrote for an hour before he realized that he was answering the wrong question.

_F_ 5. Never believing anyone would come to my rescue *I gave up hope.*

_F_ 6. No matter if we won or lost *we still played fair*

_F_ 7. Causing the streets in the inner city to be more dangerous than those in the suburbs

_F_ 8. Going to meetings that served no purpose, *Jill decided she was wasting her time.*

_S_ 9. He decided to take charge of his life.

_F_ 10. Doing only the things that he wanted to do *didn't make his mother very happy*

□EXERCISE 2

_F_ 1. Confidence that was built up after each win *made our team spirit soar.*

_F_ 2. If he were someone whom I could sit down and talk to *we might settle our difference.*

_F_ 3. Training that he'll get only at home *will help him in later life.*

_S_ 4. Learning to say no has been difficult for me.

_F_ 5. How living on your own can become a hassle *would be a good topic for a discussion.*

_F_ 6. Writing a clear thesis statement and backing it up with reasons *is what a college professor expect*

_F_ 7. That we'll all have to work together if we're going to make a go of it *is something the whole group will have to understand*

_F_ 8. With every step making my tired aching muscles come alive with pain *I tried to think of pleasant thots to occupy my mind*

_F_ 9. Being able to walk in a peaceful atmosphere without the constant fear of being mugged *is something everyone should be able to do*

_S_ 10. She looked in shop windows at the many things that she did not want

□EXERCISE 3

_S_ 1. Begin at the beginning .

_F_ 2. If you do things for other people without being asked *they'll return the favor*

_F_ 3. Then, of course, the many interesting people in this job *have all had higher education*.

_F_ 4. Something that will take years of experience to learn *is something guff didn't want to learn*;

_F_ 5. People competing with one another to be the best *is good as long as sportsmanship is exercised*

_F_ 6. How to make your own decisions instead of letting someone make

them for you *is a good policy to learn*

_F_ 7. Words that say what I want said in less time and in less space *are words I don't know the meaning of*

_F_ 8. Caring enough about a person that you do not wish to interfere

with her development *is sometimes hard to do*

_S_ 9. Making a summary is excellent training in writing briefly .

_S_ 10. Writing a journal is good training too.

□EXERCISE 4

_F_ 1. This being Friday and with nothing to do *we decided to do our homework*

_S_ 2. When depression comes, tackle yourself instead of blaming

circumstances ,

_S_ 3. Just watching the game on television was exciting ,

_F_ 4. Many times when I'm on edge because I've had a bad day *I snap at my father & mother*

_F_ 5. All day walking, boating, and generally having a good time *tends to make one very sleepy*

_F_ 6. For instance taking care of my financial needs *is a rather trying job*.

_F_ 7. As if he really knew what he was talking about, *he stood in front of the class & talked for 2 hrs.*

_S_ 8. Making my own decisions was easy for me ,

_F_ 9. When I suddenly heard a car door slam and the sound of many

excited voices *I realized my brother had come home*

_F_ 10. Trying to prevent the man you are guarding from scoring a

basket *doesn't always prove successful*

72 SENTENCE STRUCTURE AND AGREEMENT

☐EXERCISE 5

F 1. Trudging through the snow over miles of windy prairie

F 2. *We* Went to the store Saturday and bought most of my Christmas presents.

F 3. Speeding down the highway at 70 miles an hour

S 4. Although we didn't hear all of his speech, we liked what we heard.

F 5. Not having anything to do but rest all day and wait for the phone to ring

F 6. Sitting there breathlessly watching all afternoon

F 7. The singer then coming down to the footlights *bowed at the applause he received.*

F 8. Having studied really hard and wanting desperately to pass that test, *I was pleased when I saw my grade*

F 9. Driving past her house a dozen times a day, *the boy couldn't get up enuf courage to stop*

F 10. Had to live on yogurt for a week

☐EXERCISE 6

F 1. Lillian working toward her premed degree

F 2. Didn't know what to do

F 3. The new rule that we didn't think was democratic *caused many problems.*

F 4. No matter whose business it was, *she should have never interfered*

S 5. Giving her help was always rewarding.

F 6. Giving her the help that she needed *gave him a feeling of usefulness*

F 7. When he realized exactly what had happened *he was extremely shocked*

F 8. As is always the case when you are in a hurry *you forget something*

F 9. Having driven 600 miles that day *his legs were cramped*

F 10. The speaker trying to ignore the interruption *became flustered*

□EXERCISE 7

F   1. Finding that little things no longer bothered her

S   2. Thinking well of himself was the most important thing to him ,

F   3. The president giving his employees a pep talk

F   4. While he turned on the oven and set the table , *she cooked the rest of the meal.*

S   5. The Hospital Volunteers meeting was postponed until another

day ,

F   6. Having worked at painting that room all day without even stopping

for lunch , *Jill was famished by dinnertime*

S   7. Working steadily, he finished painting the room that evening ,

S   8. He stopped me at a time when I was too busy to talk ,

F   9. My hobby being one which not many people are interested in

F 10. Hoping all the time that he would call her

The following excerpts are from recent advertisements. For various reasons, the writers have chosen to use fragments. Change each one, getting rid of the fragments, so that it would be acceptable as college writing. In some you may need only to tack the fragment onto the independent clause before or after it by crossing out the period and capital letter. In others you will also need to add the proper punctuation between independent and dependent clauses.

□EXERCISE 8

1. Some of the new compact, automatic cameras seem very easy to use. Until you start using them. (Minolta XG-7)
2. Get tough. Get a tough Case Lawn and Garden Tractor. We're looking for tough customers who'll ask a lot of hard questions. Because we've got the right answers. (Case, a Tenneco Company)
3. I went back home. To see it for the first time. (Pan Am)
4. Discover a new Horizon. A breakthrough in American automobiles. Plymouth Horizon comes alive with new comforts. New confidence. Room for four big people. And front wheel drive for excellent stability. (Chrysler Corporation)

☐ **EXERCISE 9**

1. The last place your banker ought to be is in the bank. He ought to be in your office, your plant, on your farm. Learning your markets, your processes, your business. (Jefferson Bank, Peoria)

2. If you don't plan your estate, someone else will. The Government will decide who gets what. Federal and state laws will determine what your estate is worth, how much of it will go for taxes and any other claims against it. And, most importantly, how much will be left for your beneficiaries. (The Prudential Insurance Company of America)

3. We invite you to claim your inheritance. The village where your father was born. The marketplace where your great grandmother shopped. The streets they walked as children. They're all part of the memories your ancestors brought to America. They can be your memories for the price of a tour. (Pan Am)

4. In fact, 1978 promises to be the most colorful year in Time's history. Because Time has just dramatically increased its use of color photography. (Time, Inc.)

☐ **EXERCISE 10**

1. Inside this GE set is advanced computer-like circuitry that uses this VIR signal. To let the broadcaster automatically adjust all of the color on many programs. (General Electric)

2. Outward Bound is a shot of high adventure in the wilderness. And a lot more. It's a trip that'll show you what you're made of. You can discover you can do almost anything you want—if you try. Our 3-week experience in self-confidence sure isn't easy. But it might just last you the rest of your life. We have special managers' courses, courses for women, courses for your sons and daughters. All in varying lengths. (Outward Bound)

3. Delta is an airline run by professionals. Like Arlan Ellmaker, Weather Analyst. He's earned a degree in meteorology. Spent four years with the Air Force weather service. And he's been plotting Delta flights for the past seven years. (Delta Airlines, Inc.)

4. At Americana, we think getting well is a beautiful thing. Which should happen in an exceptional place. That's why people like us. We're exceptional. Our equipment is exceptional. Our attitude is exceptional. For example: we believe in fine health care at a reasonable cost. For both short, post-hospital stays and long stays. (Americana Healthcare Corporation)

Review of Run-together Sentences and Fragments

Put periods and capital letters in these selections so that there will be no run-together sentences or fragments.

1. Robert Frost is undoubtedly the most beloved American poet people who are indifferent to most poetry can often quote "Birches" or "Stopping by Woods on a Snowy Evening" he writes about the countryside and the country people of Vermont and about his own choice to take the road less traveled by.

2. There's a place set deep in the woods of northern Minnesota which is very special to me every time I go there I'm surrounded with feelings of serenity the quietness of the area is something that I don't find anywhere else there's an occasional cry of a hawk circling up above, and sometimes I hear chipmunks scurrying around in the leaves on the ground these noises always make me feel closer to nature I sometimes wish that I could be as free as that hawk or as carefree as that chipmunk.

3. I began wrestling seriously my freshman year the head wrestling coach was walking around and talking to the kids playing football he was looking for recruits for the upcoming wrestling season several of my friends had decided that they would go out for the team I decided wrestling would be a good way to keep busy through the winter looking back over my wrestling years, I feel it was good for me I learned that through hard work I could accomplish my goals my career in wrestling is something that I can take pride in.

4. I know what the chances of survival from cancer are, but I can't give up I learned as a child during the Depression that it isn't what you've lost but what you've got left that counts the important thing in any setback is whether you can pick yourself up one reason I can keep going is that I have an interest in tomorrow, something to live for.

—Hubert Humphrey

Here are the first four paragraphs of Martin Luther King's speech "I Have a Dream," given to 200,000 people gathered in front of the Lincoln Memorial in Washington on August 28, 1963. As King spoke, the audience could see the huge statue of Lincoln in the background.

The four paragraphs are printed here without the periods and capital letters that separate the sentences. Read the speech aloud and put in the periods and capital letters. Remember that each sentence must have at least one independent clause. If a dependent clause comes first in a sentence, put a comma after it. Correct your work by that at the back of the book.

"I Have a Dream . . ."

Martin Luther King, Jr.

Five score years ago, a great American, in whose symbolic shadow we stand, signed the Emancipation Proclamation this momentous decree came as a great beacon light of hope to millions of Negro slaves who had been seared in the flames of withering injustice it came as a joyous daybreak to end the long night of captivity

But one hundred years later, we must face the tragic fact that the Negro is still not free one hundred years later, the life of the Negro is still sadly crippled by the manacles of segregation and the chains of discrimination one hundred years later, the Negro lives on a lonely island of poverty in the midst of a vast ocean of material prosperity one hundred years later, the Negro is still languished in the corners of American society and finds himself an exile in his own land so we have come here today to dramatize an appalling condition

In a sense we have come to our nation's Capital to cash a check when the architects of our republic wrote the magnificent words of the Constitution and the Declaration of Independence they were signing a promissory note to which every American was to fall heir this note was a promise that all men would be guaranteed the unalienable rights of life, liberty, and the pursuit of happiness

It is obvious today that America has defaulted on this promissory note insofar as her citizens of color are concerned instead of honoring this sacred obligation, America has given the Negro people a bad check, a check which has come back marked "insufficient funds" but we refuse to believe that the bank of justice is bankrupt we refuse to believe that there are insufficient funds in the great vaults of opportunity of this nation so we have come to cash this check—a check that will give us upon demand the riches of freedom and the security of justice we have also come to this hallowed spot to remind America of the fierce urgency of now this is no time to engage in the luxury of cooling off or to take the tranquilizing drug of gradualism now is the time to make real the promises of Democracy now is the time to rise from the dark and desolate valley of segregation to the sunlit path of racial justice now is the time to open the doors of opportunity to all of God's children now is the time to lift our nation from the quicksands of racial injustice to the solid rock of brotherhood

USING STANDARD ENGLISH VERBS

This chapter and the next are for those who need practice in using Standard English verbs. Even though you may not make most of the errors discussed in these two chapters, it may be a good idea to work through the exercises because you are almost sure to find some verb forms that you use incorrectly.

Many of us grew up speaking a dialect other than Standard English, whether it was in a farm community where people said *I ain't* and *he don't* and *they was* or in a black community where people said *I is* and *it do* and *they has*. Such dialects are colorful and powerful in their place, but in college and in the wider world, everyone must use Standard English so that English-speaking people all over the world can understand. Frequently, though, after a student has learned to speak and write Standard English, he goes back to his home community and is able to slip back into his old dialect while he is there. Thus he has really become bilingual, able to use two languages—or at least two dialects.

The following tables compare four verbs in one of the community dialects with the same four verbs in Standard English. Memorize the Standard English forms of these important verbs. Most verbs have endings like the first verb *walk*. The other three verbs are irregular and are important because they are used not only as main verbs but also as helping verbs. We'll be using them as helping verbs in the next chapter.

Don't go on to the exercises until you have memorized the forms of these Standard English verbs.

REGULAR VERB: WALK

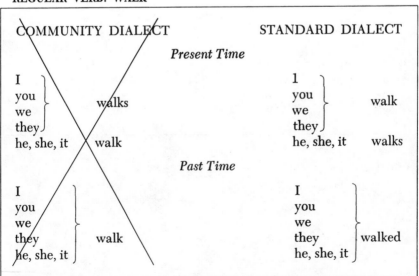

IRREGULAR VERB: HAVE

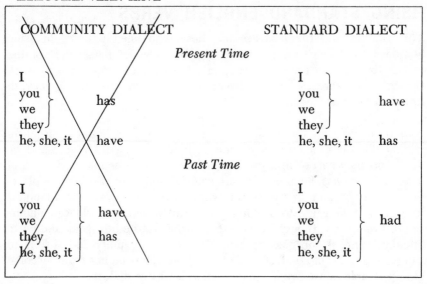

IRREGULAR VERB: BE

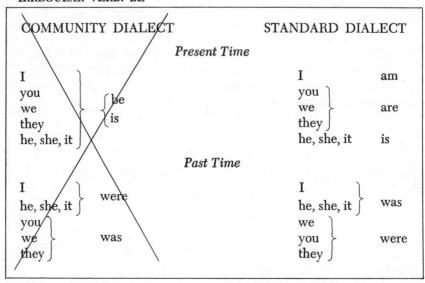

IRREGULAR VERB: DO

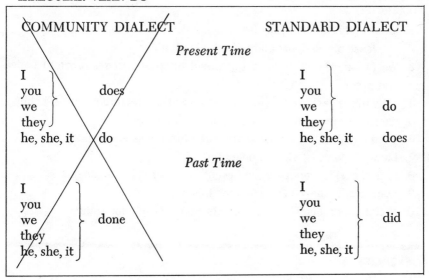

COMMUNITY DIALECT   STANDARD DIALECT

Present Time

| I, you, we, they | does |
| he, she, it | do |

| I, you, we, they | do |
| he, she, it | does |

Past Time

| I, you, we, they, he, she, it | done |

| I, you, we, they, he, she, it | did |

EXERCISES

Underline the Standard English verb form. All of the verbs follow the pattern of the regular verb **walk** (Table p. 77) except for the three irregular verbs **have, be,** and **do** (Tables pp. 78–79). Keep referring to the tables if you are not sure which form to use. Don't guess! Correct your answers for each exercise before going on to the next.

□EXERCISE 1

1. Yesterday when I (walk walked) to class, I (happen happened) to see Tony.
2. Tony (doesn't don't) know what he (want wants) to be.
3. Last year he (drop dropped) out of college, but this fall he (return returned).
4. He (do does) better now in all his courses.
5. He (ask asked) me to listen to the history paper he had written.
6. He read it to me, and that (help helped) him catch some errors.
7. We (finish finished) class early, and afterward I (talk talked) to the professor.
8. We (discuss discussed) my term paper, and his comments (help helped) me.
9. He (enjoy enjoyed) reading my paper.
10. I (work worked) hard on that paper; everyone (work works) hard in that class.

□EXERCISE 2

1. Later that afternoon Tony (ask asked) me to go out for coffee.
2. It (please pleased) me that he (ask asked) me.
3. We (walk walked) down to the Sweet Shop and (order ordered) coffee and pizza.
4. Tony (like likes) pizza now, but last year he always (order ordered) chili.
5. We (was were) at the Sweet Shop until six o'clock.
6. Then I (had has) to go home because I (need needed) to study.
7. I always (do does) all my homework.
8. I (has have) to work because I (want wants) an A in that course.
9. I (suggest suggests) that you read this book.
10. Historical novels (interest interests) you, (doesn't don't) they?

□EXERCISE 3

1. We (was were) at Dick's housewarming last week.
2. You (was were) there too, (wasn't weren't) you?
3. Most of the guests (was were) from out of town.
4. Everything I (observe observed) at the museum was interesting.
5. We (start started) our campaign last week.
6. You (are is) welcome to join our group; he (be is) welcome too.
7. They (ask asked) me to help with the balloting.
8. I (do does) what I (want wants) to do; he (do does) what he (want wants) to do.
9. I (did done) all my homework last night before I (watch watched) TV.
10. She (was were) at the movies last night, and she (be is) there again tonight.

□EXERCISE 4

1. She (do does) whatever (please pleases) her.
2. She (loan loaned) me the picture but (ask asked) that I return it.
3. One of my sisters (take takes) math; the other two (take takes) biology.
4. We (jog jogged) all the way to the cafeteria yesterday.
5. André and I both (like likes) to ski.
6. We (want wanted) to go skiing last weekend, but it (was were) too warm.
7. Since it (be is) snowing today, we (hope hopes) to go tomorrow.
8. I (have had) not met André until last month when our friends (invite invited) us to go skiing.
9. He (do does) good work in college.
10. He (want wants) to do something worthwhile with his life.

□EXERCISE 5

1. The small box (contain contains) pencils; the big boxes (contain contains) chalk.
2. Next week I (hope hopes) to write an application for a job.
3. I (enjoy enjoys) chemistry, but Dennis (drop dropped) his chemistry course last week.
4. I (wonder wonders) why he (did done) that.
5. I (talk talked) to my cousin on the phone yesterday.
6. I (stop stopped) at his house last evening, and he (cook cooked) dinner for me.
7. I always (has have) a good time at his house because I (agree agrees) with him about most things.
8. I (use used) to know him when we (was were) little fellows.
9. I (play played) the piano when I (was were) small, and I still (play plays) a little.
10. I never (perform performs) in public though.

□EXERCISE 6

1. I (doze dozed) off during that lecture yesterday.
2. The taxi driver (scare scared) me with his fast driving last night.
3. We (finish finished) dinner early and (decide decided) to go for a walk.
4. I (discover discovered) who my real friends were that day.
5. She (appear appears) happy these days.
6. She (seal sealed) the envelopes and put them in the mailbox.
7. The class (discuss discussed) the essay in small groups.
8. The instructor then (hand handed) out questions to be answered.
9. I (did done) my best, and I think I (answer answered) them all correctly.
10. That class period (benefit benefited) all the students.

□EXERCISE 7

1. The policeman (walk walked) up to me and (ask asked) my name yesterday.
2. I (happen happened) to witness the car accident.
3. He (suppose supposed) I would be a witness.
4. I (learn learned) that the trial would take several days.
5. I (ask asked) if I could be excused.
6. He said no and (walk walked) away.
7. My mother never (complain complained) about her lack of money during those years.
8. Now she (has have) all the money anyone could want.
9. She (help helps) me all she can.
10. She (do does) the best she can for all her children.

□EXERCISE 8

1. It (occur occurs) to me that I should study more.
2. This book (contain contains) the rules you (need needs) to know about English.
3. If you (do does) all the exercises, you'll gain confidence.
4. If you (do does) a lot of writing, your writing is sure to improve.
5. I (listen listened) to the instructor's explanation yesterday and now (has have) no more trouble.
6. My friends (doesn't don't) always get to class on time.
7. They always (manage manages) to get to parties on time though.
8. They (are is) determined they (are is) going to do better.
9. The instructor's criticism (bother bothers) them.
10. They (are is) determined to get to class on time from now on.

□EXERCISE 9

1. You (perform performed) very well with the rock band last night.
2. You (perform performs) well on the football field every day too.
3. The coach (influence influences) his students.
4. He (insist insists) on good sportsmanship.
5. His students (endeavor endeavors) to win, but they (want wants) mainly to play a good game.
6. I (hope hopes) someday to be a coach, so I (has have) to work hard.
7. My parents (celebrate celebrated) their silver wedding anniversary last month.
8. We (surprise surprised) them with a party.
9. I (work worked) with a lawn crew during the summer, but I (doesn't don't) work now.
10. The other day I (volunteer volunteered) to help with a day camp.

□EXERCISE 10

1. I (attend attended) a music camp last summer.
2. I (play plays) the French horn now, but I (play played) the trombone a year ago.
3. I (expect expects) to go to the camp again this coming summer.
4. We (work worked) hard there last summer, and we (learn learned) a lot.
5. It (be is) fun to be with so many other musicians.
6. I (plan plans) to major in music and (want wants) to be a professional musician.
7. If I (change changes) my mind, I still (has have) a good hobby for all my life.
8. Playing cards (bore bores) me, but I (enjoy enjoys) dancing.
9. Her paper really (impress impressed) me when it was read in class.
10. It (contain contained) plenty of specific details that (was were) interesting.

STANDARD ENGLISH VERBS (compound forms)

In the last chapter we talked about the present and past forms of the regular verb *walk*. Other forms of the regular verb may be used with helping verbs. Here is a table showing all the forms of some regular verbs and the various helping verbs they are used with.

REGULAR VERBS

BASE FORM (Use with *can, may, shall, will, could, might, should, would, must.*)	PRESENT	PAST	PAST PARTICIPLE (Use with *have, has, had.* Or use with some form of *be* to make a passive verb.)	ING FORM (Use with *am, is, are, was, were.*)
ask	ask (s)	asked	asked	asking
dance	dance (s)	danced	danced	dancing
decide	decide (s)	decided	decided	deciding
enjoy	enjoy (s)	enjoyed	enjoyed	enjoying
finish	finish (es)	finished	finished	finishing
happen	happen (s)	happened	happened	happening
learn	learn (s)	learned	learned	learning
like	like (s)	liked	liked	liking
need	need (s)	needed	needed	needing
open	open (s)	opened	opened	opening
start	start (s)	started	started	starting
suppose	suppose (s)	supposed	supposed	supposing
walk	walk (s)	walked	walked	walking
want	want (s)	wanted	wanted	wanting

Sometimes a past participle is used with some form of the verb *be* (or verbs that take the place of *be* like *appear, seem, look, feel, get, act, become*) to describe the subject.

He is dissatisfied.
He was confused.
He has been disappointed.
He appeared frustrated. (He was frustrated.)
He seems interested in her. (He is interested in her.)
He looked surprised. (He was surprised.)
He feels frightened. (He is frightened.)
He gets bored easily. (He is bored easily.)
He acts concerned. (He is concerned.)
He became disillusioned. (He was disillusioned.)
He was supposed to go with her.

Usually these past participles are called describing words that describe the subject rather than being called part of the verb of the sentence. What you call them doesn't matter. The only important thing is to be sure you use the correct form of the past participle (*ed* for regular verbs).

And still one more verb form must be mentioned. Sometimes the subject of the sentence neither *does* nor *is* anything. It just stays there passive in the sentence and is acted upon.

The lesson was studied by the children.

The subject is *lesson.* It doesn't do anything. It is passive. It is acted upon by the children Thus we say that *was studied* is a passive verb. All you really need to remember is that whenever a form of *be* is used with a past participle, you must be sure to use the correct past participle form (*ed* for regular verbs).

This is what the compound verbs tell:

1. *Have* or *has* + past participle
   tells about something that began in the past and continues into the present:

   I have walked to school every day this year.

2. *Had* + past participle
   tells about something that began and was completed in the distant past:

   I had walked to school before I broke my leg.

3. *Am, is,* or *are* + the *ing* form
   tells about something that is happening now:

   I am walking for my health now.

4. *Was* or *were* + the *ing* form
   tells about something that was happening in the past:

   I was walking for my health last year.

5. *Can, may, shall, will, could, might, should, would, must* + the base form
   tells about something that could, might, should, would, or must happen:

   I can walk; I may walk; I shall walk; I will walk; I could walk; I might walk; I should walk; I would walk; I must walk.

6. Any form of the verb *be* + the past participle
    either describes the subject:

    I was frightened.

or shows the subject being acted upon (passive voice):

    The lesson was studied by the children.

All the verbs in the table on page 83 are regular. That is, they are all formed in the same way—with an *ed* ending on the past form and on the past participle. But many verbs are irregular. Their past and past participle forms change spelling instead of just adding an *ed*. Here is a table of some irregular verbs. (The present and the *ing* forms are not usually given in a list of principal parts because they are formed easily from the base form and cause no trouble.) Refer to this list when you are not sure which verb form to use. Eventually you should memorize the entire list.

IRREGULAR VERBS

BASE FORM	PAST	PAST PARTICIPLE
be	was, were	been
become	became	become
begin	began	begun
break	broke	broken
bring	brought	brought
buy	bought	bought
build	built	built
catch	caught	caught
choose	chose	chosen
come	came	come
do	did	done
drive	drove	driven
eat	ate	eaten
fall	fell	fallen
feel	felt	felt
fight	fought	fought
find	found	found
forget	forgot	forgotten
forgive	forgave	forgiven
give	gave	given
go	went	gone
grow	grew	grown
have	had	had

IRREGULAR VERBS (continued)

BASE FORM	PAST	PAST PARTICIPLE
hold	held	held
keep	kept	kept
know	knew	known
lead	led	led
leave	left	left
lose	lost	lost
make	made	made
meet	met	met
ride	rode	ridden
rise	rose	risen
run	ran	run
say	said	said
see	saw	seen
sell	sold	sold
shine	shone	shone
sing	sang	sung
sleep	slept	slept
speak	spoke	spoken
stand	stood	stood
take	took	taken
teach	taught	taught
tell	told	told
think	thought	thought
throw	threw	thrown
wake	woke	waked
wear	wore	worn
win	won	won
write	wrote	written

EXERCISES

Write in the correct form of the verb. Refer to the tables on pages 83 and 85 and to the explanations if you are not sure which form to use with a certain helping verb. Be sure not to do more than ten sentences at a time before checking your answers.

□EXERCISE 1

walk   1. I have _____ ten miles since morning.

walk   2. She has _____ downtown twice today.

walk   3. My mother had _____ to her meeting.

walk   4. I am _____ more these days.

walk   5. We could _____ if you prefer.

walk   6. We might _____ through the orchard.

walk   7. I should _____ more for exercise.

walk   8. I can't _____ that far.

walk   9. I have _____ farther than anybody.

walk   10. They had _____ most of the way.

□EXERCISE 2

finish   1. I have _____ my outside reading in biology.

finish   2. Now I must _____ my term paper.

finish   3. I will _____ it by Saturday, I think.

finish   4. I _____ my last term paper in a week.

finish   5. It was _____ even before it was due.

finish   6. I may _____ this one early too.

finish   7. I could _____ it early if I worked steadily.

finish 8. I can _____ it easily by next week.

finish 9. I should _____ it before that though.

finish 10. Well, I'm _____ with talking about that paper.

□EXERCISE 3

invite 1. I am _____ to a dance tonight.

dance 2. I have _____ a lot this fall.

go 3. I have _____ to dozens of parties.

open 4. I haven't _____ a book since yesterday.

start 5. I _____ my history assignment last week.

suppose 6. I have read all I was _____ to read.

do 7. I haven't _____ as much reading as I had intended to though.

confuse 8. He was _____ by the instructions.

depress 9. He felt _____ after he heard the news.

surprise 10. My friends were _____ that I won the trophy.

□EXERCISE 4

prepare 1. A fancy lunch was _____ for the guests.

eat 2. All my cookies were _____ in five minutes.

suppose 3. She was _____ to call me last night.

come 4. Someone has _____ to see you.

disappoint 5. He seems _____ that you aren't ready.

finish 6. Are you almost _____ with your shower?

begin 7. He has _____ to get impatient.

fall 8. The ball had _____ into the stands.

catch 9. She had _____ it as it fell.

happen 10. She just _____ to be sitting where it fell.

□**EXERCISE 5**

go

1. Albert has _____ away to college.

need

2. He _____ to get away from home.

do

3. He has _____ well in his studies.

enjoy

4. Also he has _____ the athletic program.

decide

5. He has _____ to return there for his sophomore year.

sing

6. Sabina _____ in the choir now.

sing

7. She may _____ a solo in the musical next month.

sing

8. She has _____ solos several times.

recommend

9. She was _____ for a scholarship.

sing

10. I think she could _____ professionally if she wished.

□**EXERCISE 6**

tell

1. I have _____ her she has a good voice.

think

2. I had _____ she would major in music.

surprise

3. She appeared _____ when I told her that.

break

4. I _____ my glasses yesterday.

break

5. It's the first time I've ever _____ them.

shatter

6. They were _____ to pieces.

drive

7. We _____ to a snack bar after the movie.

eat

8. We had _____ only a light dinner.

have

9. Therefore we _____ some sandwiches and coffee.

want

10. We decided that we also _____ some dessert.

□EXERCISE 7

like   1. I have always _____ train trips.

meet   2. I have always _____ such interesting people on trains.

meet   3. Yesterday I _____ a man who designs model airplanes.

build   4. He has _____ some too.

suppose   5. His models are _____ to be the top of the line.

teach   6. On another trip I met a girl who has _____ handicapped children for three years.

devote   7. She seemed _____ to her work.

enjoy   8. The children have _____ her classes.

give   9. Another person whom I met _____ flute lessons now.

give   10. He has _____ flute lessons for many years.

□EXERCISE 8

design   1. Then I met an engineer who now _____ bridges.

concern   2. She is _____ about not damaging the environment.

catch   3. I have _____ the morning train to Terre Haute every weekend this spring.

suppose   4. I was _____ to meet my cousin at the train station yesterday.

surprise   5. I was _____ to find my uncle there also.

surprise   6. He looked _____ to see me too.

overwhelm   7. He appears _____ by his new job.

train   8. He isn't _____ for that job.

embarrass   9. She was _____ because she was late.

frighten   10. The child was _____ by the thunder.

☐**EXERCISE 9**

open   1. I had _____ the window too wide last night.

fall   2. The covers had _____ off my bed.

begin   3. It had _____ to get cold in the room by morning.

catch   4. I am _____ a cold.

discourage   5. I feel _____ about my health.

start   6. My friends have _____ their morning jogging.

go   7. They have _____ every morning this week.

ask   8. They have _____ me to go with them.

suppose   9. I was _____ to meet them this morning.

decide   10. But I have _____ to get my exercise by walking to the refrigerator.

☐**EXERCISE 10**

learn   1. I am _____ about the nesting habits of cranes.

learn   2. I have also _____ about the routes of various migrating birds.

speak   3. I _____ to her yesterday about her summer plans.

speak   4. I have _____ to her before about them.

speak   5. I will probably _____ to her about them again.

wear   6. That night she _____ the locket her daughter had given her.

wear   7. She has _____ it many times before.

like   8. She has always _____ it more than her other jewelry.

have   9. Do you think man _____ a free will?

determine   10. Or are his decisions _____ by what has happened to him in the past?

WRITING YOUR OWN SENTENCES

Write five sentences using verbs that you now realize you have been using incorrectly.

Avoiding Dialect Expressions

While verbs cause the most trouble for those who have grown up speaking a dialect other than Standard English, certain other expressions, more common in speech than in writing, should be avoided. Some (such as *he don't, you was*) have been discussed in previous chapters. A few others are listed here. Avoid them if you want to speak Standard English.

DIALECT	STANDARD ENGLISH
anywheres, nowheres, somewheres	anywhere, nowhere, somewhere
anyways	anyway
hisself, theirselves	himself, themselves
this here book, that there book, those there books	this book, that book, those books
he did good, she sang good	he did well, she sang well
my brother he plays ball	my brother plays ball
haven't no, haven't none, haven't never, haven't nothing, wasn't no, wasn't never (These are called double negatives.)	have no, have none, have never, have nothing, was no, was never

MAKING SUBJECTS, VERBS, AND PRONOUNS AGREE

All parts of a sentence should agree. In general if the subject is singular, the verb should be singular; if the subject is plural, the verb should be plural.

Each of the boys has his own room.

Over by the fireplace were two chairs.

There were two places at the long table.

The following words are singular and almost always take a singular verb:

(*one* words)	(*body* words)	
one	nobody	each
anyone	anybody	either
someone	somebody	neither
everyone	everybody	

One of my friends is a freshman.

Each of the students is responsible for one report.

Either of the girls is a good choice.

Sometimes, though, the verb agrees with the *intent* of the subject rather than with its actual form.

Neither of them were in. (The sentence means that both were not in.)

Such exceptions to the rule occur more often in conversation than in writing. Especially in college writing, it's wise to follow the correct grammatical form.

Here are some subject-verb pairs you can *always* be sure of:

you were	(*never* you was)
we were	(*never* we was)
they were	(*never* they was)
he doesn't	(*never* he don't)
she doesn't	(*never* she don't)
it doesn't	(*never* it don't)

The following "group" words take a singular verb if you are thinking of the group as a whole, but they take a plural verb if you are thinking of the individuals in the group:

group	band	heap
committee	flock	lot

crowd	class	audience
team	dozen	jury
family	kind	herd
number	public	

The group *is* planning a show. . . . . The group *are* giving their reports.
My family *is* behind me. . . . . My family *are* all scattered.
The number present *was* small. . . . A number *are* going to the rally.
A dozen *is* enough . . . . A dozen *are* going.
A lot *was* accomplished. . . . . A lot *were* late to class.

Not only should subject and verb agree. A pronoun, too, should agree with the word it refers to. If that word is singular, the pronoun should be singular; if that word is plural, the pronoun should be plural.

Each of the boys has *his* own room.

The pronoun *his* refers to the singular subject *Each* and therefore is singular.

Both of the boys have *their* own rooms.

The pronoun *their* refers to the plural subject *Both* and therefore is plural.

Modern usage, however, allows many exceptions to this rule, especially in conversation. When the word referred to is plural in *meaning*, even though singular in form, a plural pronoun may be used.

Everybody took off *their* hats as the parade went by.
Everyone was here, but *they* all went home early.
Everybody has *their* faults.

In all of these sentences the intent of the subject is to show that many people were involved. Therefore the plural pronouns are used even though the singular forms would be grammatically correct.

Today many people write *he or she* and *him or her* in an attempt to avoid sex bias, but such writing is often awkward and wordy. To avoid such wordiness, the pronouns *they, them,* and *their* are being used more and more frequently, particularly in conversation.

If *anyone* wants a ride, *they* can go in my car (less awkward than the grammatically correct *he or she can go in my car*).

If *anybody* calls, tell *them* I've left (less awkward than the grammatically correct tell *him or her* I've left).
Somebody has left *their* textbook here (less awkward than the grammatically correct *his or her* textbook).

Recently there has been a swing back to using *he, him,* and *his* to mean both sexes. For example, the new president of the University of Chicago, Hana Holborn Gray, said before her inauguration, "A university president doesn't give orders. He must persuade." In this book the universal pronouns *he, him,* and *his* are used to mean both sexes.

EXERCISES

Cross out the prepositional phrases so that you can find the subject. Then underline the correct verb in the parentheses. In some sentences you will also need to underline the correct pronoun. Use the correct grammatical form even though an alternate form may be acceptable in conversation. Check your answers ten at a time.

□EXERCISE 1

1. Nobody in our family (is are) going away this summer.
2. Donna and Wendy (was were) in the country for the weekend.
3. A number of us (is are) going on a bus trip to Santa Barbara next week.
4. There (was were) 30 people on the last trip we took.
5. Most of my friends (has have) traveled more than I have.
6. One of my friends (has have) just come back from Jacksonville.
7. Another one of my friends (goes go) to college in Corsicana, Texas.
8. I never knew that you (was were) from Kentucky.
9. I'll bet that they (was were) glad to see you down there.
10. We (was were) wondering whether you'd get back today.

□EXERCISE 2

1. Each of these chapters (presents present) an important rule.
2. And all of the exercises (helps help) you apply the rule.
3. Everyone who takes this course (is are) sure to improve (his their) writing.
4. If a person is serious about learning to write, (he they) will improve rapidly.
5. It (doesn't don't) matter to me whether I write beautifully; I just want to write clearly.
6. Only one of the members of the class (has have) finished (his their) paper.

7. Everybody in the class (is are) looking forward to hearing some of the papers read aloud.
8. One of my dreams (has have) always been to have a college degree.
9. Each one of my family (is are) wishing me success.
10. On my study table (stands stand) my typewriter and my books.

□**EXERCISE 3**

1. There (is are) two doctors and a dentist in that building.
2. Across the street (is are) a pharmacy and a clinic.
3. If a person agrees to do something, (he they) should do it.
4. You (was were) here first.
5. It (doesn't don't) matter; go ahead.
6. The reason that we (was were) late was that the sitter didn't come on time.
7. Nobody (knows know) much about the candidate except that he's a good tennis player.
8. Two of my absences from class (was were) because of my trip to Alabama.
9. You (was were) absent several days too, (wasn't weren't) you?
10. It's too bad that we (was were) absent for the panel discussions.

□**EXERCISE 4**

1. Each of Cheryl's brothers (is are) making something for her birthday.
2. Each of them (has have) been spending all of (his their) spare time on (his their) project.
3. There (is are) three kinds of dessert in the refrigerator.
4. Both of the boys (seems seem) too busy to think about eating though.
5. Each of them (needs need) more time on (his their) project.
6. You (was were) at the play last night, (wasn't weren't) you?
7. There (was were) many elaborate stage sets.
8. All of the characters (was were) well cast.
9. A couple of the main characters (hopes hope) to make a career of acting.
10. Each of them (has have) a desire to play on Broadway.

□**EXERCISE 5**

1. Everybody in our family (is are) going to the contest this afternoon.
2. Not a one of us (wants want) to miss it.
3. Each of the contestants (performs perform) best before an audience.
4. Each of the women (is are) presenting (her their) own interpretation of the novel.
5. (Wasn't Weren't) you amazed at her winning?
6. There (is are) fifteen horses in the featured race.

7. Each of the polo teams (is are) good in (its their) own way.
8. Luckily it (doesn't don't) look like rain today.
9. Each of those girls (claims claim) experience in mountain climbing.
10. Only one of them (has have) ever climbed this mountain before though.

□EXERCISE 6

1. One of my friends (intends intend) to go into law.
2. But another of my friends (plans plan) to drop out of college.
3. He (doesn't don't) intend to finish his education.
4. Two of my cousins (attends attend) Mars Hill College.
5. One of my cousins (has have) a job on weekends as well.
6. (Doesn't Don't) he ever sleep?
7. Each of my brothers (owns own) (his their) own car now.
8. Both of them (plans plan) to finish college in three years.
9. There (is are) two things I want to learn from this course.
10. Neither of them (is are) easy.

□EXERCISE 7

1. She goes to college in Conway, (doesn't don't) she?
2. I thought her brothers (was were) going to college there too.
3. I thought you (was were) majoring in music.
4. (Doesn't Don't) he work here any more?
5. All of them in the choir (is are) ready to go on stage.
6. If one of the substations (is are) knocked out, we can resort to the reserve station.
7. Each of the bird stamps (comes come) from a different country.
8. An all-day hike alone through the wilderness will teach a person a lot about (himself themselves).
9. Some of those math problems (is are) easy; most of them (is are) hard.
10. Now that we have heard his lecture, there still (remains remain) a number of questions.

□EXERCISE 8

1. One of my friends (has have) been selected to be on the committee to promote Bill 19, which is against age discrimination.
2. She really (doesn't don't) want to be on the committee.
3. All of her friends (was were) trying to persuade her to accept.
4. There (was were) two reasons for her reluctance to be on the committee.
5. She (doesn't don't) have time for it, and she (doesn't don't) feel qualified.
6. A number of people (is are) fighting Bill 19.

7. The members of the committee (intends intend) to work hard to see that it is passed.
8. It (doesn't don't) seem important to some people, and they may not vote.
9. Each of the committee members (has have) (his their) own way of arguing for the bill.
10. Each of them (stresses stress) a different aspect of the important problem.

□**EXERCISE 9**

1. At the opening of the new YMCA building there (was were) speakers from all over the country.
2. There (was were) gifts from all over the country too.
3. There (was were) a carved table and an old bookcase from the Historical Society.
4. All of the rooms in the building (was were) decorated by various organizations.
5. A person (doesn't don't) have to belong to the Y to enjoy its facilities.
6. (Was Were) you at the opening?
7. Two of the good aspects of the building (is are) its central location and its facilities for older as well as younger people.
8. Most of the townspeople (intends intend) to join.
9. All of the things that he did for me (has have) made me realize what I owe him.
10. You (was were) most helpful to me too.

□**EXERCISE 10**

1. Every one of the students in this class (gets get) to class on time.
2. If one of the students (is are) late, (he they) (miss misses) the one-sentence quiz given at the beginning of the hour.
3. The instructor dictates a sentence, and each of the students (writes write) it on a piece of paper and (hands hand) it in.
4. The sentence includes several of the points that (is are) in the day's assignment.
5. If a student gets the sentence correct (he they) (gets get) a mark in the instructor's record book.
6. If he misses any part of the sentence, he (doesn't don't) get a mark.
7. Most of the students (likes like) those quizzes because they are short and easy.
8. If a student has done all of (his their) exercises, (he they) usually (passes pass) the quiz.

9. The quiz (doesn't don't) take long, but it (gives give) a good idea of the student's progress.
10. If one of the students (comes come) in late, (he they) of course (misses miss) the test.

WRITING YOUR OWN SENTENCES

On a separate sheet write five sentences with correct agreement that you may formerly have had trouble with.

WRITING ASSIGNMENT

As you do the writing assignments that begin on page 182, are you keeping a list of your misspelled words on page 285?

CHOOSING THE RIGHT PRONOUN

Of the many kinds of pronouns, the following cause the most difficulty:

SUBJECT GROUP	NONSUBJECT GROUP
I	me
he	him
she	her
we	us
they	them

A pronoun in the Subject Group may be used in two ways:

1. as the subject of a verb:

    He is my brother. (*He* is the subject of the verb *is.*)

    We girls gave a party. (*We* is the subject of the verb *gave.*)

    He is taller than *I.* (The sentence is not written out in full. It means "He is taller than I am." *I* is the subject of the verb *am.*)

2. as a word that means the same as the subject:

    That boy in the blue jeans is *he.* (*He* is a word that means the same as the subject *boy.* Therefore the pronoun from the Subject Group is used.)

    It was *she* all right. (*She* means the same as the subject *It.* Therefore the pronoun from the Subject Group is used.)

    Modern usage allows some exceptions to this rule however. *It is me* and *it is us* (instead of the grammatically correct *It is I* and *it is we*) are now established usage, and *it is him, it is her,* and *it is them* are widely used, particularly in informal speech.

Pronouns in the Nonsubject Group are used for all other purposes. The following pronouns are not subjects, nor are they words that mean the same as subjects. Therefore they come from the Nonsubject Group.

He came with Lynn and *me.*

A good way to tell which pronoun to use is to leave out the extra name: *He came with me.* You would never say *He came with I.*

We saw Lynn and *him* last night. (We saw *him* last night.)

He gave *us* boys a pony. (He gave *us* a pony.)

He gave Stan and *them* some tickets. (He gave *them* some tickets.)

EXERCISES

Underline the correct pronoun. Remember the trick of leaving out the extra word in order to decide which pronoun to use. Use the correct grammatical form even though an alternate form may be acceptable in conversation.

□EXERCISE 1

1. The instructor asked Jessica and (I me) to organize a panel discussion.
2. Since Glenn is such a good speaker, we asked (he him) and Brian to be the leaders.
3. (He Him) and Brian got some pointers from the instructor.
4. Between you and (I me), I think it was a good program.
5. Everyone told Jessica and (I me) that it was interesting.
6. The instructor asked if Jessica and (I me) would organize another panel.
7. Most of (we us) students think we should have panel discussions often.
8. My aunt asked my sister and (I me) to go to Virginia Beach with her.
9. My aunt asked whether my sister and (I me) would go to Virginia Beach with her.
10. Naturally both my sister and (I me) were pleased.

□EXERCISE 2

1. My uncle sent my fiancé and (I me) a record player.
2. Now my fiancé and (I me) are collecting records.
3. We're going to invite (he him) and Aunt Linda to our wedding.
4. This is strictly between you and (I me).
5. We received a gift from (he him) and his wife.
6. If I were (they them), I'd do some traveling.
7. It was a bad week for (he him) and his family.
8. Most of the criticism was directed at (we us) newcomers.
9. The instructor praised Barry and (I me) for having good details in our papers.
10. The instructor asked if Barry and (I me) would give him copies of our papers.

□EXERCISE 3

1. Carol and (I me) went to a play at the university last night.
2. Carol thought Betty would be there, and at intermission we saw (she her) and Bob.
3. Bob and (I me) have always been good friends.
4. They came over and spoke to Carol and (I me) and asked us to go out for pizza afterward.
5. When we went out for pizza, Bob and (I me) fought over the check.
6. Then they rode home with Carol and (I me) in my car.

7. They asked Carol and (I me) to go skiing with them next weekend.
8. It didn't take long for Carol and (I me) to accept.
9. (Bruce and I, Me and Bruce) have gone out for the boxing team.
10. The coach says both (he and I, him and me) should make it.

□EXERCISE 4

1. (My brother and I, Me and my brother) take turns shoveling our walks.
2. He is younger than (I me).
3. He thinks the family car should be available to both (he and I, him and me).
4. It was a problem my dad and (I me) had to work out.
5. Dad and (I me) sat down to talk it over.
6. Dad thought the car should be available equally to my brother and (I me).
7. My brother and (I me) now have an agreement about it.
8. There never has been any trouble between (we us) two.
9. The speaker said, "On behalf of my wife and (I me), I want to thank you for your hospitality."
10. The committee had entertained (he him) and his wife at dinner.

□EXERCISE 5

1. The committee asked (we us) guys to do the decorating for the spring party.
2. Most of it was left up to Carl and (I me), but we didn't mind.
3. Carl and (I me) played pinochle all evening, and the last game was a tie between (he him) and (I me).
4. There was plenty of food left for Carl and (I me) even though we were late getting around to eating.
5. Carl and (I me) then told Irma we'd do the dishes.
5. We gave the extra cokes to (she her) and Jane.
7. Then we asked (she her) and Jane if they wanted a ride home.
8. They told Carl and (I me) that they already had a ride.
9. I think both (they them) and their swimming coach will get awards this year.
10. At least I hope (they them) and their coach get awards.

WRITING YOUR OWN SENTENCES

On a separate sheet write three sentences using pronouns you may formerly have used incorrectly.

MAKING THE PRONOUN REFER TO THE RIGHT WORD

When you write a sentence, *you* know what it means, but your reader may not. What does this sentence mean?

Joe told his father he would have to take the car to the garage.

Who would have to take the car? We don't know what word the pronoun *he* refers to, whether to Joe or to father. The sentence might mean

Joe said that his father would have to take the car to the garage.
or
Joe told his father he was planning to take the car to the garage.

A simpler way to get rid of such a faulty reference is to use a direct quotation:

Joe said to his father, "I will have to take the car to the garage."

Here is another sentence with a faulty reference:

I have always been interested in nursing and finally have decided to become one.

Decided to become a nursing? There is no word for *one* to refer to. We need to write

I have always been interested in nursing and finally have decided to become a nurse.

Another kind of faulty reference is a *which* clause that refers to an entire idea:

No one could tell him where the bike had been left which made him angry.

Was he angry because no one would tell him or because the bike had not been left in its proper place? The sentence should read

It made him angry that the bike had not been left in its place.
or
It made him angry that no one would tell him where the bike had been left.

EXERCISES

Most of the following sentences are not clear because we do not know what word the pronoun refers to. Revise each sentence, making the meaning clear. Remember that using a direct quotation is often the easiest way to clarify what a pronoun refers to. Since there are more ways than one to rewrite each sentence, yours may be as good as the one on the answer sheet. Just ask yourself whether the meaning is perfectly clear.

□**EXERCISE 1**

1. When Irwin showed the dented fender to his father, ~~he~~ was upset. *his father*

2. He said ~~he would~~ have to get it repaired. *"You will"*

3. The instructor showed us a conch shell and explained how they ~~live in~~ them. *the molusk lives in it*

4. The parents take turns supervising the park playground, where ~~they~~ have free use of the swings and slides. *the kids*

5. He told his instructor that he didn't think he understood the novel. *"I don't understand the novel"*

6. His instructor said ~~that~~ maybe he hadn't read it carefully enough. *you haven't*

7. The salesman ~~told~~ his boss he was too old for the job. *said to* *"I am"*

8. When the professor talked with Roland, he was really worried. *Roland*

9. She ~~told~~ her girlfriend ~~that her~~ record collection needed reorganizing. *said to* *"your"*

10. She ~~asked~~ the job applicant, ~~to~~ come back after she had given more thought to the question. *said to* *"you have"*

□**EXERCISE 2**

1. His motorcycle hit a parked car, but it wasn't damaged. *the motorcycle*

2. As I went up to the baby's carriage, it began to cry. *the baby*

3. Anita ~~told~~ her mother, ~~that her~~ wardrobe ~~was~~ completely out of date. *said to* *"my"* *is*

4. As soon as the carburetor of my car was adjusted, I drove ~~it~~ home. *my car*

5. I couldn't find the catsup bottle, and I don't like a hamburger without it. *catsup*

6. I ignored his advice, which turned out to be a good thing. *Ignoring his advice turned out to be a good thing*

7. Margo ~~told~~ Edna ~~that she had~~ failed the exam. *said to* *"I have"*

8. She was shy, and it kept her from moving ahead in her profession. *Her shyness kept her from moving ahead in her profession*

9. She served Black Mountain cake, which is my favorite dessert.

10. In our physics course, we had to do only three experiments which made
me happy. *I was happy we only had to do three experiments*

□EXERCISE 3

1. When the dentist pulled the child's tooth, it screamed. *the child*

2. I finished my paper, put down my pen, and handed it in. *my paper*

3. I have always been interested in politics and would like to become a
politician.

4. She told her mother she needed a new car. *said to*

5. When I opened the dog's carrying case at the airport, it ran away. *my dog*

6. The cars streamed by without paying any attention to the stalled motorist.

7. Oliver told Max that his parakeet was loose in his room. *said to," your parakeet is loose in your room "*

8. She likes ballet dancing and would like to study to be one. *a ballerina*

9. When Gilbert phoned his father, he was quite ill. *his father*

10. He asked the salesman to come back when he wasn't so rushed. *said to* *I am not*

□EXERCISE 4

1. He told his father that his car was in need of a tune-up.

2. After I read about Tom Dooley's career in medicine, I decided that that's
what I want to be.

3. They gave me a new schedule that was much easier.

4. He loves to wrestle and spends most of his time doing it.

5. The park commission established a hockey rink where they can play free.

6. The doctor told the orderly he had made a mistake.

7. She tried to persuade her sister to take her car.

8. I refused the waitress job, which displeased my father.

9. She told her mother she was working too hard.

10. I have always enjoyed helping teach preschoolers, and now I'm actually
going to be one.

☐EXERCISE 5

1. She told her daughter that she had always been too shy.

2. Elizabeth's mother let her wear her mink coat to the party.

3. No one had finished his paper, which annoyed the instructor.

4. Last week I wrote a paper which the instructor liked.

5. She told her sister that her alarm had not gone off.

6. The president told the chief accountant that he had made an error in reporting his income.

7. He told the cashier that he had made a mistake.

8. I was offered a job which boosted my ego.

9. He told his father he thought he should go back to college for a year.

10. His father told him he didn't have enough money.

GETTING RID OF MISPLACED
OR DANGLING MODIFIERS

A modifier explains some word in a sentence, and it should be as close to that word as possible. In the following sentence the modifier is too far away from the word it modifies to make sense:

Leaping across the road we saw two deer.

Was it *we* who were leaping across the road? That is what the sentence says becauset the modifier *Leaping across the road* is next to *we*. Of course it should be next to *deer*.

We saw two deer leaping across the road.

Now the sentence is clear. The next example has no word at all for the modifier to modify:

At the age of six my family moved to North Dakota.

Obviously the family was not six when it moved. The modifier *At the age of six* is dangling there with no word to attach itself to, no word for it to modify. We must change the sentence so there will be such a word:

At the age of six I moved to North Dakota with my family.

Now the modifier *At the age of six* has a proper word—I—for it to modify. Or we could get rid of the dangling modifier by turning it into a dependent clause:

When I was six, my family moved to North Dakota.

Here the clause has its own subject—I—and there is no chance of misunderstanding the sentence.

The following sentences contain similar dangling modifiers—dangling because there is no word for them to modify:

Looking down over the valley, a wisp of smoke appeared. (Was the wisp of smoke looking down over the valley? Who was?)
After running six blocks, the bus pulled away as I reached it. (Had the bus run six blocks? Who had?)

Rewrite each of the above two sentences in two ways to get rid of the dangling modifier. Cover the right-hand column until you have done your rewriting.

1. First change each sentence so there is a word for the modifier to modify:

_____ Looking down over the

_____ valley, I saw a wisp

_____ of smoke appear.

_____ After running six blocks,

_____ I saw the bus pull away

_____ as I reached it.

2. Then turn the dangling modifier into a dependent clause:

_____ While I looked down

_____ over the valley, a

_____ wisp of smoke appeared.

_____ After I had run six

_____ blocks, the bus pulled

_____ away as I reached it.

Either way of getting rid of the dangling modifier makes the sentence clear.

EXERCISES

Most—but not all—of these sentences contain misplaced or dangling modifiers. Some you may correct simply by shifting the modifier so that it will be next to the word it modifies. Others you will need to rewrite. Since there is more than one way to correct each sentence, your way may be as good as the one at the back of the book.

□EXERCISE 1

1. Garbed in a brief bikini, he watched her walk along the beach.

2. After finishing the English assignment, that pizza tasted great.

3. Glowing in the dark garden, we watched hundreds of fireflies.

4. You'll be glad you stuck with college in years to come.

5. After cleaning the cage and putting in fresh water and seed, my canary began to sing.

6. Sound asleep in the hammock, I discovered my boyfriend.

7. Jerking the leash, I brought my dog to heel.

8. At the age of six, my mother had another baby.

9. I gave away that blue suit to a charity that I didn't care about any more.

10. While answering the doorbell, my cookies burned to a crisp.

□EXERCISE 2

1. Hundreds of colorful tropical fish could be seen cruising in the glass-bottomed boat.

2. While playing on the floor, I noticed that the baby seemed feverish.

3. After being wheeled out of the operating room, a nurse asked me how I felt.

4. While watching the football game, Mark's bike was stolen.

5. The bank will make loans to responsible individuals of any size.

6. Rounding a bend in the road, a huge glacier confronted me.

7. I could see more than a hundred lakes flying at an altitude of 5,000 feet.

8. Having finished mowing the lawn, the lawn chair looked comfortable.

9. Before planting my garden, I consulted a seed catalog.

10. Having broken my right arm, the instructor let me take the test orally.

□EXERCISE 3

1. After doing all the outside reading, the term paper practically wrote itself.

2. Flitting among the apple blossoms, I spotted a monarch butterfly.

3. After drinking a lot of coffee, the lecture became less boring.

4. Standing there being milked, we thought the cows looked contented.

5. The Museum of Science and Industry is the most interesting museum in the city that I have visited.

6. She was going to dinner with a man who owned a Pinto named Harold.

7. We gave all the meat to the cat that we didn't want.

8. Speeding down the slope, our toboggan hit a rock.

9. Determined to learn to write, the textbook was slowly mastered.

10. After a quick lunch, our train left for Pomona.

□EXERCISE 4

1. The little town is in the middle of a prairie where I was born.

2. Having grown up in a strict family, I had never encountered such a problem.

3. At the age of three I saw my first circus.

4. She put the clothes back in the traveling bag that she had not worn.

5. Although almost ten years old, he still hangs onto his old car.

6. Completely smashed, I saw that my little car was beyond repair.

7. Barking furiously, I went to see what was the matter with my puppy.

8. Sitting there looking out over the water, her decision was finally made.

9. Crying pitifully, I tried to find the child's mother.

10. Being a boring conversationalist, I always try to avoid him.

□EXERCISE 5

1. I bought a secondhand car from a man with generator trouble.

2. I read that the hit-and-run driver had been caught in the evening paper.

3. We gave all the newspapers to the Boy Scouts that have been lying around for months.

4. She left the meat on the table that was too tough to eat.

5. A report was made about the holdup by the police.

6. Twittering delightfully, I watched the wren building its nest.

7. Being a conceited fool, I didn't much care for his company.

8. After smelling up the whole house, I finally gave my dog a bath.

9. While watering the geraniums, a bee stung me.

10. Being unsure of the way to correct dangling modifiers, my instructor gave me a low grade.

10-15

USING PARALLEL CONSTRUCTION

Your writing will be clearer if you use parallel construction. That is, when you make any kind of list, put the items in similar form. If you write

I enjoy *swimming, skiing,* and *to hunt.*

the sentence lacks parallel construction. The items do not all have the same form. But if you write

I enjoy *swimming, skiing,* and *hunting.*

then the items are parallel. They all have the same form. They are all *ing* words. Or you could write

I like *to swim, to ski,* and *to hunt.*

Again the sentence uses parallel construction because the items all have the same form. They all use *to* and a verb. Here are some more examples. Note how much easier it is to read the column with parallel construction.

LACKING PARALLEL CONSTRUCTION	HAVING PARALLEL CONSTRUCTION
I enjoy *sewing* and *to plan* wardrobes.	I enjoy *sewing* and *planning* wardrobes. (Both items start with *ing* words.)
It's important *to make* good grades as well as *having* fun.	It's important *to make* good grades as well as *to have* fun. (Both items start with *to* and a verb.)
She expected a man *to have* a good job, *to be* good-looking, and *who* would pamper her every whim.	She expected a man *to have* a good job, *to be* good-looking, and *to pamper* her every whim. (All three items start with *to* and a verb.)
His experience made him *sullen, bitter,* and *a cynic.*	His experience made him *sullen, bitter,* and *cynical.* (All three are words describing him.)
She asked me *whether I could take shorthand* and *my experience.*	She asked me *whether I could take shorthand* and *what experience I had had.* (Both items are dependent clauses.)

By hard work and *because I invested my savings* in the company, I won a promotion.	*By hard work* and *by investing my savings* in the company, I won a promotion. (Both start with prepositional phrases.)
She wanted a house with *seven rooms, a two-car garage,* and *it should be in a good location.*	She wanted a house with *seven rooms, a two-car garage,* and *a good location.* (All three are words that can be read smoothly after the preposition *with.*)

Here are examples of thesis statements (see pp. 185–187 for an explanation of thesis statements), which of course should always use parallel construction. Note how each item in the last column can be read smoothly after the main statement. Those in the first column cannot.

My summer job at a resort was worthwhile because it gave me 1. money for college. 2. I hadn't had a full-time job before. 3. had time for recreation	My summer job at a resort was worthwhile because it gave me 1. *money* for college. 2. *experience* in a full-time job. 3. *time* for recreation.
A college student should not live at home because 1. he needs to be independent. 2. friendships in a dorm 3. waste time commuting	A college student should not live at home because 1. *he needs* to be independent. 2. *he will make* more friends in a dorm. 3. *he won't waste* time commuting.

EXERCISES

Many of these sentences lack parallel construction. Cross out the part that is not parallel and write the correction above.

□EXERCISE 1

1. I like living in Vancouver because I can go fishing, sailing, or ~~take a ski~~ *skiing* ~~trip~~ without driving very far.

2. Vancouver has a great climate, excellent parks, posh hotels, and ~~you~~ ~~can go to~~ good plays and concerts.

3. He can ski, sail a catamaran, play baseball, and ~~he has even learned to~~ *can even* fly a plane.

4. The goals of this course are critical reading, careful writing, and ~~being~~ ~~able to think clearly.~~ *clear thinking*

5. I haven't decided whether to go into medicine or be a ~~lawyer~~. *law*

6. I like hiking, mountain climbing, and ~~I~~ especially ~~like~~ camping out overnight.

7. It's not only what you do but ~~the way in which~~ *how* you do it.

8. Expecting a phone call, dreading it, and yet wanting it, I sat there all evening.

9. The orchestra leader asked us to come to practice at 7:00, that we should get ~~our instruments tuned immediately~~, and to be ready to start practicing at 7:15.

10. I admire her, I love her, ~~I find that~~ I need her.

□EXERCISE 2

1. This course teaches you how to limit your subject, how to form a thesis statement, how to back it up with several points in well-developed paragraphs, how to write an introduction and conclusion, and ~~then you~~ *how* ~~should think~~ *to think* up a good title.

2. When you have finished your paper, proofread it for spelling, fragments, run-together sentences, and see whether it has any lack of parallelism.

3. He liked being the boss and that people came to him for advice.

4. I am learning how to study, the way to organize my time, and how to concentrate.

5. A good salary, that I have pleasant working conditions, and good fringe benefits are among the assets of my job.

6. Since I live 200 miles from campus, since I'm eager to make the most of my time here, and since I really have nothing to go home for, I've decided not to make any weekend trips.

7. I have promised myself to work harder and fewer parties.

8. The instructor expects us to do all the exercises, to study the spelling list, and that we should get our papers in on time.

9. I have done all the exercises, written all the papers, and I am expecting a good grade.

10. To have knowledge is more important than having money, so they say.

□EXERCISE 3

1. The Senator works in Washington, lives in Maryland, and he often goes home to Minnesota for weekends.

2. His talk was interesting, practical, and inspired the audience.

3. In many homes parents are living in harmony and raise their children responsibly.

4. My uncle is a Democrat, a Mason, and he belongs to the Methodist church.

5. Our system for controlling crime is ineffective, unjust, and it costs too much.

6. We believe in a government of the people, by the people, and for the people.

7. I like to go to bed early and getting up early the next morning to study.

8. The article made me consider quitting college and go to work instead.

9. When I started college, I was shy, ill at ease, and I was really scared of everybody.

10. Now I'm outgoing, confident, and unafraid.

□EXERCISE 4

1. His dream was to get his degree, get a good job, and then he would help his younger brother and sister.

2. When I was a child, I was expected to keep my room clean, had to help with the dishes, and to carry out the garbage.

3. To have a study schedule and sticking to it will help any student.

4. The speed reading course has taught me not only to read faster but comprehending more of what I read.

5. The do-it-yourself psychology book sets out to help the reader handle everyday problems as well as understanding himself better.

6. He looked at his daughter over his newspaper, put the paper down, got up, walked to the hall closet, and he indulgently handed the car keys to her.

7. The weather was perfect with the sun shining, no clouds in the sky, and a cool breeze was coming down from the mountain.

8. The traffic in San Diego is heavier than San Bernardino.

9. In this country we are promised life, liberty, and the pursuit of happiness.

10. Going to summer camp is important for a child because it will give him self-confidence, teach him about nature, and he will learn to live with a group of his peers.

□EXERCISE 5

1. They want to move to the country because they want to be near nature, live simply, and to spend less money.

2. They are looking for a house with a prestige location, with land around it, and a view.

3. They were thinking of buying a lot that was a hundred feet wide and three hundred feet in length.

4. They decided it was too big, too wooded, and that it was more expensive than they needed.

5. They found a house on a smaller lot and decided to buy it and that they would move at the end of the month.

6. Before they move in, they will paint the walls, wash the cupboards. clean the rugs, and the windows have to washed inside and out.

7. Moving to a new community, making new friends, and to find work for everyone in the family may prove difficult.

8. Her course in interior decorating has taught her how to choose the right colors, how to make draperies, and the various kinds of period furniture.

9. I like a movie that has strong characters, a good plot, and that has a message.

10. He is succeeding through hard work, persistence, and maybe he's also having a bit of luck.

☐ EXERCISE 6

1. The patients all had fever, sore throats, weakness, and their heads ached.

2. My doctor specializes in internal medicine, has a huge practice, charges huge fees, and it's usually hard to get an appointment with him.

3. My doctor tells me to cut down on calories and more exercise.

4. My wife does volunteer work at the hospital, helps the handicapped at the Y, and she also drives for Meals on Wheels.

5. Her hobbies of doing Japanese cooking, making unusual desserts, and creating artistic centerpieces all add interest to her life.

6. The room contained an old treadle sewing machine, a barrel-top trunk, and there was an old cabinet made with square nails.

7. My suede coat is warm, good-looking, and I find it easy to take care of.

8. Each of the women was asked to serve on a committee, take part in one program, and she was also supposed to act as hostess for one meeting.

9. The dog was barking and stood guard at the door.

10. Most important to me are my family, my work, and having friends.

□EXERCISE 7

1. She was the kind of employee any boss would like—efficient, knowledgeable, friendly, and she always got to work on time.

2. You can depend on her to work hard, introduce new ideas, and she will promote the firm.

3. Your credentials file should include a transcript of your credits, letters of recommendation, and you ought to include a summary of your experience.

4. Travel lets one learn about other cultures, see distant places, meet other nationalities, and one also gets a better understanding of one's own country.

5. The visitors to the island were impressed with the quiet friendliness of the people, the lack of hard-sell tactics in the stores, the absence of billboards and neon lights, and of course they liked the balmy weather.

□EXERCISE 8

1. What worries American business leaders is persistent inflation, rising interest rates, expectation of an economic slowdown, threats of energy shortages, and that the government threatens to do more regulating.

2. A million years ago man's ancestor, Homo erectus, hunted in organized bands, mastered the uses of fire, made specialized tools, housed and clothed himself against the cold, and he developed the ability to speak.

3. Firemen may have to do many things besides put out fires; they may have to lure a child out of a locked bathroom, rescue a cat from the top of a tree, draw water from a flooded basement, or they may even have to deliver a baby that can't make it to the hospital.

4. To the feeder outside the picture window came evening grosbeaks with their yellow and black coats, juncos with their slate-colored jackets, pine siskins with their neat stripes, and the goldfinches had their winter plumage of pale yellow.

5. Money may be the husk of many things, but not the kernel. It brings you food, but not appetite; medicine, but not health; acquaintance, but not friends; servants, but not loyalty; days of joy, but not peace or happiness.

—Henrik Ibsen

□EXERCISE 9

1. My grandfather had only an eighth-grade education, began to work on a farm when he was twelve, and yet he eventually got to the top of his profession.

2. My grandmother never complained about their lack of money, their isolation on that farm, nor the fact that she was separated from all her family.

3. In those days the country school teacher cleaned the schoolroom, built the fire, shoveled a path to the outhouses, and he had to teach eight grades in one room.

4. The children memorized their lessons, listened to other grades recite, brought their lunches from home, and they always played ball with the teacher at recess.

5. The teacher was usually patient, kind, and he gave lots of encouragement to his pupils.

□EXERCISE 10

Make the parts of these thesis statements parallel.

1. Recycling cans and bottles has been worthwhile because
    1. it has reused valuable resources.
    2. prevents littering
    3. it has made Americans conscious of ecological problems.

2. Inflatable seat bags should be standard equipment on new cars because
    1. tests have proved them effective.
    2. they would cut casualty rates.
    3. worth the cost

3. My summer job on the playground for the handicapped was valuable because

    1. it provided funds for my first year of college.

    2. it provided experience for my career.

    3. opportunity to do something for society

4. A camping trip in Estes Park gave me some new insights.

    1. I now know I'm capable of coping with hardship.

    2. new interest in nature

    3. ecology

5. Improving one's vocabulary is important because

    1. it will lead to improvement in academic grades.

    2. lead to a more successful career

    3. give one personal satisfaction

WRITING YOUR OWN SENTENCES

On a separate sheet write five sentences using parallel construction.

AVOIDING SHIFT IN TIME

If you begin writing a paper in past time, don't shift now and then to the present; and if you begin in the present, don't shift to the past. In the following paragraph the writer starts in the present and then shifts to the past.

> In *The Old Man and the Sea* there are various conflicts. The Old Man has to fight not only the marlin and the sharks; he has to fight the doubts in his own mind. He wasn't sure that he still had the strength to subdue the giant marlin.

It should be all in the present:

> In *The Old Man and the Sea* there are various conflicts. The Old Man has to fight not only the marlin and the sharks; he has to fight the doubts in his own mind. He isn't sure that he still has the strength to subdue the giant marlin.

Or it could be all in the past:

> In *The Old Man and the Sea* there were various conflicts. The Old Man had to fight not only the marlin and the sharks; he had to fight the doubts in his own mind. He wasn't sure that he still had the strength to subdue the giant marlin.

EXERCISES

In these sentences there are shifts in time, either from past to present or from present to past. Change the verbs in each example to agree with the first verb used. Cross out the incorrect verb and write the correct one above it.

□ EXERCISE 1

1. Only a few feet in front of me I saw a quail, and I ~~walk~~ *walked* quietly forward, hoping not to frighten it away.

2. Kent stopped me and ~~says~~ *said* he'll see me later.

3. We were enjoying the game tremendously, and then it ~~begins~~ *began* to rain.

4. I tried to keep a study schedule, but sometimes I ~~give~~ *gave* up.

5. I closed my book, had a snack, and ~~then decide~~ *decided* to call it a day.

6. I wanted to register for that course, but it was full, so I ~~register~~ *registered* for this one.

7. He thought he wanted to take a job, but then he finally ~~come~~ *came* back to college.

8. I go into the kitchen, raise the shade, look out into the garden, and there ~~I saw~~ *see* a rabbit eating my lettuce.

9. He takes all the tests, writes all the papers, and then he ~~got~~ *gets* only a C.

10. When I was seven, I ran away and stayed away until dark; then I ~~come~~ *came* home.

□ **EXERCISE 2**

1. We walked along the shore hunting for shells, and finally we ~~are~~ *were* lucky enough to find a perfect specimen of a helmet shell.

2. We found lots of limpets, and before we finally give up for the day, we discovered a beautiful sea fan coral.

3. We took our specimens home, wash them, and then we identified each one accurately and wrote a label for it.

4. I worked all that summer boning up on my math, and then I am rewarded by passing the proficiency exam.

5. The book gives an account of Dickens' life, but it didn't tell much about his novels.

6. After we had driven about 50 miles on the freeway, we discover we are going the wrong direction.

7. Here we are minding our own business when a cop came along and asks to see my driver's license.

8. The Two Solitudes is a novel by Hugh MacLennan which told about the social conflict between the French- and English-speaking people in Canada.

9. We drove to the top of the hill to watch the sunset, and then we come back in time for supper.

10. I locked the door and then realize I have left my keys inside.

□EXERCISE 3

1. I brought the leaves home, pressed them hard and long with a warm iron, then pressed them in wax paper on both sides, and finally place them under a heavy book for a week or so.

2. By then they were ready to be mounted, and I add them to my collection.

3. I added something to my knowledge of nature today; I learn the difference between cumulus and nimbostratus clouds.

4. In the movie the heroine has one misfortune after another, but naturally she overcame them all in the end.

5. John Steinbeck wrote in Grapes of Wrath about the dust bowl days; he describes how one family left their home in Oklahoma and migrated to California.

6. I started out the door, but then I remembered that I haven't closed all the windows.

7. The story begins with a great problem, but the hero solved it at the end.

8. I started taking guitar lessons in the fall, and I finish in June.

9. I wake up, take one look at my clock, and realized that I have missed my class.

10. I learn a new word almost every day, and I always tried to use it in conversation when I can.

□EXERCISE 4

1. When I arrived in Atlanta, I lost my bearings and can't find the street I was looking for.

2. I stopped for a moment, and a cop came up to me and says I couldn't park there.

3. Then he gave me some directions, and I drive off to see if I can follow them.

4. The next morning I got up early and decided to leave before daylight.

5. After I had been driving a couple of hours, I see a roadside park.

6. I decided to stop to have some food, and also I need a bit of exercise.

7. While I was sitting there eating the sandwiches I had brought with me, a car pulls up beside me.

8. It was my next-door neighbor from Carrollton; he didn't even know I have been away.

9. After another couple of hours of driving, I decided to get off the freeway to have lunch, but I can't find an off-ramp.

10. Finally I found one, but when I got off, I find I'm in the middle of nowhere with no restaurants to be seen; therefore I simply get back on the freeway again.

□EXERCISE 5

1. Eric Berne's Games People Play shows how people play games instead of acting frankly. It explained that people play the game of Blemish by pointing out other people's faults in order to enhance their own image.

2. We visited the old one-room schoolhouse that had been built in 1877 and now has been restored. Even old books of that day are lying on the desks, and the coal oil lamps in brackets on the wall had oil in them.

3. Mark Twain gives us a saga of the Mississippi River in his novel Huckleberry Finn. The story was told by Huck and recounts the adventures of the two most famous boys in American literature.

4. Hans Selye, a world authority on stress, says that life without stress would be boring and meaningless, but he also said that it must be the right kind of stress.

The following student papers shift back and forth between past time and present. Change the verbs to agree with the first verb used, thus making the whole paper read smoothly.

□**EXERCISE 6**

MY BEAR SKIN BLANKET

One cold March evening I came home late and got ready for bed. I think I must have switched myself onto automatic as I went through the familiar routine of taking off my clothes, brushing my teeth, and setting my clock radio. At least I know I must not have been very aware of anything.

I turned out the lights, crawled into bed, and reach for my bear skin blanket, which keeps me toasty warm on the coldest of nights. I reach but can't find it. I check the floor to see if it has fallen off the bed. Nothing. My mind wakes out of its half-asleep-already state. I pause and try to think where in my room it was. I shook my head and peered into the darkness, but I can't see a thing.

"Something strange here," I thought.

I get up, grope for the light switch, and see that my desk drawers are all open and ransacked. And there is no bear skin blanket anywhere.

"What's been going on? Someone's been in my room," I thought.

Now my mind races as I scan the room. My stereo was still there, and my TV is OK, and I haven't anything else valuable, but someone has been in my room. I found a few other things missing: my camera, some change from a jar, and a half bottle of wine from the cupboard. I was furious. I had left my door unlocked, so I really was angry at myself too. But the worst part was the idea that someone has been looking through my things. I felt like my privacy had been invaded.

Well, after a few days of rage, I finally calmed down and give up ever recovering my bear skin blanket. Now I lock my door when I go out.

□**EXERCISE 7**

THE DAY I FLEW

I had always wanted to fly a plane, so I grab at my chance. I had saved the money for lessons, and I had enough enthusiasm to fly a jumbo jet.

That first time I flew I remember the sensation of leaving the ground and feeling the air pull us off the runway and float us upward and cushion us from the effects of gravity. It was an amazing sensation, a feeling of escaping the ground and of leaving gravity behind. It was a wonderful feeling to hear the engine drone as we moved higher and see the earth get smaller below.

My instructor let me do most of the flying even on my first lesson. It seems so easy and yet so impossible that a little plane could get off the ground. I kept trying to remember just what kept us up, and I nervously try to reassure myself that airplanes do work and we aren't going to suddenly fall out of the sky.

I learn to turn left and right and go up or down. In only half an hour I learn the thrill of flying. Then I am reminded how much more there is to flying when my instructor asks me if I know where we are. It has been only a few minutes since we were over the airport, but now I have no idea how to get back.

"There's a lot more to learn," he said as he took over and flew us back.

And he was right. I learned a lot more in future lessons, but that first time I flew will always be special to me.

WRITING YOUR OWN SENTENCES

Write a brief paragraph in past time describing your arrival at a vacation spot. Now describe the same arrival as if it is happening at this moment.

AVOIDING SHIFT IN PERSON

You may write a paper in

First person—*I, we*
Second person—*you*
Third person—*he, she, one, anyone, a person, they*

but do not shift from one group to another. You may shift from *one* to *he* because they are both in the third person group, but do not shift from one group to another.

Wrong: In making experiments in chemistry *one* should read the directions carefully. Otherwise *you* may have an explosion.

Right: In making experiments in chemistry *one* should read the directions carefully. Otherwise *one* may have an explosion.

Right: In making experiments in chemistry *you* should read the directions carefully. Otherwise *you* may have an explosion.

Wrong: Few *people* get as much enjoyment out of music as *they* could. *One* need not be an accomplished musician to get some fun out of playing an instrument. Nor do *you* neeed to be very far advanced before joining an amateur group of players.

Right: Few *people* get as much enjoyment out of music as *they* could. *One* need not be an accomplished musician to get some fun out of playing an instrument. Nor does *one* (or *he* or *she*) need to be very far advanced before joining an amateur group of players.

Too many *one*'s in a paper make it sound stilted. If you begin a sentence with *one*, it usually sounds more natural to use *he* in the rest of the sentence. For example, it sounds stilted to say

One should follow a study schedule if one wants to be efficient.

It's more natural to say

One should follow a study schedule if he wants to be efficient.

Since *one* and *he* are both in the third person group, you can shift between them as you wish.

Often an inexperienced writer lets a *you* creep into his writing even though he does not really mean *you, the reader* (Exercise 5 below is an example.).

Sometimes, however, a shift to *you* is permissible. Increasingly the indefinite *you* is being used in good writing. The first paragraph of Exercise 4 on page 175 begins with *I* and continues quite satisfactorily with *you*, and the paper beginning on page 179 shifts in the next to the last sentence to *your* and *yourself*. The shift seems more natural than using the correct *my* and *myself*.

As a rule, though, a shift in person should be avoided.

EXERCISES

Change the pronouns (and verbs when necessary) so that there will be no shift in person. Cross out the incorrect words and write the correct ones above.

☐**EXERCISE 1**

1. I enjoy jogging because ~~you~~ feel so good when ~~you~~ quit.
   (I)   *(I)*

2. In high school our English teacher wouldn't give you more than a C.

3. I like going out with her because she really makes you feel important.

4. I used to think my parents were fussy, but as you grow older, you become more tolerant.

5. I'm finding you have to do a lot of memorizing if you want to be a good speller.

6. I like living in Gainsville because you have good weather all year long.

7. As a rule a person can find work if you are willing to take what you can get.

8. It's wise for a beginning driver to stay out of heavy traffic until you have more experience.

9. If you want to play the guitar well, one really needs lessons.

10. All those who intend to graduate should order your gowns immediately.

□EXERCISE 2

1. Anyone who doesn't have a reservation is taking a chance unless you don't really care whether you have a place to stay.

2. If one has done all his exercises in this book, he should be able to get a perfect score on the final grammar test.

3. At the Oriental Institute one can see the great Winged Bull from Iraq, and you can also see many other Middle East antiquities.

4. When we looked down, you could see the little farms growing smaller and smaller.

5. We were on the plane for six hours, and you get tired of sitting that long.

6. We tried to move around, but there was not too much you could do.

7. Our car was in the midst of a traffic jam, and you could see that we weren't going to make our appointment.

8. When they opened the door that morning, one could see rabbit tracks in the snow.

9. One should always look up the spelling of a word he isn't sure of.

10. I like being with a person you can talk perfectly frankly with.

When students write **you** in a paper, they usually don't mean **you**, the reader. Rewrite these sentences eliminating the **you** and stating the sentences as simply as possible. Getting rid of the **you** will usually get rid of wordiness also.

□EXERCISE 3

1. You should have seen the mess my room was in.

2. You can imagine how terrified I was.

3. Swimming is the best exercise you can take.

4. You don't need to be a member of the Kiwanis Club to attend their breakfast.

5. Your paper will always be more interesting if you put in specific details.

6. Her paper was excellent; you could tell she had spent time on it.

7. If you want to succeed in college, you really need to have a good vocabulary.

8. Your vocabulary will improve if you read widely.

9. You feel absolutely foolish after you have said such a thing.

10. You can imagine how I looked forward to that weekend.

□ EXERCISE 4

1. When you watch television for a whole evening you realize how much violence is on the programs.

2. After you finish that course in psychology, you're an entirely different person.

3. I spent two days in Williamsburg, but you really need more time if you want to see everything.

4. You need to exercise every single day if you want to keep fit.

5. Anyone interested can call this number if you want more information.

6. If you want to prevent air pollution, you should take your car in for a tune-up twice a year.

7. From the above facts you can see that many companies still discriminate in their hiring.

8. You can't imagine how frustrating it was to be unable to get there on time.

9. You should have seen the elegant costume she wore to the masquerade.

10. After an escape like that, you feel pretty lucky to be alive.

Get rid of the shift in person toward the end of this paragraph.

□EXERCISE 5

As I drove on a deserted black top road, I saw horned larks feeding on the surface of the road and along the shoulders. This road, used by farmers for transporting grain from fields to elevators, furnished a bountiful table for these little cold-weather birds. As I came along, the larks rose up from the road and with a low, slightly undulating flight disappeared into a plowed field. I drove to the side of the road and waited. In a few moments the larks came circling back and dropped down to the road again, running all over the road and in the ditches searching for food. As I slowly approached, some of the larks raised their heads seeming to gauge how close they could let me approach before they again circled off. You could see the black mark or "whisker" on each side of the head and the black collar below the light throat. On a few of them you could even see the tiny feather "horns" and, as they flew off, the black feathers in the tail, which distinguish them from other birds of the open fields.

GETTING RID OF WORDINESS

Good writing is concise writing, writing that uses no unnecessary words. Don't say something in ten words if you can say it just as well, or better, in five. "In this day and age" is not as effective as simply "today." "At the present time" should be "at present" or "now."

Another kind of wordiness comes from saying something twice. There is no need to say "in the month of July" or "7 A.M. in the morning" or "my personal opinion." July *is* a month, 7 A.M. *is* the morning, and my opinion obviously *is* personal. All you need to say is "in July," "7 A.M.," and "my opinion." Below are more examples of wordiness.

WORDY WRITING	CONCISE WRITING
at that point in time	then
refer back	refer
repeat again	repeat
personally I think	I think
he was there in person	he was there
a person who is honest	an honest person
40 acres of land	40 acres
11 P.M. at night	11 P.M.
very unique	unique
three different kinds	three kinds
usual custom	custom
my father he	my father
field of sociology	sociology
brown in color	brown
and etc.	etc.

EXERCISES

Cross out the unnecessary words or rewrite parts of each sentence to get rid of the wordiness. Doing these exercises can almost turn into a game to see how few words you can use without changing the meaning of the sentence.

□ **EXERCISE 1**

An experienced player would have known what to do.

1. ~~A player who had experience would have had an idea about what he should do.~~

2. The girl who had roomed with me during my college years now was going to make a trip to see me.

3. Personally I think that the field of electronics is a good field to go into.

4. In the month of May two of the members of our family have birthdays.

5. The story I am going to tell you is a story that I heard from my grandfather.

6. It seems to me that the government should be able to work out some way to speed up the judicial process in the courts of our land.

7. What I'm trying to say is that I think justice should be swift and sure.

8. I grew up as a child in an ordinary small town.

9. Owing to the fact that I had a lot of work to do, it wasn't possible for me to accept their invitation.

10. I was unaware of the fact that she was leaving.

□EXERCISE 2

1. History is a subject that interests me a great deal.

2. The professor is a man who makes his subject interesting to everyone.

3. I have no doubt but that he spends a great deal of time preparing each lecture and getting ready to present it to the class.

4. He was arrested for driving his car in an intoxicated condition.

5. A personal friend of mine has a very unique invention.

6. A total of ten people were stranded by that avalanche.

7. I am of the opinion that she has done just about as much work as you can expect her to do under the circumstances.

8. My final conclusion is that she really and truly is not much interested in the work she is doing.

9. One of those suits is equally as good as the other on you.

10. The barber who cuts my hair has been away from the shop where he works for almost a week.

□EXERCISE 3

1. The purple martin circled around and around the martin house for half an hour and then disappeared from view.

2. By the time I arrived on the scene there wasn't much left to do.

3. At the present time modern present-day medicine has practically wiped out polio from our country.

4. There were a number of spectators who couldn't get seats.

5. It is my opinion that the grandstand is not as large as it should be.

6. As you may be aware, a fly has a little suction cup on each of its six feet, and this enables it to walk on the ceiling without falling off.

7. The hardest exam that I had last semester was a psychology exam.

8. That exam included a number of questions about things that I had forgotten about completely.

9. The magpie is a bird that is quite large and has a black head, a long greenish tail, and white wing patches on its wings.

10. She is a person who will always do whatever she promises that she'll do.

□EXERCISE 4

1. In this modern age we have more crime than was known during the days when our grandparents were alive.

2. However, there are also many good aspects that we should remember about our life today.

3. Because of the fact that various miracle drugs have been discovered and are now in use, we do have a longer life span than did the people who lived back at the time of our grandparents.

4. Another factor which makes life easier now than life was during past generations is the fact that many labor saving devices have been invented to save people much of the drudgery of everyday tasks.

5. You should consider the arguments for the case as well as the arguments against it before you finally come to your decision.

6. There was a lot of objection on the part of the taxpayers.

7. They found three different kinds of shells that were new to them.

8. It was 5:00 A.M. in the morning when we started, and we got there at 6:00 P.M. that evening.

9. She was of the opinion that the administration was doing all in its power to correct the inequity between the salaries of the two employees.

10. The fact of the matter is that the administration had to take into account the employees' past performance as well as their present performance.

□EXERCISE 5

1. The book that I got from the library and have been reading is Brave New World.

2. It seems to me, all things considered, that much more could be done and should be done to help students find jobs that will be suitable for them.

3. All the crude remarks that she made served to make him very annoyed.

4. In this course we are learning the basic fundamentals of the art of writing.

5. If it should happen that you don't know what mark of punctuation you should use in a particular sentence, refer back to the chapters on punctuation.

6. Our instructor asks that we keep a spelling list of all our misspelled words in the back of our books.

7. We are supposed to put on the list all the words that we have misspelled in any of our papers.

8. I personally feel it was a mistake on the part of the professor to give me a grade as low as that.

9. The pendant that she was wearing was oblong in shape and blue in color.

10. It was a question as to whether we should shovel the walks now or whether we should wait until it stopped snowing.

☐EXERCISE 6

1. Owing to the fact that I don't like to play bridge, I didn't accept the invitation that she sent to me.

2. She wore a dilapidated old coat that made her look years older than she really was.

3. I personally think that she could do quite a bit more to try to make herself more presentable-looking.

4. He didn't know anything at all about history, but he was a genius as far as science was concerned.

5. She is planning to major in the field of astronomy.

6. She has such a friendly nature that she gets invited to parties all the time.

7. In this day and age there is a lot more freedom of expression than there used to be in days gone by.

8. The lecturer was speaking in reference to the new zoning law that is going to change the zoning in several suburbs of the city.

9. The fact of the matter is that I have been so busy that I haven't had time to give any thought to the question of zoning.

10. I suppose we are going to have to face the question sooner or later.

☐EXERCISE 7

1. What you will need to do is narrow down the subject to fit the particular aspect of it that you want to talk about.

2. She said she would attempt to try to teach me some office skills.

3. This one Saturday that I'm going to tell about was one of the most interesting Saturdays of my life.

4. I have seen your ad in the newspaper The Kansas City Star for the need of a coach to coach football to the boys in your summer football camp.

5. I personally think that our system of justice here in the United States is not nearly as effective as it should be.

6. No one had informed me of the fact that the speaker had arrived.

7. The story that I am about to tell you is one that I think you will find pertinent to the problem at hand.

8. In the month of August most of the employees of this institution of ours take a vacation.

9. The fact of the matter is that I have not had time to prepare an agenda for the program for our meeting this afternoon.

10. I want to repeat my final conclusion again.

□ EXERCISE 8

1. The governor was there in person to open the assembly as was his usual custom.

2. We found three different kinds of coral and all of them were very unique.

3. She is a woman who has done a great deal for the betterment of her community.

4. Each student has four minutes of time in which to tell about his own strengths.

5. At the end of the four-minute interval, the student thanks his listeners: "Thank you."

6. I would have gone except for the fact that I had a previous engagement.

7. There was an objection by some people to the new library hours.

8. The great percentage of the students on this particular campus prefer the semester system rather than the quarter system.

9. Edna St. Vincent Millay was a poet of the early years of this century. She wrote many poems, and one of the best known is "Renascence."

10. With reference to your recent letter, I beg to inform you that the article you have requested is now no longer available. If you are desirous of having a substitute, please let us know at your earliest convenience.

□EXERCISES 9 and 10

These paragraphs are from a university publication about a new library. Revise them to get rid of the wordiness and see how much more effective they will be. The material as it stands has 241 words; the revision at the back of the book has 126—just about half as many. Can you make your revision that concise and still keep the essential information?

1. Whatever has been accomplished has been made possible because of the cooperation of the University administration, faculty, students and the library staff working together.

2. Periodicals do not circulate because of the heavy use by all students and this provision guarantees that they will always be available. Many divisions provide photoduplication facilities so that articles from the periodicals can be easily reproduced.

3. The Information Center is a general reference area which assists faculty and students in the use of the card catalogue, basic reference books, bibliographies, and indexes. There is an orientation program for the purpose of instructing students on library procedures as well as the Inter-Library Loan service.

4. The Reserve Reading Room houses and circulates those books and materials which the faculty has chosen as required reading for current courses.

5. In the Music Division there are at present ten listening stations, and six of these are equipped with cassette recorders which can be used to record a particular piece of music so that the listener can play it back several times in order to study it.

6. Much of the material essential to a new Library is no longer available in printed form. Technology has overcome this problem with the development of microfilms, microcards, and microfiche. The Library contains over one million items of microfilms, and the students soon discover the very attractive rooms which house the latest equipment for accommodating these items, as well as microprint machines if copies are required.

Review of Sentence Structure and Agreement

One sentence in each pair is correct; the other is incorrect. Read *both* sentences carefully before you decide. Then write the letter of the *correct* sentence in the blank. You may find any one of these errors:

fragment
run-together sentence
wrong verb form
lack of agreement between subject and verb
lack of agreement between pronoun and word referred to
wrong form of pronoun
dangling modifier
lack of parallel construction
shift in time or person

_____ 1. A. They invited Lawrence and me to go along.
        B. They invited Lawrence and I to go along.

_____ 2. A. He ask his parents for more money, and they gave it to him.
        B. They gave an award to him and his brother.

_____ 3. A. One cannot make people learn; you can only show them the way.
        B. I've worked really hard and think I'll pass the course.

_____ 4. A. The director asked Ed and me to help with the publicity.
        B. I can't decide whether to be a secretary, a nurse, or go into teaching.

_____ 5. A. Having finished washing the car, I found the swimming pool inviting.
        B. Kirk told the professor that his watch was wrong.

_____ 6. A. Have you finish your assignment yet?
        B. He invited my brother and me to go for a ride in his boat.

_____ 7. A. Most of the class were prepared for the exam.
        B. I finished my math then I spent the rest of the evening watching TV.

_____ 8. A. Racing down the hill, I fell and sprained my ankle.
        B. You're suppose to turn in a paper every Friday.

_____ 9. A. He has walk to campus ever since his car broke down.
        B. We got an invitation from him and his wife.

_____ 10. A. A list of required readings was posted in the library.
        B. They asked whether you was intending to come.

_____ 11. A. Making the most of every opportunity that came his way.
        B. When I turned in for the night, I fell asleep immediately.

_____ 12. A. There's no use to complain it's too late now.
        B. I certainly didn't choose an easy course.

_____ 13. A. The instructor gave A's to both Sara and me.

B. It don't make any difference to me what you do.

_____ 14. A. Most of my friends are going to work this summer.

B. I was driving along at the speed limit when I see a cop following me.

_____ 15. A. He likes classical music he doesn't like rock.

B. Of course they blamed my friend and me.

_____ 16. A. There was nothing more to do the outcome was settled.

B. Our team had worked hard but simply couldn't compete with them.

_____ 17. A. Getting an A made me happy and caused me to have more self-confidence.

B. Each of my sisters have their own phone now.

_____ 18. A. When one writes a thesis statement, you should make the points parallel.

B. I worked until midnight and even then didn't finish.

_____ 19. A. She's beautiful, talented, and has lots of money.

B. The car belongs to my fiancé and me.

_____ 20. A. Just having graduated from college, and then being unable to find a job.

B. Each of my three friends has a scholarship.

_____ 21. A. I had been studying since morning I had to have a break.

B. I wish they'd invite my husband and me sometime.

_____ 22. A. The rain dampen the heads but not the spirits of the cheering crowd.

B. I enjoy math and psychology, but I find history and English difficult.

_____ 23. A. Each of his children is interested in music.

B. She order an expensive suit, and then she couldn't pay for it.

_____ 24. A. The instructor asked Ross and me to lead a group discussion.

B. I came around a turn in the road, and there I see a pheasant in front of me.

_____ 25. A. You was here before I was, so you should go in first.

B. We girls helped with the program.

3

**Punctuation
and
Capital Letters**

3　Punctuation and Capital Letters

PERIOD, QUESTION MARK, EXCLAMATION MARK, SEMICOLON, COLON, DASH

Every mark of punctuation you use should help your reader. Just like Stop and Go signals at an intersection, marks of punctuation will keep the reader, like the traffic, from getting snarled up.

Here are the rules for six marks of punctuation. The first three you have known for a long time and have no trouble with. The one about semicolons you learned when you studied independent clauses (p. 54). The one about the colon will be less familiar.

Use a period at the end of a sentence and after an abbreviation.

Mr.	lbs.	Dr.	Wed.	sq. ft.
Mrs.	etc.	Jan.	P.M.	ibid.

Use a question mark after a direct question (but not after an indirect one).

Shall we go?
He asked whether we should go.

Use an exclamation mark after an expression that shows strong emotion.

Great! You're just in time!

Use a semicolon between two independent clauses unless they are joined by one of the connecting words <u>and, but, for, or, nor, yet, so.</u>

The rain came down in torrents; we ran for shelter.
I have work to do; therefore I must leave.

Use a colon after a complete statement when a list or long quotation follows.

We took the following items: hot dogs, fruit, and coffee. (*We took the following items* is a complete statement. You can hear your voice fall at the end of it. Therefore a colon is used before the list.)
We took hot dogs, fruit, and coffee. (Here *We took* is not a complete statement; it needs the list to make it complete. Therefore since we don't want to separate the list from the first part of the sentence, no colon is used.)

Use a dash when there is an abrupt change of thought.

This test includes run-together sentences, fragments, agreement—everything we've studied so far. (Here the writer, instead of going on with the list, decides to sum everything up in one statement.)
And the dash—well, don't use it too often.

EXERCISES

Add the necessary punctuation (period, question mark, exclamation mark, semicolon, colon). Correct your answers ten at a time.

□EXERCISE 1

1. Are you sure we're on the right road.
2. We agreed to meet that evening then we hurried home.
3. I try to make my long distance calls after 11 P M or before 8 A M when the rates are lower.
4. I took the following items to the exam pen, pencil, paper, and dictionary.
5. Her most prized possessions were an antique music box, a Wedgwood plate, and an old wine glass.
6. I have decided now to be independent I make all my own decisions.
7. Three things are necessary for winning in any competition discipline, desire, and dedication.
8. Stop You're on the wrong track.
9. You changed my mind you argued until I had to change my mind.
10. Did you know that right and left shoes were thought up only a little more than a century ago.

□EXERCISE 2

1. Today various textile finishes are used durable press, soil release, flame retardant, antistatic, and shrinkproof.
2. I don't study at night I get up at 5:00 A M and study when I'm fresh.
3. Amazing How do you do it.
4. Is it more wrong to steal from a little old man on a pension than to steal from a big corporation with Inc or Ltd after its name.
5. Wait I want to go with you.
6. As usual their demands were for shorter hours, more pay, and more fringe benefits.
7. Do you know what an odometer is.
8. It's the device in your car that tells how many miles you have traveled.
9. I learned the difference between two words today atheist and agnostic.
10. An atheist is sure there is no God an agnostic merely doesn't know.

□EXERCISE 3

1. Did you know there are more than half a million snowflakes in each cubic foot of snow.
2. And did you know that glaciers are formed by snowflakes being compressed for thousands of years into hard ice.
3. Snow delights children it often annoys or inconveniences adults.
4. Snow has often influenced the course of history it slowed Hannibal and nearly defeated Russia in its "winter war" with Finland.
5. People think of snow as sterile actually it teems with microorganisms.
6. There are various kinds of snow the Eskimos have more than two dozen words for snow.
7. The sign on his door read Noel Thatcher, B A , M A , Ph D.
8. Help I'm sinking.
9. Out of my wallet fell all my credit cards, my bills, and Miriam's picture.
10. Out of my wallet fell the following all my credit cards, my bills, and Miriam's picture.

□EXERCISE 4

1. If you take this action, where will it lead.
2. How will it affect others. What will it do to you.
3. Will you think well of yourself afterward.
4. There are two kinds of education the kind you get from schools and the kind you get from living.
5. He asked me what my plans are for next year.
6. Hurry. We're going to be late.
7. Money giving, says Karl Menninger, is a good criterion, in a way, of a person's mental health generous people are rarely mentally ill people.
8. I've enrolled in a class in oil painting I've always wanted to paint.
9. Great You should do what you want to do.
10. I'm not very good at it nevertheless I'm having fun.

□EXERCISE 5

1. I took the following courses last semester European history, chemistry, English, and dress design.
2. The courses I enjoyed most were history and dress design.
3. Most of my time was spent on chemistry it was my hardest course.
4. Each evening I was tired nevertheless I would study.
5. I would study until 2:00 A.M. then I would go to bed.
6. The design course was not demanding I'm sure I passed it.
7. The other courses were harder however I'm quite sure I passed them too.

8. My brother received his B A then he began work on his M A.
9. But he has other interests besides his academic field he plays a good game of tennis and a fair game of golf.
10. Also he loves to cook he says he's at home on the range.

□EXERCISE 6

1. By what are you remembered. How do people describe you.
2. Your dog's leg is still not strong it wobbles.
3. Take him home he'll be better off at home.
4. My favorite outdoor hobbies are gardening, hiking, and canoeing.
5. My indoor interests are these chess, bridge, and furniture refinishing.
6. Checkers is not an overly difficult game however it demands much concentration.
7. We have bought a place in the country it's only three miles from town.
8. It's a run-down farmhouse it's really only a shell.
9. We enjoy remodeling we'll make something of it.
10. Sure, it will take work it will take some money too.

□EXERCISE 7

1. He has become well adjusted he's really quite mature.
2. Little things no longer upset him he has ceased to be annoyed by the petty aggravations in life.
3. He used to rant when the boy didn't come early to shovel his walks now he says, "What difference?"
4. He saves his time and energy for real problems he works at things that he thinks are important and that he can help to change.
5. Is there anything you'd give your life for.
6. I wasn't asking for help I just wanted to present my side.
7. I didn't ignore her intentionally I was just too busy to go out with her.
8. Was she really hurt.
9. Among her antiques were an old photograph album, some 1890 books, and some old valentines.
10. She also treasured the following items a carved ivory paper knife, a small autograph album, and a hand-painted inkwell.

□EXERCISE 8

1. The track meet was supposed to start at 2:00 P M it began at 2:45 P M
2. I won the first race it was easy.
3. The next race was the mile it was a little more difficult.
4. Muhammad Ali refused induction into the army he said he had no quarrel with the Viet Cong.

5. He was convicted of draft evasion and given a five-year prison sentence then he started the lengthy process of appeal.
6. But he could no longer get fights in the U S he had thrown his career away for something he believed in.
7. They're going to the theater tonight, aren't they.
8. They asked us if we'd go with them.
9. There are only two lasting things we can give our children roots and wings.
10. A child is egocentric many people never mature but remain egocentric all their lives.

□EXERCISE 9

1. Will you meet me at 4:00 P M tomorrow.
2. Perhaps the best-known American poets are Frost, Sandburg, and Millay.
3. The following poets of the early half of the century also were widely read in their day Vachel Lindsay, Amy Lowell, and Edwin Arlington Robinson.
4. Our library has an exchange table people can donate magazines to it or take magazines from it.
5. It was the first time I had ever received an A on a paper formerly I had seldom had even a B.
6. He asked me whether I had registered to vote.
7. She owned an Egyptian scarab that was dated 900 B C.
8. How about going out with me for a coke.
9. Wow What an absolutely fantastic idea.
10. Well, what would you like to do then.

□EXERCISE 10

1. There are two kinds of pain the pain that leaves as soon as the wound heals and the pain that lasts a lifetime.
2. We started on our 600-mile trip each mile brought us closer to home.
3. He didn't come we'll miss him.
4. They discussed colors, fabrics, styles, etc but came to no decision.
5. Her ideas are antiquated she seems not to know that we're living in 1979 A D.
6. The program was dull I soon walked out.
7. Her table was set with sterling silver, Spode, and crystal.
8. My table is set with the following plastic dishes from Woolworth's, stainless steel flatware, and giveaway glasses from our local filling station.
9. It's amazing how he looks so young year after year it's really incredible.

10. The Scots-born veterinarian James Herriot has named his best sellers after the lines in an old hymn <u>All Things Bright and Beautiful</u>, <u>All Creatures Great and Small</u>, <u>All Things Wise and Wonderful</u>.

WRITING YOUR OWN SENTENCES

On a separate sheet write two sentences with lists, one requiring a colon and the other not requiring one.

COMMAS

Students often sprinkle commas through their papers as if they were shaking pepper out of a pepper shaker. Saying "I thought there should be one" or "There seemed to be a pause" is not a good reason for using a comma. Never use a comma unless you know a rule for it. But commas are important. They help the reader. Without them, a reader would often have to go back and reread a sentence to find out exactly what the writer meant.

Actually you need only six comma rules. MASTER THESE SIX RULES, and your writing will be easier to read. The first rule you have already learned (p. 55).

1. **Put a comma before <u>and, but, for, or, nor, yet, so</u> when they connect two independent clauses.**

We lost our oars, and that was the end of our boating.
We may leave Friday, or we may wait until Monday.
I wanted to go but could not get my car started.

The last example does not have two independent clauses (it has just one subject and two verbs); therefore no comma is needed.

2. **Put a comma between items in a series.**

Hurrah for the red, white, and blue.
She put down the phone, picked up her purse, and left.

Some words "go together" and don't need a comma between them even though they do make up a series.

The dear little old lady
The eager little boy
The dilapidated old building

The way to tell whether a comma is needed between two words in a series is to see whether *and* could be used naturally between them. It would sound all right to say *red and white and blue*; therefore commas are used. But it would not sound right to say *dear and little and old lady* or *eager and little boy*; therefore no commas are used. Simply use a comma where an *and* could be used. (It is permissible to omit the comma before the *and* connecting the last two members of a series, but more often it is used.)

If an address or date is used in a sentence, treat it as a series, putting a comma after every item, including the last.

He was born on May 17, 1959, in Salisbury, North Carolina, and grew up there.

She lived at 2340 Tenth Avenue, Doylestown, Pennsylvania, for two years.

3. **Put a comma after an introductory expression that does not flow smoothly into the sentence.** It may be a word, a group of words, or a dependent clause.

Yes, I'll go.

Well, that was the end of that.

Running down the hill, she slipped and fell.

When everyone had left, the auditorium was locked for the night.

When you studied dependent clauses, you learned that a dependent clause at the beginning of a sentence usually needs a comma after it. In the last example you can see that a comma is necessary. Otherwise the reader would read *When everyone had left the auditorium . . .* before realizing that that was not what the writer meant. A comma makes the reading easier.

EXERCISES

Punctuate these sentences according to the first three comma rules. Correct your answers ten at a time.

□EXERCISE 1

1. Our language changes slowly but it does change.
2. Not only are words added but many expressions that were considered incorrect in our parents' day are now acceptable.
3. If you have studied these sentences should be easy.
4. When a dependent clause comes first in a sentence I keep forgetting to put a comma after it.
5. I never studied much in high school but I'm studying now.
6. When I was in high school spelling wasn't stressed.
7. If it had been I'd not be having trouble today.
8. By looking up every single word that I'm not sure of I'm learning to spell.
9. I wasn't upset by the spelling quiz for I was well prepared.
10. Having done all the exercises and finished all the writing for the course I feel satisfied.

□EXERCISE 2

1. Outward Bound gives students experience in rafting mountaineering canoeing sailing and wilderness backpacking.
2. I sent my application for admission to Indiana Vocational Technical College Indianapolis Indiana.
3. Because the lecture had not been well advertised there was a small attendance.
4. The speaker said that applause before a speech is faith during a speech is hope and after a speech is charity.
5. After the lecture people went up to ask questions.
6. When everyone had left the auditorium thermostat was turned down.
7. She was born on November 2 1960 in Charleston Illinois but her family moved the next year to Spokane Washington.
8. He bought an expensive stereo system but forgot that a good system reproduces all the sounds on a record including dust and scratches.
9. Since he hadn't cared for his records properly the new system sounded far worse than his old one.
10. Scientists dream of discovering an easy efficient economical way of harnessing the sun's clean energy.

□EXERCISE 3

1. Carl Sandburg was born in Galesburg Illinois on January 6, 1878.
2. Between the ages of 13 and 17 he was successively a driver of a milk wagon porter in a barbershop scene shifter in a theater and truck operator at a brick kiln.
3. Then he went west where he pitched wheat in the Kansas wheat fields washed dishes at hotels in Kansas City Omaha and Denver and worked as a carpenter's helper in Kansas.
4. After he returned he went to college became a newspaper reporter and began writing poetry.
5. Because we didn't set our clocks ahead we almost missed the bus.
6. We almost missed the bus because we didn't set our clocks ahead.
7. Well I promised her I'd pick her up and I must do it.
8. Her job involves giving travel information planning trips for people and writing out their tickets.
9. The wettest place on earth is Mt. Waialeale Kauai Hawaii where there is rain 350 days a year and the average yearly rainfall is 451 inches.
10. On the shelf were a tea set from Japan a vase from China and a piece of coral from Australia.

□EXERCISE 4

1. For every ton of newspaper recycled 17 trees are not cut down.
2. No I would never vote for a man who says that when you've seen one redwood you've seen 'em all.
3. The Nature Conservancy the Wilderness Society the Sierra Club and other conservation groups are making some headway in saving the redwoods.
4. The lowest temperature ever recorded was −126.9 degrees Fahrenheit in Vostok Antarctica on August 24 1960.
5. Yes and we're complaining that it's cold here.
6. Oswego New York was buried under 56 inches of snow during the winter of 1978.
7. The first power-driven air flight occurred at Kitty Hawk North Carolina on December 17 1903 when Orville Wright flew at a speed of 30–35 m.p.h.
8. The official air speed record now is 2070 m.p.h. made over Edwards Air Force Base California on May 1 1965.
9. Since the era of manned space flight people everywhere are taking a more active interest in the sky.
10. Jupiter is the largest planet and Mercury is the smallest.

□EXERCISE 5

1. The most important thing in life, he felt, was to leave something for future generations: a child a law an invention a book even a garden.
2. As he worked away in his garden he felt that it would be there forever that someone after him would enjoy it that someone after him would care for it.
3. He was liked for his honesty morality and intelligence and he was respected for his hard work.
4. The number of people who are poorly nourished or undernourished can only be roughly estimated but they probably represent an eighth of the human population.
5. She got the breakfast got the children off to school and still got to her own class on time.
6. We get along well and we get things done.
7. When it comes to eating people differ in their tastes.
8. Her fiancé is handsome personable and intelligent.
9. I'm considering various career possibilities: nursing secretarial work or teaching.
10. He is attending George Brown College Casa Loma Campus Toronto Ontario Canada.

□EXERCISE 6

1. The tallest inhabited building in the world is the Sears Tower on Wacker Drive Chicago with 110 stories.
2. They are tearing down that lovely old brick building in the park.
3. The earliest parking meters ever installed were those put in the business district of Oklahoma City Oklahoma on July 19 1935.
4. Working most of the night she finally finished the task.
5. When oxygen water and iron come together rust is produced.
6. For recreation you can go to the Student Union, where you can bowl play billiards or watch a movie.
7. By pruning the roses drastically I hope to have better roses next year.
8. America needs to add order to liberty and Russia needs to add liberty to order.
9. The Gesell Institute is located at 310 Prospect Street New Haven Connecticut.
10. People who died in 1929—just 50 years ago—had never heard of jet airplanes Polaroid cameras food freezers frozen vegetables radar V-8 engines electric razors electric typewriters drive-in movie theaters color television the United Nations the atomic bomb or bubble gum.

□EXERCISE 7

1. We heard a carillon recital from the Bok Singing Tower at Lake Wales Florida.
2. The carillon was designed built and installed in 1928 by a company in England.
3. It is composed of 53 tuned bronze bells ranging in size from the largest weighing 22,300 pounds to the smallest weighing 17 pounds and they play a chromatic scale.
4. While the history of carillons in Europe dates back more than 300 years it is only in this century that carillons have become popular on this continent.
5. A Chinese proverb says that when the moon is fullest it begins to wane and when it is darkest it begins to grow.
6. The only way to reach him is through American Express Paris France.
7. As you probably know someone like that is valuable to a company.
8. The accountant's address is 410 Main Street and he will see you at 10:00 A.M. on Monday February 19.
9. If you didn't do it right the first time the dancing instructor made you do it again and again.
10. The highest temperature ever reached in the shade was 136.4 degrees Fahrenheit in Azizia Libya on September 13 1922.

□EXERCISE 8

1. I used to think great writers just sat down and wrote without errors but now I understand that they have to write and write and rewrite.
2. In preparation for each class hour we write either a complete thesis statement a rough draft or a final draft.
3. A few rough drafts are read aloud and we all learn from hearing them.
4. We turn our final drafts in on Friday and we get them back on Monday.
5. I like getting my paper back promptly for then I still remember my struggles with it.
6. A few papers are read aloud to the class but the instructor never reads the writer's name.
7. Sometimes my paper sounds better than I thought it was and sometimes it sounds worse.
8. One thing is sure and that is that each paper I write is an improvement over the last one.
9. I now no longer fear writing a paper for I know how to go about it.
10. If I work out a good thesis statement the rest comes easy.

□EXERCISE 9

1. No one is fool enough to choose war instead of peace for in peace sons bury fathers but in war fathers bury sons.　　　　—Herodotus
2. I spoke to the professor about my absence and he gave me some make-up work.
3. The boring wordy self-centered speaker finally sat down.
4. The charming little antique music box was on sale for a thousand dollars.
5. We love old china old silver old furniture and old prints but we haven't learned to treasure old folks.
6. As of September 1 1979 their address will be changed to 2936 Capital Avenue Sacramento California.
7. I went shopping for a cheap little cotton shirt but I couldn't find one that I liked.
8. Beyond a doubt he'll win that golf tournament.
9. The U.S. is rather presumptuous in calling itself America. A big chunk of America is Canada and a big chunk is Mexico and if you look at a map of the North American continent, you'll see that the U.S. is really just a swath across the middle.
10. History is what man has done philosophy is what man has thought art is what man has created science is what man has discovered and literature is what man has felt and expressed. (Punctuate as a series.)

□**EXERCISE 10**

1. In the issue of <u>Saturday Review</u> that came on the newsstands the week before Robert Kennedy was killed Richard L. Tobin gave the following report of an eight-hour monitoring of three networks and half a dozen local outlets: "We marked down ninety-three specific incidents involving sadistic brutality murder cold-blooded killing sexual cruelty and related sadism. . . . We encountered seven different kinds of pistols and revolvers three varieties of rifle three distinct brands of shotgun half a dozen assorted daggers and stilettos two types of machete one butcher's cleaver a broadax rapiers galore a posse of sabers an electric prodder and a guillotine. Men (and women and even children) were shot by gunpowder burned at the stake tortured over live coals trussed and beaten in relays dropped into molten sugar cut to ribbons (in color) repeatedly kneed in the groin beaten while being held defenseless by other hoodlums forcibly drowned whipped with a leather belt. . . . By the end of the stint we were quite insensitive, almost immune to the shock of seeing a human being in pain."

WRITING YOUR OWN SENTENCES

On a separate sheet write the first three comma rules. Then write a sentence to illustrate each.

COMMAS (continued)

4. Put commas around the name of a person spoken to.

I think, Bianca, you are absolutely right.
Craig, how about a game of tennis?
I've finished washing the car, Phil.

5. Put commas around an expression that interrupts the flow of the sentence (such as however, moreover, finally, therefore, of course, by the way, on the other hand, I am sure, I think).

He thought, however, that I should wait.
I hope, of course, that they will come.
We took our plates, therefore, and got in line.
It should, I think, take only an hour.

Read the above sentences aloud, and you will hear how those expressions interrupt the flow of the sentence. Sometimes, however, such expressions flow smoothly into the sentence and don't need commas around them. Whether a word is an interrupter or not often depends on where it is in the sentence. If it is in the middle of a sentence, it is more likely to be an interrupter than if it is at the beginning or the end. The expressions that were interrupters in the above sentences are not interrupters in the following sentences and, of course, don't require commas.

However hard she tried, she could not please him.
Of course I hope they'll come.
Therefore we took our plates and got in line.
I think it should take only an hour.

Remember also that the above expressions (however etc.) often come between two independent clauses and then require a semicolon in front of them.

He was busy; however he took time to help.
It's an important meeting; therefore I'm going.

Thus words like *however* are used in three ways:

1. as an interrupter (put commas around it)
2. as a word that flows into the sentence (no commas)
3. as a connective between two independent clauses (semicolon in front of it)

6. Put commas around nonessential material.

The material may be interesting, but the main idea of the sentence would be clear without it. In the following sentence

Gladys Nolan, who is heading the United Fund drive, broke her ankle.

the clause *who is heading the United Fund drive* is not essential to the main idea of the sentence. Without it we still know exactly who the sentence is about and exactly what she did: Gladys Nolan broke her ankle. Therefore the nonessential material is set off from the rest of the sentence by commas to show that it could be left out. But in the following sentence

The woman who is heading the United Fund drive broke her ankle.

the clause *who is heading the United Fund drive* is essential to the main idea of the sentence. Without it the sentence would read: The woman broke her ankle. We would have no idea which woman. The clause *who is heading the United Fund drive* is essential because it tells us which woman. It could not be left out of the sentence. Therefore commas are not used around it. In this sentence

The Grapes of Wrath, a novel by John Steinbeck, was a best seller.

the words *a novel by John Steinbeck* could be left out, and we would still know the exact meaning of the sentence: *The Grapes of Wrath* was a best seller. Therefore the nonessential material is set off by commas to show that it could be left out. But in this sentence

John Steinbeck's novel *The Grapes of Wrath* was a best seller.

the title of the novel is essential. Without it the sentence would read: John Steinbeck's novel was a best seller. We would have no idea which of John Steinbeck's novels was a best seller. Therefore the title could not be left out, and commas are not used around it.

EXERCISES

The first four exercises make use of Comma Rules 4 and 5. You will need to decide whether an expression is really an interrupter or whether it flows smoothly into the sentence. Also you will have to watch for sentences in which words like **however** are not interrupters at all but merely come between independent clauses and require a semicolon.

□EXERCISE 1

1. The person I admired most of course was my mother.
2. Naturally I liked my father too.
3. The lecture was on the whole quite informative.

 4. The audience though was small.
 5. Those who did hear the lecture however were impressed.
 6. I wish I could help you however I'm busy.
 7. I'll help you next time however if you'll ask me earlier.
 8. However much I'd like to help, I'm simply too busy now.
 9. This time though you'd better ask someone else.
10. You need help immediately therefore you shouldn't wait for me.

□EXERCISE 2

 1. Yes Gregg I know the car needs washing.
 2. I'm too busy this evening however to wash it.
 3. It will have to wait therefore until tomorrow.
 4. Therefore it will have to wait until tomorrow.
 5. I can't do it now therefore it will have to wait.
 6. I wish Gregg that I could be out surfing right now.
 7. Surfing however won't get you a college degree Jay.
 8. Neither will watching television Gregg.
 9. OK, OK, I'll turn it off however I do want to get the news at ten.
10. I do too nevertheless we'd better not watch it long.

□EXERCISE 3

 1. I tell you Jackie I don't like what's happening in our office.
 2. The boss has cut our coffee breaks to half an hour, and he's asking moreover that we work overtime.
 3. I don't want to, but I've decided nevertheless that I'd better.
 4. Hey Kristin how about a game of table tennis?
 5. Most students I think take Friday nights off.
 6. A few students on the other hand study on Friday nights.
 7. I decided by the way to invite him after all.
 8. He will I'm sure jump at the invitation.
 9. I've just heard however that the Calhouns can't come.
10. We'll have a good time nevertheless.

□EXERCISE 4

 1. Maturity the lecturer explained is the ability to establish helping relationships.
 2. The immature person is egocentric as a rule and thinks of the other person only as someone who will enhance the immature person's ego.
 3. The mature person on the other hand is concerned about the development, the well being, and the happiness of the other person.
 4. The great difference in people therefore is in their ability to care.
 5. Also the speaker continued it is in their ability to sustain a caring relationship.

6. I'm afraid Andrea that we're going the wrong way.
7. But we followed the signs Fred.
8. I know Andrea but we're back where we started from.
9. I shouldn't have come she thought as she sat through the boring talk.
10. There comes a time however when you've done all you can.

The rest of the exercises include not only Comma Rules 4 and 5 but also Comma Rule 6. Make sure you understand the explanation of Rule 6 before you begin the exercises.

□EXERCISE 5

1. This is the car that I bought three years ago.
2. This car which I bought three years ago has gone 50,000 miles.
3. We're going to our cottage which is near Muskegon.
4. The cottage that we bought last summer is near Muskegon.
5. Frederick Stock the great conductor of the Chicago Symphony always tried to fix the mistake, never the blame.
6. The Door into Summer a novel by Robert A. Heinlein is a good introduction to science fiction.
7. Carl Sandburg's best prose work is The Prairie Years a biography of Lincoln.
8. "Chicago" which first brought Sandburg recognition is his best-known poem.
9. "Fog" however is the poem most people memorize.
10. The early winter months are good for viewing the Milky Way which stretches high overhead early in the evenings.

□EXERCISE 6

1. Most of the class I think now avoid misspelled words in their writing.
2. I think most of the class now avoid misspelled words in their writing.
3. The trick is I've found never to let yourself spell a single word wrong.
4. After I left Simpkins Hall the English building I went to Sherman Hall the Administration building.
5. One half of the college graduates who were interviewed by a large corporation inquired about retirement benefits.
6. The back stroke which I am just learning requires a lot of practice.
7. My instructor who has had lots of experience is really helping me.
8. He tries moreover to let me work at my own speed.
9. I have worked hard therefore I feel satisfied.
10. I have decided nevertheless not to enter the tournament.

□EXERCISE 7

1. The reason students can't write some people say is that they haven't been taught enough grammar.
2. They should some think learn to diagram sentences the way their grandparents did.
3. Authorities tell us however that extensive drill on grammar has virtually no effect on writing skills.
4. Too much drill on grammar can in fact be harmful because it will take time that should be spent on writing.
5. Of course students need to know the fundamentals of grammar.
6. But more important than a lot of grammar drill we are told is giving students more opportunity to write.
7. The standardized test which can be graded by a computer has virtually replaced the essay exam.
8. Students do not therefore write as much as they used to.
9. What is necessary it seems clear is for students to write more in all of their classes and not only in English.
10. Hayakawa says that a person doesn't know anything clearly unless he can state it in writing.

□EXERCISE 8

1. It is important therefore that students have opportunities to write in all their courses so that they will learn more.
2. When a student writes about a subject he learns more undoubtedly than if he merely reads about it and answers some true-false questions.
3. A student who studies two hours a night for each subject will probably get good grades.
4. Martin Fisher who studies two hours a night for each subject will probably get good grades.
5. A parent who is too dependent on a child's love cannot be a good parent.
6. Likewise a teacher who is too dependent on students liking him will not be a good teacher.
7. Lars Larson who isn't concerned about popularity with students is a good teacher.
8. Dedicated teachers not fancy equipment make the difference in education.
9. That book I assure you will help you with your writing.
10. It's the book that our professor recommended at the beginning of the term.

□EXERCISE 9

1. Cherry cobbler which is really easy to make is always a popular dessert.
2. Cherry pie on the other hand takes longer to make and isn't any better.
3. Foods that take a long time to prepare I have found are often no tastier than simpler recipes.
4. Spending a lot of time in the kitchen as you can see isn't my idea of the good life.
5. Most American homes it seems to me are cluttered with too many things.
6. We could take a lesson I think from the Japanese whose homes are decorated simply.
7. The traditional Japanese room is decorated with only one picture which is changed frequently so that it won't become monotonous.
8. One picture and one vase of flowers are as a rule the sole ornaments in a room.
9. Western ways however are rapidly gaining popularity in Japan.
10. Before long I fear much of the traditional beauty of Japanese life will be gone.

□EXERCISE 10

1. Anthropologist Mary Leakey wife of famed Louis Leakey has made some new discoveries in Africa about the origin of man.
2. Forty years ago she and Louis worked for a time in Laetolil a remote area of northern Tanzania but found little of interest.
3. They moved on to Olduvai Gorge 25 miles to the north where they made most of their discoveries.
4. Now however Mrs. Leakey has returned to Laetolil and has uncovered jawbones, teeth, and other fossils of manlike origin.
5. Her greatest find is the footprint of a man-ape that may be the oldest-known direct ancestor of man.
6. The footprint according to radioactive dating was made more than three million years ago.
7. It is wider than the footprints of Neanderthal man which were left 80,000 years ago and have been generally accepted as the earliest human footprints.
8. Children who are not taught unselfishness will not likely become unselfish adults.
9. A new synthetic material that has been brought out by Du Pont closely resembles silk.
10. The whooping crane one of the first species of birds to be recognized as endangered has now reached a population of more than 100.

WRITING YOUR OWN SENTENCES

On a separate sheet write two sentences, one including essential material that must not be set off with commas and the other including nonessential material that must be set off.

Review of the Comma

THE SIX COMMA RULES

1. Put a comma before **and, but, for, or, nor, yet, so** when they connect two independent clauses.

2. Put a comma between items in a series.

3. Put a comma after an introductory expression that doesn't flow smoothly into the sentence.

4. Put commas around the name of a person spoken to.

5. Put commas around an interrupter, like **however, moreover**, etc.

6. Put commas around nonessential material.

Add the necessary commas to these sentences.

☐**EXERCISE 1**

1. Initiative hard work and quality output have been rewarded with generous bonuses.
2. My father who hasn't had a vacation for three years is on his way to Puerto Rico.
3. My little sister searched for my love letters but she couldn't find them.
4. While I was watching a pretty face at the curb the light turned green and cars behind began to honk.
5. Yes I'd like to go along Luella if you can wait a few minutes.
6. After mending Peggy's mitten finding lunch money for Tim and locating a lost workbook I finally sent the children on their way.
7. Much of my time moreover was spent in merely keeping records.
8. If you don't like your work you'd better quit.
9. A good thesis statement is not only helpful but essential for a good paper.
10. Grammar is language as it is and not as someone thinks it should be.
11. The book that I had requested at the library came in.

12. A chimpanzee can aim a ball at a target almost as well as a man can but he can't concentrate as long.

13. If the first few shots are unsuccessful the man tries harder.

14. The chimpanzee however rapidly loses patience and his aim deteriorates.

15. If the aiming tests are made too difficult the chimpanzee may even wreck the apparatus.

QUOTATION MARKS

Put quotation marks around the exact words of a speaker (but not around an indirect quotation).

> He said, "I will go." (his exact words)
> He said, "Man is mortal." (his exact words)
> He said that he would go. (not his exact words)
> He said that man is mortal. (not his exact words)

Whenever *that* precedes the words of a speaker (as in the last two examples), it indicates that the words are not a direct quotation and should not have quotation marks around them.

If the speaker says more than one sentence, quotation marks are used only before and after his entire speech.

> He said, "I will go. It's no trouble. I'll be there at six."

The words telling who is speaking are set off with a comma, unless, of course, a question mark or exclamation mark is needed.

> "I will go," he said.
> "Do you want me to go?" he asked.
> "Come here!" he shouted.

Every quotation begins with a capital letter. But when a quotation is broken, the second part does not begin with a capital letter unless it is a new sentence.

> "A little learning," wrote Alexander Pope, "is a dangerous thing."
> "I object," he said. "We've worked hard. We deserve more."

Begin a new paragraph with each change of speaker.

> "May I have the car?" I asked.
> "What for?" Dad said.
> "To go see Kathy," I replied.

Put quotation marks around the name of a story, poem, essay, or other short work. For longer works such as books, newspapers, plays, or movies, use underlining, which means they would be italicized in print.

> We read Robert Frost's "The Road Not Taken."
> I read Margaret Mitchell's *Gone with the Wind*.
> I saw the movie *Animal Crackers*.
> Thurber's essay "Here Lies Miss Groby" may be found in his book *My World and Welcome to It*.

EXERCISES

Punctuate the quotations, and add any other other necessary punctuation marks. Underline or put quotation marks around each title. Correct each group of ten sentences before going on.

□EXERCISE 1

1. A college education is one of the few things a person is willing to pay for and not get said William Lowe Bryan former president of Indiana University.
2. Honest writing helps a person discover himself the psychologist said.
3. Americans have more timesaving devices and less time than any other group of people in the world wrote Duncan Caldwell.
4. When you write our instructor said you produce something new, something that didn't exist before.
5. You'll get satisfaction out of writing he continued.
6. Then he asked me how I was getting along with my paper.
7. Just understanding a rule of writing isn't enough he said you must practice it.
8. You must practice it he continued until using it becames automatic.
9. Education said Robert Frost is the ability to listen to almost anything without losing your temper or your self-confidence.
10. Marcus Aurelius wrote no matter what happens, you can control the situation by your attitude.

□EXERCISE 2

1. What's the most important thing you've learned in this class Brenda asked.
2. Learning to write a complete thesis statement Alex said because it's going to help me in my writing for other courses.
3. I know that's important she replied but I think my biggest improvement has been learning to write concisely my papers used to be so wordy.
4. That never was my problem he said my biggest achievement besides learning about thesis statements is that I finally decided to learn to spell.
5. And have you improved?
6. Tremendously he said now I just spell every other word wrong I used to spell every word wrong.
7. Come on you're not that bad I read one of your papers and there wasn't a single misspelled word.
8. I'll admit I have improved he said now when I'm not sure of a word I look it up.
9. What dictionary do you use?
10. American Heritage he said it's fun to use because of the illustrations.

□EXERCISE 3

1. I had three chairs in my house: one for solitude two for friendship and three for society wrote Henry David Thoreau in his book Walden.
2. If a man does not keep pace with his companion perhaps it is because he hears a different drummer he continued.
3. The mass of men lead lives of quiet desperation Thoreau said.
4. Sometimes wrote Thoreau as I drift idly on Walden Pond I cease to live and begin to be.
5. Our sense of humor wrote Harvey Mindess is one of our most valuable faculties.
6. It can help us contend with adversity derive greater joy out of living and maintain our sanity he continued.
7. In an art gallery a man said to his wife I know what that artist is trying to say he's trying to say he can't paint worth a damn!
8. By working faithfully eight hours a day, you may eventually get to be a boss and work twelve hours a day said Robert Frost.
9. Golf is a good walk spoiled said Mark Twain.
10. Marriage said the toastmaster is oceans of emotions surrounded by expanses of expenses.

□EXERCISE 4

1. Do commas and periods go inside the quotation marks he asked.
2. Of course she replied they'd look lost on the outside.
3. What do you do if you want to quote a whole paragraph from a book he asked.
4. If the quotation is more than five lines long, then you punctuate it differently from ordinary quotations she said.
5. What do you do he asked.
6. You indent the whole quotation five spaces, single-space it, and forget about the quotation marks she said.
7. I suppose that makes it stand out clearly as quoted material.
8. Exactly she said.
9. Victor Hugo wrote the greatest happiness of life is the conviction that we are loved, loved for ourselves, or rather loved in spite of ourselves.
10. The important thing in life is not the person one loves it is the fact that one loves said Marcel Proust in his novel Remembrance of Things Past.

□EXERCISE 5

1. No one can make you feel inferior without your consent said Eleanor Roosevelt.
2. It isn't that I have so much energy continued Mrs. Roosevelt it's just that I never waste any of it on indecision or regret.
3. A man who uses a great many words to express his meaning is like a bad marksman who instead of aiming a single stone at an object takes up a handful and throws at it in hopes he may hit said Samuel Johnson.
4. A Danish proverb says that faults are thick where love is thin.
5. We're just now beginning to discover some of the causes of birth defects the speaker said.
6. Ralph Lapp wrote we are aboard a train which is gathering speed, racing down a track on which there are an unknown number of switches leading to unknown destinations. . . . Most of society is in the caboose looking backward.
7. No one can make me do something I don't want to do my father said.
8. Happiness wrote William R. Sheldon is essentially a state of going somewhere, wholeheartedly, one-directionally, without regret or reservation.
9. Genius wrote Carlyle is the art of taking infinite pains.
10. We have made a good start in turning the gobbledygook of federal regulations into plain English that people can understand said President Carter.

□EXERCISE 6

1. How about going out for coffee Lee asked.
2. Sure why not when shall we go Jill replied.
3. Oh, in a few minutes Lee said.
4. My mother used to say whatever is worth doing is worth doing well.
5. She also used to say what isn't in your head must be in your heels.
6. In describing the Taj Mahal, Rufus Jones said only a few times in one's earthly life is one given to see absolute perfection.
7. Oliver Wendell Holmes wrote many people die with their music still in them.
8. If fifty million people say a foolish thing said Anatole France it is still a foolish thing.
9. Flight Number 485 is now ready for boarding at Gate 60 the airport loudspeaker announced.
10. More coffee asked the flight attendant.

☐EXERCISE 7

1. And what have you been doing with yourself Kevin wanted to know.
2. Oh, I've been doing a lot of reading for one thing Natalie said.
3. Still learning new words Kevin asked.
4. Sure, I'm always learning new words Natalie said yesterday I learned what energize means.
5. And what does it mean?
6. Well, the root erg means a unit of energy or work, and energize means to give energy to. For example, some people find cold showers energizing Natalie said.
7. I prefer to get my energy some other way Kevin said I suppose that same root erg is in energy and energetic.
8. Right. And it's also in metallurgy, which means working with metals. Another interesting word is George. Geo means earth, and erg means work. Therefore George is an earth worker or farmer.
9. I never knew that before Kevin said it really helps to know word roots, doesn't it.
10. It helps me Natalie replied.

☐EXERCISE 8

1. You can't undo history all you can do is be just in your own time wrote John F. Kennedy.
2. I have been reading an essay entitled Gobbledygook from the book The Power of Words by Stuart Chase.
3. If all misfortunes were laid in a common heap said Socrates whence every one must take an equal portion, most people would be content to take their own and depart.
4. Habits are first cobwebs, then cables says a Spanish proverb.
5. I have been brought up to believe that how I see myself is more important than how others see me said Anwar Sadat.
6. People always get what they ask for the only trouble is that they never know, until they get it, what it actually is that they have asked for wrote Aldous Huxley.
7. An excellent plumber is infinitely more admirable than an incompetent philosopher says John Gardner.
8. Alfred North Whitehead said that education is a movement of the mind from freedom through discipline to freedom again.
9. The weather and my mood said Blaise Pascal have little connection.
10. The secret of happiness is not in doing what one likes said James M. Barrie but in liking what one has to do.

□**EXERCISE 9**

The table was a large one, but the three were all crowded together at one corner of it.

No room! No room! they cried out when they saw Alice coming.

There's <u>plenty</u> of room! said Alice indignantly, and she sat down in a large arm-chair at one end of the table.

Have some wine the March Hare said in an encouraging tone.

Alice looked all around the table, but there was nothing on it but tea. I don't see any wine she remarked.

There isn't any said the March Hare.

Then it wasn't very civil of you to offer it said Alice angrily.

It wasn't very civil of you to sit down without being invited said the March Hare.

I didn't know it was <u>your</u> table said Alice it's laid for a great many more than three.　　　　　　　　　　　　　　—Lewis Carroll, <u>Alice in Wonderland</u>

□**EXERCISE 10**

Are we nearly there Alice managed to pant out at last.

Nearly there! the Queen repeated why, we passed it ten minutes ago! Faster! And they ran on for a time in silence, with the wind whistling in Alice's ears, and almost blowing her hair off her head, she fancied.

Now! Now! cried the Queen Faster! Faster! And they went so fast that at last they seemed to skim through the air, hardly touching the ground with their feet, till suddenly, just as Alice was getting quite exhausted, they stopped, and she found herself sitting on the ground, breathless and giddy.

The Queen propped her up against a tree, and said kindly you may rest a little now.

Alice looked round her in great surprise why, I do believe we've been under this tree the whole time! Everything's just as it was!

Of course it is said the Queen what would you have it?

Well, in <u>our</u> country said Alice, still panting a little, you'd generally get to somewhere else—if you ran very fast for a long time as we've been doing.

A slow sort of country! said the Queen now, <u>here</u>, you see, it takes all the running you can do to keep in the same place. If you want to get somewhere else, you must run at least twice as fast as that.

　　　　　　　　　　　—Lewis Carroll, <u>Through the Looking-Glass</u>

WRITING YOUR OWN SENTENCES

Write a conversation that might be heard at your breakfast table any morning. Start a new paragraph with each change of speaker.

CAPITAL LETTERS

Capitalize

1. The first word of every sentence.

2. The first word of every direct quotation.

> He said, "This is the end."
> "This is the end," he said, "and I'll have no more to do with him." (The *and* is not capitalized because it is not a new sentence.)
> "Why do you ask?" she said. "You know the answer." (*You* is capitalized because it begins a new sentence.)

3. The first, last, and every important word in a title. Don't capitalize short prepositions, short connecting words, or *a, an, the.*

> What a Property Owner Needs to Know
> What's the World Coming To?

4. Names of people, places, languages, races, and nationalities.

Grandfather Smith	England	Chicano
Uganda	English	Indian

5. Names of months, days of the week, and special days, but not the seasons.

February	Fourth of July	spring
Wednesday	Thanksgiving	summer
Labor Day	winter	fall

6. A title of relationship if it takes the place of the person's name, but not otherwise. If *my* is used before the word, a capital is not used.

Do you mind, Mother?	but	My mother doesn't mind.
I think Mother will come.	but	I think my mother will come.
I'm sorry, Grandfather.	but	My grandfather is seventy.
Come on, Sis.	but	My sister is coming.
I visited Aunt Martha.	but	I visited my aunt.

7. Names of particular people or things, but not general ones.

Call Dr. Simmons.	but	Call the doctor.
I spoke to Professor Olson.	but	I spoke to the professor.
We sailed on the Hudson River.	but	We sailed on the river.
I walked down Third Street.	but	I walked down the street.
1 met President Cox.	but	I met the president of Sears.
Are you from the Middle West?	but	We turned west.

Her accent shows she's from the South.	but	She lives in the south part of town.
I take History 301 and French 10.	but	I take history and French.
I went to Trenton High School.	but	I was in high school last year.
He goes to Kingsboro Community College.	but	He is going to college now.

EXERCISES

Add the necessary capital letters.

□EXERCISE 1

1. I subscribe to both time and newsweek.
2. Last year I attended St. Louis community college.
3. Next year I'm going to go to eastern Illinois university.
4. Many people now attend community colleges and later transfer to universities.
5. This summer I'm taking european history, english, mythology, social science, and gym.
6. My most difficult subjects are english 101 and social science 220, both of which meet in Simpkins hall.
7. My mythology professor, who has traveled in the near east, is professor Hazelton.
8. For my english class I have professor Pex, who has really helped me with my writing.
9. The professor who teaches social science makes the course interesting.
10. We had a good discussion with captain Smith at the canteen last night.

□EXERCISE 2

1. On labor day we decided to go fishing in the Mississippi river.
2. I had never fished in a river before; I had always fished in lakes.
3. One lake where I have fished is lake Bemidji in Minnesota.
4. I went fishing there one fourth of July and by the fifth of July I had my quota of fish.
5. My sister graduated from high school in Hopkinsville.
6. Then she attended Hopkinsville community college for two years.
7. Now she is at western Kentucky university at Bowling Green.
8. Yesterday dean Taylor gave a talk at the Kiwanis club luncheon.
9. They called for a doctor, and dr. Snelling was there in ten minutes.
10. Anne Morrow Lindberg's book gift from the sea is still popular.

□EXERCISE 3

1. My brother went to high school in Pineville.
2. Now he's a freshman at Xavier university in New Orleans.
3. We heard a talk by senator Van Etten in the elks hall last night.
4. We rowed slowly down the river and finally came out on the bay.
5. Did I get any mail this morning, mom?
6. Do you know Edna St. Vincent Millay's poem "my candle burns at both ends"?
7. More social rights legislation was passed under President Johnson than under any other president.
8. His mother is president of the school board; his father is president of the lions club.
9. She creates quite a splash when she walks down the avenue.
10. Her clothes look as if they came from fifth avenue.

□EXERCISE 4

1. My uncle, mr. Osborn, is a novelist.
2. For years cousin Tina has been my favorite cousin.
3. She has just returned from a vacation in the south.
4. We live at 2100 second avenue, Boca Raton, Florida.
5. All the houses on our avenue are on quarter-acre lots.
6. At the end of our street is a high school building.
7. Our children, however, go to Lincoln school several blocks away.
8. I have been reading Kenneth Clark's civilisation for my art history class.
9. Art history 201 requires a lot of reading.
10. My english and history courses require a great deal of reading too.

□EXERCISE 5

1. I tell you, mom, I'm not going to make it on time.
2. "I learned a long while ago," said Eleanor Roosevelt, "not to make judgments on what other people do."
3. I've been rereading a doll's house by Ibsen.
4. The Belleville community college offers a number of courses in adult education.
5. Many adults are going to night school at community colleges.
6. My mother is going to a community college and is preparing for a new career.
7. We are all proud of what mom's doing.
8. We drove almost due north for 600 miles; then we followed the shore of lake ontario for another hundred miles.
9. Hey, dad, that left rear tire is down.
10. Well, son, what are you going to do about it?

□EXERCISE 6

1. We have been using Bulfinch's <u>age of fable</u> as a text in our mythology course.
2. We spoke to professor Niva about our assignment.
3. All of the freshmen are required to take english and math.
4. He got his degree in english literature from the university of New Orleans.
5. Would you mind, uncle Dave, if I borrow your golf clubs for the afternoon?
6. We don't have a family doctor, but we usually go to dr. Sweazy.
7. I was on my way to rocky mountain national park.
8. I had never been in the rockies before.
9. Somehow I got turned around; I thought I was going west, but I was actually going south.
10. Don't you want me to do that mowing, dad?

□EXERCISE 7

1. Do you remember the old brick building at the corner of main and second avenue?
2. Do you mean the old Garwood building?
3. He speaks three languages: english, german, and spanish.
4. We spend our summer at the lake every year.
5. We have a cottage at lake Minnetonka.
6. On memorial day weekend we went to visit my wife's parents.
7. They live 600 miles north of here.
8. Originally they lived on the west coast, but they moved to the northwest two years ago.
9. You can see where they live by consulting an atlas. Here's the Rand McNally atlas.
10. My cousin is a sophomore at central Y.M.C.A. college in Chicago.

□EXERCISE 8

1. I always thought I'd like to live in the deep south.
2. "I'm going south," Ms. Pearson said, "for the entire winter."
3. He sent her a poem on valentine's day.
4. She has memorized the preamble to the constitution.
5. William Lyon Phelps said, "this is the final test of a gentleman: his respect for those who can be of no possible service to him."
6. All the networks carried the president's fireside chat.
7. They elected him president of their club.

8. They are sending their daughter to a school in the east.
9. There is a small public park west of our house.
10. She grew up in the midwest but went to the west coast after her marriage.

□EXERCISE 9

1. I think, professor, that I misunderstood the assignment.
2. I am pleased that professor Schiebold is giving me another chance.
3. You can always get extra help from professor Johnson, who teaches greek drama.
4. My father spends his leisure time at the country club.
5. I think dad is almost a pro at golf.
6. Shall I paint the ceiling, mom, or just the walls?
7. We went fishing in the river every saturday when I was a youngster.
8. Then on saturday nights we would go to a movie or just stand in front of Honstead's grocery on main street.
9. A famous arctic explorer is speaking at the Presbyterian church tonight.
10. My aunt and I visited the art institute on Michigan avenue.

□EXERCISE 10

1. Dan and Allison went for a walk along Keweenaw bay, which is a part of lake superior.
2. I was given some good advice by mr. MacLean, who is our lawyer.
3. My father said, "don't let anyone make your decisions for you."
4. I have been rereading Rachel Carson's the sea around us.
5. I think, grandfather, we should write down some of those stories.
6. I'd like to have a record of how you and grandmother pioneered in McDonough county.
7. "What happens," she said, "is not so important as how you react to what happens."
8. Canada is a bilingual country with both english and french as official languages.
9. We had open house on new year's day.
10. Of all my professors I owe the most to professor France.

Review of Punctuation and Capital Letters

Punctuate these sentences and paragraphs. They include all the rules for punctuation and capitalization you have learned. Correct your answers carefully by those at the back of the book. Most sentences have several errors.

□EXERCISE 1

1. A comma is required when a dependent clause comes first in a sentence.
2. When an independent clause comes first no comma is required.
3. In other words if the dependent clause comes first use a comma if the independent clause comes first don't use a comma.
4. Stop I'll go with you can you wait until 5:00 P M.
5. Yes Phyllis you can do it that way it will take longer the coach said.
6. I think as a rule it's better to begin at the beginning she continued.
7. He memorized William Butler Yeats' poem The Lake Isle of Innisfree.
8. Eric Heiden a sophomore at the university of Wisconsin in Madison is the first skater to win three world championships in one year.
9. Heiden an 18-year-old skated his way to three world championships in one stunning season against the best speed skaters of Europe.
10. While they have a high current income the arabs have almost none of the real assets found in any prosperous nation the schools hospitals roads banks factories and farms that are the true bases of national wealth.
11. Over 200 colleges and universities throughout the U S are now giving credit for knowledge gained outside the classroom.
12. Commas are like pounds you either have too many or too few or you have them in the wrong places.

□EXERCISE 2

1. A study has shown that children whose TV viewing was cut back to no more than one hour a day improved their grades in school and seemed happier they played more with other kids and increased their concentration in school one child changed from a passive loner into a friendly playmate then when the study was concluded she went back to her former TV habits and became a loner again.
2. A hundred years ago when Edison was working on his first tin horn phonograph he wasn't even thinking about music he just wanted to make a dictating machine in fact it took almost a whole generation for musicians to get interested in recordings fortunately Edison lived long enough (until 1931) to get the first inkling of the big change his invention was making in the world of music.

□EXERCISE 3

1. An Assyrian stone tablet of about 2800 B C makes the following statements our earth is degenerate in these latter days bribery and corruption are common children no longer obey their parents the end of the world is evidently approaching.

2. Russia is building a railway across northern Siberia to bring out the riches of that remote region petroleum coal iron ore gold diamonds salt asbestos copper tin and bauxite. The route covers mountainous regions areas of permafrost and many bogs where the ground heaves during the short summer thaw. Some 3,700 bridges and culverts must be built across rivers and streams and tunnels must be drilled through mountain ranges much of the time the temperature is 50 degrees below zero F. by the time the project is finished in 1983 the cost may reach $15 billion—twice the price of the Alaska pipeline.

□EXERCISE 4

1. Yesterday I had my first solo flight at the Flying Club it's an amazing feeling when your instructor tells you to go flying alone then after you take off you look around and find you really are alone at that point it's too late to change your mind you've got to land by yourself sooner or later it's a great sensation it's like the time you first rode a bicycle— quite a thrill.

2. The federal budget speaks in terms of billions but how much **is** a billion dollars if a man stood over a big hole in the ground and dropped in a $20 bill every minute day and night it would take him 95 years to throw a billion dollars into the hole.

Punctuate the following selection, which is based on a news story in Time, January 9, 1978.

□EXERCISE 5

Most furniture is expensive clumsy to carry costly to move and uninteresting now there is a move to make your own cheap furniture does not necessarily mean orange crates and constructions of boards on bricks.

Recently many Americans have discovered that they can assemble stylish comfortable totable furnishings with paper cardboard plywood Masonite rough lumber foam rubber epoxy glue a staple gun and unlimited imagination almost any piece of furniture can be constructed inexpensively and almost instantly.

Spiros Zakas who teaches in Manhattan's Parsons School of Design has written Furniture in 24 Hours with diagrams and photographs to help the beginner.

Probably the biggest single element in the new trend is the development of urethane foam which has done away with the necessity for springs the new supergrip glues are also a boon they will hold wood joints together durably one of the most important technical innovations is the staple gun which can be used for upholstery by tacking the material over foam and onto the frame.

Very simple but attractive furniture can be put together to sit on eat at or store in.

Comprehensive Test on Entire Text

In these sentences you will find all the errors that have been discussed in the entire text. Correct them by adding punctuation and capital letters and by crossing out incorrect expressions and writing corrections above. Work carefully. Most sentences have several errors. A perfect—or almost perfect—score will mean that you have mastered the text.

1. We girls made the deserts for the party everyone like them.

2. She ask my brother and me to wash the dishes we was glad to help.

3. We lose that game nevertheless we still had hopes for the championship.

4. When we got to the end of the detour we turn south and then West.

5. Which turned out to be the wrong thing to do.

6. Each of her trophies are displayed in it's proper place on the shelf.

7. Working hard that semester my grades improved.

8. I enjoy math social studies and gym but I find chemistry and english difficult.

9. Making the most of every opportunity that came her way.

10. He spends most of his time however reading comic books and you cant do that and get satisfactory grades.

11. I cant decide whether to get a job take a trip or whether I should just loaf this summer.

12. Yes personally I think Jeanettes costume is more striking than Robertas.

13. She took to many cloths along on her trip party dresses beach wear and half a dozen other outfits.

14. Her mother and father send her to a exclusive school but she dont appreciate it.

15. Kurt told his father he was embarrassed by his old car.

16. Their quiet pleased with there new car but I think it was to expensive.

17. Jerry you was driving to fast when we past that cop.

18. We didnt know what she was talking about we had never heard of the proposal.

19. Huberts invitation to my girlfriend and me came as a surprise.

20. Each of the leaves are quite unique in their vein patterns.

21. Ive been wondering about you and hoping for a letter.

22. She memorized Masefield's poem Sea Fever from his book Salt Water Ballads.

23. John Masefield who became Poet Laureate of England was born on June 1 1878 in Ledbury Herefordshire England.

24. Life's always a struggle if anything's easy it's not likely to be worthwhile said Hubert Humphrey.

25. When you get to the end of your rope said Franklin D. Roosevelt tie a knot and hang on.

Proofreading Exercise

Proofread this student paper. You will find only a few errors—thirteen in fact—but correcting those few errors will improve the paper (the shift to *your* and *yourself* in the last paragraph is not counted an error). This is the kind of careful proofreading you should do before you call your own papers finished.

THE BIG GRIN ON MY FACE

One afternoon I was driving my car when I notice a pinging noise in my engine. In a few days the pinging grew to a thumping and then to a loud clunking that couldn't be ignored.

My knowledgeable friends broke the news to me that it was undoubtedly my main engine bearings and in the same breath they mentioned sums like four or five hundred dollars. Being a poor student, I had only two alternatives—walk or fix it myself.

Necessity force me to chose the latter alternative and I found myself up to my elbows in grease and grime for the next few days. With the help of a lot of free advice from friends, who claimed to be undiscovered mechanical geniuses, and from a good library book on engines, I removed and disassembled the whole thing.

An engine is something I take for granted as long as it goes, and only when it fails, do I really appreciate how intricate and complicated it is. Their are all kinds of odd-shaped highly polished parts, each one for some function. My taking the engine apart was like a little boy fixing an alarm clock each new piece was so interesting and so completely unfathomable.

Then when it was all in pieces the reassembly with new parts began, along with the job of trying to remember where each nut and bolt belonged. This work was a lot slower and required more help but it was encouraging to watch the motor grow with each new piece.

Finally it was all connected in the car and ready to be tested. It had taken weeks of late evenings of work but now it was ready at last. My friends stood around offering final advice and checking to make sure I had remembered everything. I held my breath and turned the key—the engine started and turned, a little rough at first, but soon it ran smoothly.

"Eureka! I've done it!" I shouted.

I was overwhelm with a great feeling of accomplishment and I couldn't hide the big grin on my face.

There's an indescribable feeling of pride in having rebuilt your own engine yourself. It was worth it, not just for saving money but for the experience.

Writing

4 Writing

FREE WRITING

"Writing is good for us," said Oliver Wendell Holmes, "because it brings our thoughts out into the open, as a boy turns his pockets inside out to see what is in them." Try "turning your pockets inside out" by writing as fast as you can for five minutes. Write anything that comes into your mind —no one is going to read what you write. Put your thoughts down as fast as they come. If you can't think of anything to write, just write words. Write anything, but keep writing for five minutes without stopping. Look at your watch and begin.

This free writing should limber up your mind and your pen. Try it at home. Besides helping you write more freely, it will help you sort out your ideas. Sometimes after you have discussed a problem on paper, it suddenly becomes less of a problem.

Now try another kind of free writing—focused free writing. Write for ten minutes as fast as you can and say anything that pops into your head, but this time stick to one subject—music. Look at your watch and begin.

Did you focus your thoughts on music for that long? Did you think not only of music you like but of music you don't like, of music your mother tried to interest you in as a child, of music you've heard on special occasions, of your struggles to play some instrument, of conflicts you've had with someone concerning music?

You didn't have time to include all those things of course. Once more write for ten minutes and add more to your discussion of music. Begin.

Focused free writing is a good way to begin writing a paper. When you are assigned a paper, write for ten minutes putting down all your thoughts on the subject. It will help you figure out what aspect of the subject to write about, and it will let you see what material you have.

As an out-of-class assignment, choose any subject that interests you and write for fifteen minutes without stopping. Time yourself. No one will read what you write.

GETTING RID OF CLICHÉS

A cliché is an expression that has been used so often it has lost its originality and effectiveness. Whoever first said "light as a feather" had thought of an original way to express lightness, but today that expression is outworn and boring. Most of us use an occasional cliché in speaking, but clichés have no place in writing. The good writer thinks up fresh new ways to express his ideas.

Here are a few clichés. Add at least four more to the list.

all work and no play	quick as a flash
apple of his eye	sadder but wiser
as luck would have it	short but sweet
as white as snow	skin of our teeth
better late than never	slowly but surely
blue in the face	too funny for words
bright and early	work like a dog
by leaps and bounds	
center of attraction	
cool as a cucumber	
die laughing	
easier said than done	
few and far between	
heavy as lead	
last but not least	

One way to become aware of clichés so that you will not use them in your writing is to see how many you can purposely put into a paragraph.

Assignment 1   The Morning I Left for College

Write a paragraph describing the morning you left home to come to college, using all the clichés possible while still keeping your account smooth. You might begin: "I was up bright and early, raring to go. Everyone else was cool as a cucumber, but I was busy as a bee. . ." What title will you give such a paper? Why, a cliché of course! Writing such an account should make you so aware of clichés that they will never again creep into your writing.

USING SPECIFIC DETAILS

Specific details often make the difference between effective and ineffective writing. If you are describing the moment you won a prize in a grade school contest, you have to do more than tell your reader it was a great moment for you. You have to tell him what you saw, what you heard, how you felt so that he will experience the incident with you. In the next assignment you will have a chance to use specific details to help your reader.

Assignment 2   A Moment I'd Like to Relive

What moment in your life, if you could live one moment over again, would you most enjoy reliving? It might be a moment when you won a sports event, a moment when you made a big decision, a moment when you achieved something you didn't think you could do, a moment when you did something courageous. . . . It need not be a dramatic moment; it might be a very simple one, but it should be a moment that had great meaning for you. Write an account of that moment giving specific details so that your reader will experience it with you and feel its importance.

Here is a student paper on this assignment. The writer was having so much trouble with sentence structure and wordiness that the paper was at first difficult to read, but after four rewritings, it is now clear. The writer had something interesting to say, and it was worth her while to get rid of errors so that her paper can be read easily.

I TOLD HER OFF

When we moved from one side of Elk Grove to the other, everyone seemed to have their own friends, and I wasn't one to go out of my way to meet people. From the first day of fourth grade until the beginning of junior high, I kept my mouth shut. Then I met Suzette.

Suzette tried to gain popularity by making fun of people, this time someone who wouldn't talk back, someone who was shy. She ridiculed me in front of her friends, who in turn ridiculed me in front of the whole school. She pointed out how I dragged my feet on the ground, how I had a soft voice, and how unattractive I was.

At the end of eighth grade came the most embarrassing moment of my life. At our junior high graduation, where my father was one of the speakers, Suzette had planned for everyone to clap for me. Although clapping is usually good, this time everyone, including my father, realized it wasn't meant for praise.

As I walked home that evening, I knew I couldn't take being ridiculed any more. Despite my shyness I had to tell Suzette what I thought. The next day as I stood at her doorstep trying to get courage to ring the bell, I knew I wasn't shaking because of the cold. Suddenly, with the next shiver, my finger jerked far enough forward for the bell to ring. As the door opened, I must have looked confident because Suzette didn't. None of her friends were there to back her up, and the impossible happened. I told her how she had ruined three years of my life. I explained how, because I was shy, I had no close friends, no one to talk over my problems with.

I got my point across because Suzette ridiculed me no more. But what makes me feel even better is that if I hadn't spoken to Suzette, I would still be that shy little girl who wouldn't speak up for herself.

LIMITING THE SUBJECT

Finding the right subject is sometimes the hardest part of writing. For one thing, you need to limit your subject so that you can handle it in a 300-500-word paper. The subject music, which you used for free writing, was obviously too big. You could limit it by saying

My Stereo Collection
Music I Hate
The Important Place Music Had in Our High School

but even those topics are too big. Keep making your topic smaller

Our High School Marching Band

and smaller

My First Week with Our High School Marching Band

and smaller

The Day I Won the Tryout for the Marching Band

Now you have a topic that is limited enough to write about in a short paper.

Which of the following topics are small enough to be handled in a short paper?

The Energy Crisis	One Way to Save Gas
Dieting	How I Lost Twenty Pounds
Exercise for Health	Jogging My Way Back to Health
The Spring Track Meet	Winning the Broad Jump
Sewing Your Own Clothes	My $4.50 Dress
Refinishing Antiques	Refinishing an Old Picture Frame

Obviously the topics in the first column are too big; those in the second column would be more manageable. Usually the more you limit your topic, the better your paper will be, for then you will have room for plenty of specific details.

WRITING A THESIS STATEMENT

Even after you have limited your subject, you are still not ready to write. You now have to decide what point you want to get across to your reader. The topic "The Day I Won the Tryout for the Marching Band" doesn't say anything. It doesn't make any point. What about that day? What did it do to you? What point about that day would you like to get across to your reader? You might write

Making the Marching Band Gave Me New Confidence

or

The Day I Made the Marching Band I Decided to Major in Music

or

Making the Marching Band Gave Me Something to Work For

Now you have said something. When you write in one sentence the point you are going to try to get across to your reader, you have written a thesis statement.

What was your thesis statement for the paper "A Moment I'd Like to Relive"? If your paper was effective, you had a thesis statement in mind even though you may not have been aware of it. It would have been something like this one:

Telling off Suzette was my first step in getting over my shyness.

Write a thesis statement for your "Moment I'd Like to Relive."

SUPPORTING THE THESIS WITH REASONS OR POINTS

Now you are ready to support your thesis statement with reasons or points. That is, you will think of ways to convince your reader that your thesis statement is true. How could you convince your reader that making the marching band gave you new confidence? You might say

Making the marching band gave me new confidence because
1. it was the first competition I ever won.
2. I won over peers I had always felt inferior to.
3. it was an achievement to get into one of the best bands in the state.

Notice that each of the reasons can be read smoothly after the *because* of the thesis statement.

Now think of some problem you are presently trying to decide, and write a thesis statement for *each side* of the problem. For example, if you are wondering whether to drop out of college for a semester, you might write

I've decided to drop out of college for a semester and take a job.
I've decided to stick with college.

These statements now need to be supported with reasons. Put a *because* at the end of each thesis statement and list your reasons underneath. You might write

I've decided to drop out of college for a semester and take a job because
1. I need to make some money.
2. I want some experience in my field.
3. I might come back to college with more purpose.

I've decided to stick with college because
1. I don't want to waste time merely making money.
2. I'm now getting used to studying.
3. if I left, I might never come back.

Three reasons usually work well, but you could have two or four. Be sure that your reasons are all in the same form. All of the above reasons can be read smoothly after the *because* of the thesis statement:

because   I need to make some money.
because   I want some experience. . . .
because   I might come back. . . .

A thesis statement does not have to end with *because*. All that is necessary is to make sure all the reasons are in the same form. You might write.

I've decided to drop out of college for a semester.
1. I want to make some money.
2. I want some experience in my field.
3. I want to sort out my values.

When the reasons are in the same form, we say they are parallel. Be sure that the supporting reasons you write for any thesis statement are in parallel form. For a fuller explanation of parallel form, see page 111.

Perhaps the most important thing you can learn in this course is to write a good thesis statement. Most writing problems are not really writing problems but thinking problems. Whether you are writing a term paper or merely the answer to a test question, working out a thesis statement is always the best way to organize your thoughts. If you take enough time to think, you will be able to write a clear thesis statement, and if you have a clear thesis statement, your paper will almost write itself.

WRITING A PAPER FROM A THESIS STATEMENT

Once you have a good thesis statement worked out, writing your paper won't be difficult.

First you will need an introductory paragraph. It should catch your reader's interest and suggest in some way your thesis statement. It will not include the supporting points because it is more effective to let them unfold paragraph by paragraph rather than to give them all away in your introduction. (Your instructor may ask you to write your complete thesis statement with supporting points at the top of your paper above the title so that it may be referred to easily.) Even though your complete thesis statement will not appear in your paper, your reader will be perfectly aware of it if your paper is properly constructed.

Your second paragraph will present your first supporting point—everything about it and nothing more. And be sure to use specific examples to prove your point.

Your next paragraph will be about your second supporting point—all about it and nothing more.

Your next paragraph will be about your third supporting point. Thus each of your points will have its own paragraph. Keep everything about one point in its own paragraph, and don't let anything else creep in.

Finally you will need a brief concluding paragraph. In a short paper it isn't necessary to restate all your points. Even a single clincher sentence to round out the paper is sufficient.

Here are the introductory and concluding paragraphs from a student paper. Note that the introductory paragraph arouses the reader's interest and suggests but does not state the thesis statement. And the concluding paragraph simply wraps the paper up in one good sentence.

Introductory paragraph	My superman doesn't soar through the sky or leap tall buildings in a single bound. My superman is my dad. I think my dad is super because he shows that he cares with the little things he does.
	(The paper tells in three paragraphs the kinds of little things the father does.)
Concluding paragraph	My dad may not change clothes in a telephone booth or rescue the earth from alien attack, but he's still superman to me.

Thus your paper will have five paragraphs. (If you have two or four supporting points rather than three, that of course will change the number of your paragraphs.)

---

1. Introduction arousing your reader's interest
2. Your first supporting point
3. Your second supporting point
4. Your third supporting point
5. Conclusion

Next you will need to spend some time figuring out a title. Just as you are more likely to read a magazine article with a clever title, so your reader will be more eager to read your paper if you give it a good title. (And remember that every important word in a title is capitalized.) Which of these titles from student papers would make you want to read further?

It's Not Just Pumping Gas
Ready! Wrestle!
An Interesting Experience
A Place I'll Never Forget
Birth on a Sidewalk

Assignment 3   A Problem I'm Trying to Solve

Now return to the two thesis statements you wrote about a problem you are trying to solve and choose one to write about. Even if your mind is not completely made up, take a stand on one side. You may mention in your introduction that there are arguments on the other side, but you must take a stand on one side if your paper is to be effective.

As you write, imagine you are talking to your reader. Then when you have finished writing, read your paper *aloud* slowly word by word to catch omitted words, errors in spelling or punctuation, run-together sentences, fragments, wordiness. Finally, read it aloud once more at normal speed to see whether it reads smoothly.

Assignment 4   A Letter to Someone Who Has Influenced Me

What person, other than a parent, has been of great influence in your life? Has someone—perhaps a teacher or a counselor or a coach—encouraged you in athletics or music, influenced you in the choice of a career, given you confidence in yourself? Write a thesis statement saying that a certain person has influenced you, and organize under two or three main points the ways in which you were influenced. Then write a letter to that person telling him what he has done for you, remembering to use specific examples. Even though you are writing a letter, it will still be in essay form, with an introduction, a paragraph for each supporting point, and a conclusion.

Assignment 5   In Praise of Something

Write a paper praising something. It might be a job you enjoyed, an activity such as dramatics or music from which you have benefited, a sport that has done something for you, a kind of motorcycle or car you think is superior. Be sure to limit your subject. Basketball for example would not be a possible subject because it's too broad. You might limit it to what a particular basketball game did for you. After you have limited your subject, work out a good thesis statement with two or three supporting points. Then write your paper using plenty of specific details.

Before you hand your paper in, read it aloud *slowly* word by word to catch errors.

Assignment 6   A Letter to Myself

One reason for writing is to gain knowledge about ourselves. For this assignment instead of looking outward, look inward. Have a talk with yourself. What are some things you've been telling yourself you should or should not do? Ten minutes of free writing will be a good way to find out what material you have. Then work out a thesis statement and write a letter to yourself. One student began his letter "Dear Ben, Why don't you wise up?" Then he went on to tell three things he knew he should be doing. It's always harder to analyze oneself than someone else, but it can be fun and perhaps productive.

Assignment 7   The Meaning of Maturity

In groups of three or four, discuss what maturity means. Does it have much to do with chronological age? Are there certain qualities every mature person has? After your discussion, write a thesis statement listing the two or three outstanding qualities you think any mature person will have. Then write a paper giving specific examples from your own experience or observation.

Assignment 8   My Opinion on a Current Problem

Choose one of the problems below and present your arguments for one side. Write a carefully thought out thesis statement, supported by reasons, before you begin to write your paper. In your introduction or conclusion you may want to mention briefly the reasons you can see for the opposite side.

A. A couple, both alcoholics and totally unable to care for their infant son, were forced by the court to place him in a foster home. Ten years later the couple, by then completely rehabilitated, asked to have their child returned to them. The boy had come to think of his foster parents as his real parents, and they in turn thought of him as their son. But the courts gave the boy, against his wishes, back to his natural parents. If you had been the judge, what would you have done?

B. The most important football game of the season is coming up, with the outcome depending largely on one top player. Unfortunately that player, although he has put forth considerable effort, has been flunking chemistry all term and now has failed the final exam. He is eager to play because he hopes to have a career in professional football and knows that scouts from professional teams will be watching. If he receives an F or even an Incomplete, he will be ineligible. If you were the chemistry professor, what grade would you give him?

C. A bill is before Congress to create a national park in an area where a commercial lumbering company is ready to move in. The congressman from that district, a conservationist, strongly favors the park and would like to vote for the bill. His constituents, however, are writing him asking that he oppose the bill because they want the commercial lumbering company to come in and create jobs. If you were the congressman, what would you do?

WRITING A SUMMARY

A good way to learn to write concisely is to write 100-word summaries. Writing 100 words sounds easy, but actually it is not. Writing 200 or 300 or 500 words isn't too difficult, but crowding all the main ideas of an essay or article into 100 words is a time-consuming task—not to be undertaken the last hour before class. If you work at writing summaries conscientiously, you will improve your reading ability by learning to spot main ideas, and your writing ability by learning to construct a concise, clear, smooth paragraph. Furthermore, your skill will carry over into your reading and writing for other courses.

Assignment 9   A 100-Word Summary

As you read the following article, jot down any points that seem important enough to include in a summary. Note that difficult words are defined in the margin.

The Jeaning of America—and the World
Carlin C. Quinn

This is the story of a sturdy American symbol which has now spread throughout most of the world. The symbol is not the dollar. It is not even Coca-Cola.

It is a simple pair of pants called blue jeans, and what the pants symbolize is what Alexis de Tocqueville called "a manly and legitimate passion for equality. . . ." Blue jeans are favored equally by bureaucrats and cowboys; bankers and deadbeats; fashion designers and beer drinkers. They draw no distinctions and recognize no classes; they are merely American. Yet they are sought after almost everywhere in the world—including Russia, where authorities recently broke up a teen-aged gang that was selling them on the black market for two hundred dollars a pair. They have been around for a long time, and it seems likely that they will outlive even the necktie.

de Tocqueville (1805–1859)—a French historian who wrote about America

This ubiquitous American symbol was the invention of a Bavarian-born Jew . . . Levi Strauss. He was born in Bad Ocheim, Germany, in 1829, and during the European political turmoil of 1848 decided to take his chances in New York, to which his two brothers already had emigrated. Upon arrival, Levi soon found that his two brothers had exaggerated their tales of an easy life in the land of the main chance. They were landowners, they had told him; instead, he found them pushing needles, thread, pots, pans, ribbons, yarn, scissors, and buttons to housewives. For two years he was a lowly peddler, hauling some 180 pounds of sundries door-to-door to eke out a marginal living. When a married sister in San Francisco offered to pay his way West in 1850, he jumped at the opportunity, taking with him bolts of canvas he hoped to sell for tenting.

ubiquitous—present everywhere

eke out—to make with great effort
marginal—low quality

It was the wrong kind of canvas for that purpose, but while talking with a miner down from the mother lode, he learned that pants—sturdy pants that would stand up to the rigors of the diggings—were almost impossible to find. Opportunity beckoned. On the spot, Strauss measured the man's girth and inseam with a piece of string and, for six dollars in gold dust, had them tailored into a pair of stiff but rugged pants. The miner was delighted with the result, word got around about "those pants of Levi's," and Strauss was in business. The company has been in business ever since.

lode—a vein of mineral ore between rocks

When Strauss ran out of canvas, he wrote his two brothers to send more. He received instead a tough, brown cotton cloth made in Nîmes, France—called *serge de Nîmes* and swiftly shortened to "denim" (the word "jeans" derives from *Gênes*, the French word for Genoa, where a similar cloth was produced). Almost from the first, Strauss had his cloth dyed the distinctive indigo that gave blue jeans their name, but it was not until the 1870's that he added the copper rivets which have long since become a company trademark. The rivets were the idea of a Virginia City, Nevada, tailor, Jacob W. Davis, who added them to pacify a mean-tempered miner called Alkali Ike. Alkali, the story goes, complained that the pockets of his jeans always tore when he stuffed them with ore samples and demanded that Davis do something about it. As a kind of joke, Davis took the pants to a blacksmith and had the pockets riveted; once again, the idea worked so well that word got around; in 1873 Strauss appropriated and patented the gimmick—and hired Davis as a regional manager.

appropriate—to take possession of

By this time, Strauss had taken both his brothers and two brothers-in-law into the company and was ready for his third San Francisco store. Over the ensuing years the company prospered locally, and by the time of his death in 1902, Strauss had become a man of prominence in California. For three decades thereafter the business remained profitable though small, with sales largely confined to the working people of the West—cowboys, lumberjacks, railroad workers, and the like. Levi's jeans were first introduced to the East, apparently, during the dude-ranch craze of the 1930's, when vacationing Easterners returned and spread the word about the wonderful pants with rivets. Another boost came in World War II, when blue jeans were declared an essential commodity and were sold only to people engaged in defense work. From a company with fifteen salespeople, two plants, and almost no business east of the Mississippi in 1946, the organization grew in thirty years to include a sales force of more than twenty-two thousand, with fifty plants and offices in thirty-five countries. Each year, more than 250,000,000 items of Levi's clothing are sold—including more than 83,000,000 pairs of riveted blue jeans. They have become, through marketing, word of mouth, and demonstrable reliability, the common pants of America. They can be purchased pre-

ensuing—following

demonstrable—capable of being proved

washed, pre-faded, and pre-shrunk for the suitably proletarian look. . . .

proletarian—working class

The pants have become a tradition, and along the way have acquired a history of their own—so much so that the company has opened a museum in San Francisco. There was, for example, the turn-of-the-century trainman who replaced a faulty coupling with a pair of jeans; the Wyoming man who used his jeans as a towrope to haul his car out of a ditch; the Californian who found several pairs in an abandoned mine, wore them, then discovered they were sixty-three years old and still as good as new and turned them over to the Smithsonian as a tribute to their toughness. And then there is the particularly terrifying story of the careless construction worker who dangled fifty-two stories above the street until rescued, his sole support the Levi's belt loop through which his rope was hooked.

Smithsonian—a musem in Washington, D.C.

Today "those pants of Levi's" have gone across the seas—although the company has learned that marketing abroad is an arcane art. The conservative-dress jeans favored in northern France do not move on the Côte d'Azur; Sta-Prest sells well in Switzerland but dies in Scandinavia; button fronts are popular in France, zippers in Britain.

arcane—secret

Though Levi Strauss & Co. has since become Levi Strauss International, with all that the corporate name implies, it still retains a suitably fond regard for its beginnings. Through what it calls its "Western Image Program," employing Western magazine advertisements, local radio and television, and the promotion of rodeos, the company still pursues the working people of the West who first inspired Levi Strauss to make pants to fit the world.

How honest can you be with yourself?

If you want to learn to write a good summary—for this course and for exam questions in other courses—follow these suggestions. Write what you are asked to write **BEFORE YOU LOOK AHEAD** so that you will do your own thinking and learning. It's always tempting to look ahead to find the right answer, but only if you work out the summary *yourself*, will you learn how to write one.

A good way to begin is to figure out the author's thesis statement. Usually it is suggested in the first paragraph. Reread the first paragraph of the article, and decide what main idea the author wanted to get across to the reader. Write that idea down **BEFORE YOU READ FURTHER.**

You probably wrote something like this: *An American symbol of equality now spreading throughout the world is a simple pair of pants called blue jeans.*

Using that thesis statement as your first sentence, summarize as briefly as you can the rest of the article, which is simply the history and present status of blue jeans.

Your aim in writing your summary should be to give someone who has not read the article a clear idea of it. Your first draft will probably be 150 words or more. Now cut it down by omitting all but the most important points and by getting rid of wordiness. Keep within the 100-word limit. You may have a few words less but not a single word more. And *every* word counts. By forcing yourself to keep within the 100 words, you will get to the very kernel of the author's thought and will gain a better understanding of the article.

When you have written the best summary you can (it may take a couple of hours), copy it to hand in. Then, and not until then, compare it with the summary on page 283. If you look at the model sooner, you will cheat yourself of the opportunity to learn to write summaries because once you read the model, it will be almost impossible not to make yours similar. So do your own thinking and writing and *then* compare.

Even though your summary is different from the model, it may be just as good. If you are not sure how yours compares, ask yourself these questions:

Did I include as many important ideas?

Did I omit all unnecessary words and phrases?

Does my summary read as smoothly?

Would someone who had not read the article get as clear an idea of it from my summary?

Assignment 10   Another 100-Word Summary

Now that you have had some practice in writing a summary, try writing one for the following essay. Keep within the 100-word limit and write so clearly that someone who has not read the essay will get all its main points. When yours is in final form, compare it with the one at the back of the book. Yours may differ and still be a good summary.

Death or Taxes

Back in the 1920's people called them coffin nails. Nobody knew exactly why cigarettes were harmful, but many thought they were. Today few people question that cigarette smoking is a health hazard, with statistics

Sources: *Newsweek*, Jan. 30, 1978, p. 74; *Science*, Feb. 17, 1978, p. 753; *Business Week*, Jan. 30, 1978, p. 23, and May 29, 1978, p. 68.

from HEW indicating that in 1977 smoking was a major factor in 220,000 deaths from heart disease, 78,000 from lung cancer, and 22,000 from other forms of cancer. But despite these statistics, smoking is decreasing hardly at all. Men have reduced their smoking, but women and teen-agers are smoking more, and twice as many teen-age girls are smoking now as were smoking ten years ago. Alarmed, various organizations are trying to get America to kick the habit.

The National Commission on Smoking and Public Policy (an offshoot of the American Cancer Society) has asked Congress to give the Food and Drug Administration the authority to regulate cigarettes. It also has asked the Department of Defense to quit selling tax-free cigarettes at PX's, where service personnel can buy a pack for from seven to ten cents. And it wants the American Cancer Society and other health organizations to spend more of their budgets on public education about smoking.

Insurance companies are offering incentives to nonsmokers. The State Mutual Life Assurance Company of America has been offering non-smokers discounts of from 3.5% to 5% since 1964, and dozens of other insurance companies have followed suit. One company, the Hanover Insurance Company of Worcester, Massachusetts, even offers discounts on homeowner and driver policies. The decrease in fire risk for homeowners is obvious, and regarding driver policies a Hanover spokesman says, "Non-smokers have fewer distractions and probably are more cautious individuals."

More and more companies are paying their workers to stop smoking on the job, finding that cutting down on smoking boosts productivity, reduces the fire hazard, and cuts absenteeism. The Speedcall Corporation of Hayward, California, which offers its employees a $7 bonus for each week they do not smoke, paid its employees $9,828 in 1977. Another company offers its 140 employees $500 to quit smoking for a year, and so far 32 workers have collected. At another company nonsmokers collect $10 a month, and at still another, employees get a 50-cents-an-hour raise after six months of non-smoking. Even the big companies—General Foods Corporation and the New York City branch of Sears—have their own plans. Money talks. People who would not quit for health reasons have quit because of dollars in their pockets.

The Department of Health, Education, and Welfare also has launched a campaign against smoking, under the direction of Secretary Joseph Califano, a three-packs-a-day man until he stopped smoking as a birthday present to his worried 11-year-old son. Although Califano calls the campaign "the most vigorous program against smoking this country has ever seen," it has turned out to be more recommendation than action. It advocates restricting smoking in public buildings, suggests a graduated tax on cigarettes that would make those with the most tar the most expensive, and asks the Civil Aeronautics Board to ban smoking on commercial airlines. The program, predictably, has not been well accepted. Naturally the tobacco interests object, but the antismoking groups are also complaining. They say the $23 million allotted to the campaign is a paltry sum compared to the estimated $400 million spent on advertising by the tobacco industry. They also claim the government is undercutting its own program by paying $65 million a year in subsidies to tobacco growers. Furthermore, the critics point out, the reason the government is not putting on a more vigorous campaign is probably because it takes in $6 billion a year in taxes from tobacco products and a billion and a half more from tobacco exports.

Where will all these campaigns to combat smoking lead? They will help many individuals no doubt, but the overall effect may depend on whether the government ever decides to launch more than a halfhearted campaign. Yes, smoking causes deaths—but smoking also brings in taxes. It's a problem the government will eventually have to come to grips with—death or taxes.

Assignment 11   One More Summary

The following article from *Time* will give you one more chance to write a summary. Keep to the 100-word limit, crowd in as many facts as possible, and give your reader the flavor of the article. When your summary is ready to hand in, compare it with the one at the back of the book.

I Am Somebody

An imposing man with the build of a football player and the command of a general strides onstage in the high school auditorium. Immediately, the audience falls silent. He captures the students expertly, first soothing them with his soft, sensuous voice, then whipping them into a frenzy with a quickening cadence. "We can be as good in academics as in athletics," he shouts, "but we've got to believe we are somebody. Repeat after me, 'I am somebody.'" Hundreds of teenagers rise to their feet, chanting, "I may be poor, but I am somebody. I may be on welfare, but I am somebody. Nobody can save us, for us, but us." He calls the captain of the basketball team to the stage. "If you're behind in the game, what do you do?" he asks. "Try harder," declares the hoopster. "Say amen!" yells the preacher. A chorus booms back.

The pep rally is in a Chicago ghetto school; the

sensuous—appealing to the senses

cadence—rhythmic flow, as of language

Adapted from "Learning to Excel in School," *Time*, July 10, 1978. Reprinted by permission from TIME, The Weekly Newsmagazine; Copyright Time Inc. 1978.

cheerleader is none other than the Rev. Jesse Jackson (he was ordained as a Baptist minister). His style is a combination of razzle-dazzle and Southern revival meeting. But the message is a very basic version of the old Protestant work ethic: work hard and aim high. In corridors where punks push dope, Jackson pushes hope. Project EXCEL, a tough self-help regimen for students and parents alike, which reached 21 schools in Chicago, Los Angeles and Kansas City during this past school year, is turning the old ghetto battle cry of "Burn, baby burn!" into "Work, brother, work!"

regimen—system

. . . [Jackson's] message to underclass blacks is that they must learn not to rely on help from the outside, that they must take responsibility for their own upward mobility and the quality of their lives.

mobility—movement

. . . .

Since Jackson blames an abdication of responsibility for the downfall of standards in U.S. schools, his strategy calls for renewed cooperation among students, teachers and parents. "We get parents to pledge four things: to meet with the child's teacher and exchange phone numbers, to pick up report cards four times a year, to pick up test scores and to make sure that their children study two hours a night without radio or television. We know that when parents' interest increases, the student's effort increases. Jackson is also advocating dress codes and student decorum to help restore school discipline and pride.

abdication—giving up

decorum—correct conduct

Many young apostles seem to be espousing Jackson's creed. During the 1976-77 school year in Kansas City's Central High School, an average of 500 students out of 1,300 were absent each day. Last month the absenteeism was down to 200 students a day. A student pride association raised money to carpet the auditorium, paint murals on the walls and plant trees.

apostle—one who leads a new cause
espousing—supporting

EXCEL high schools in Los Angeles and Chicago are enjoying similar benefits: less graffiti, fewer fights, a reduction in thefts. In Chicago's Marshall High School, where city cops not so long ago were keeping students from knifing one another, the police are becoming counselors. Another indication of the turn-around at Marshall is a sharp increase in the number of students choosing advanced English, math and science courses as electives. . . .

Part of the reason for Jackson's success is that he symbolizes black brotherhood. Jackson was beside Martin Luther King, Jr., when he died; he fought for jobs for blacks in Chicago's Operation Breadbasket twelve years ago and, at age 36, he has smoothed some of the rougher edges of his younger years and acquired substantial authority within the civil rights movement. He is also the father of five children ages 2 to 14, and knows about the problems they face. Few others, particularly whites, could emerge as heroes by telling ghetto kids to shape up. Jackson has credibility as well as charisma.

· · · · · · · ·

... Jackson and Project EXCEL have drawn national attention to the fact that reform of inner-city schools, often regarded as hopeless, actually can be achieved. HEW has awarded EXCEL $400,000 next year to expand into four more cities, and the National Institute of Education is funding a study to determine EXCEL's effectiveness. Indeed students everywhere can learn a lesson from Jesse Jackson: "When the doors of opportunity swing open, we must make sure that we are not too drunk or too indifferent to walk through."

credibility—believe-ability
charisma—ability to attract supporters

WRITING AN APPLICATION

Assignment 12 A Letter of Application

You may not need to do much writing in the career you have chosen, but almost certainly you will at some time need to write a letter of application. Write a letter of application now, either for a job this coming summer or for a job you might want to apply for after you finish college. Then on a separate sheet write a résumé. Follow the forms given here.

500 West Adams Street
Macomb, Illinois 61455
February 1, 1979

Mr. John Blank, Director
Chicago Park District
425 East McFetridge Drive
Chicago, Illinois 60605

Dear Mr. Blank:

I have seen your ad in the Chicago <u>Tribune</u> for helpers in the Park District Recreation Department for the coming summer. I would like to be considered for a position.

I am a freshman at Western Illinois University and am majoring in Special Education. Therefore I would be particularly pleased if I could work with mentally or physically handicapped children.

I have listed my training and experience on the enclosed résumé, and I shall be glad to come for an interview at your convenience.

Sincerely,

John Doe

John Doe

```
            John Doe
            500 West Adams
            Macomb, Illinois 61455
            Telephone: 000-000-0000
```

PERSONAL
      Age 18
      Height 5 feet, 10 inches
      Weight 145 pounds
      Unmarried

EDUCATION
      1978-1979   Freshman at Western Illinois Univer-
                  sity. Majoring in Special Education.
      1974-1978   Student at McKenzie High School,
                  Chicago.

ACTIVITIES
      Bowling
      Swimming. Won second place in a swimming meet
                  at Western in 1979.

WORK EXPERIENCE
      1978 summer. Helper in County of St. Louis
                   Department of Parks and Recreation.
                   Worked with mentally handicapped
                   children.
      1977 summer. Worked at a private camp at Lake
                   Minden, Wisconsin, coaching
                   swimming.
      1976 summer. Took a tour with a group from my
                   high school to Washington, D.C.,
                   and then helped at the South
                   Chicago YMCA pool, working with
                   physically handicapped children.

REFERENCES
      Mr. John Jones, Director
      County of St. Louis
      Department of Parks and Recreation
      7900 Forsyth Boulevard, St. Louis, Missouri 63105

      Mr. Henry Smith, Director
      Lake Minden Camp for Boys
      Lake Minden, Wisconsin   00000
```
```

WRITING AN EVALUATION

Assignment 13   What I've Gained from This Course
or Why I Haven't Gained What I Might Have from This Course

Do five minutes of free writing on your performance in this course. Don't evaluate the course—it may have been bad or good—but simply evaluate how you performed. Although you may need to mention some weakness or strength of the course, the emphasis must be on how you reacted to that weakness or strength.

Don't be afraid to be honest. This isn't an occasion for apple-polishing. If you've gained little, you'll write a better paper by saying so than by trying to cook up phony gains. Someone who has gained little may write a better paper than someone who has gained much. How well the paper is organized and whether there are plenty of specific examples will determine the effectiveness of the paper.

After you have written your thesis statement, list your supporting points. If you have made gains, list the kinds—gains in study habits, gains in writing skills, gains in confidence, etc. Or, if you have gained little, list the reasons why—lack of time, lack of interest, getting off to a bad start, etc.

Since no one will have all gain or all loss in any course, you may want to include in your introduction or conclusion a sentence about the other side.

Answers

Answers

Words Often Confused (p. 9)

□EXERCISE 1

1. have, course
2. an, effect
3. fourth, compliment
4. advise, accept, or
5. knew, an
6. coarse, cloths
7. advise, break
8. Our, Desert
9. conscious, dessert
10. It's, new

□EXERCISE 2

1. know, advice
2. course, chose, affect
3. all ready, except
4. compliment, effect
5. its, new
6. are, fourth
7. already
8. chose, choose
9. have, clothes
10. knew, brake

□EXERCISE 3

1. have, our
2. conscience, knew
3. choose
4. an, a
5. Our, new, all ready
6. Its, an, it's
7. forth
8. conscious, clothes
9. break, dessert
10. does, course

□EXERCISE 4

1. accept
2. course, compliment
3. It's
4. clothes, does
5. break
6. It's, its
7. effect, affect
8. conscience, desert
9. a, our, fourth
10. dose, have

□EXERCISE 5

1. new, clothes
2. course, an
3. course, have
4. doesn't, know
5. conscious, advice
6. know, our
7. have, chose
8. fourth
9. compliments, effect
10. choose, choose

□EXERCISE 6

1. forth
2. no
3. doesn't, affect
4. already, fourth
5. it's, except

6. chose, break
7. have, dessert
8. knew, choose
9. clothes, coarse, cloths
10. have, it's

□EXERCISE 7

1. conscious, advise
2. brakes, already
3. course, no
4. clothes
5. effect

6. advice, have, accept
7. chose, desert
8. It's
9. dose, effect
10. knew, break

□EXERCISE 8

1. conscious, effect
2. choose, chose
3. already, forth
4. our, its
5. doesn't, affect, except

6. conscience, doesn't, break
7. course, conscious
8. forth, its
9. It's, dessert
10. chose, except

□EXERCISE 9

1. does, advice
2. a, already
3. course, an
4. It's, our
5. have

6. knew, have
7. its
8. It's, desert
9. know, fourth
10. brake

□EXERCISE 10

1. It's, already
2. advise, accept
3. affect
4. chose, new, clothes
5. doesn't, advice

6. have, compliment
7. conscious
8. Coarse, are, our
9. desserts, coarse
10. It's, choose

Words Often Confused (continued) (p. 16)

□EXERCISE 1

1. too, conscience, doesn't
2. They're, already
3. too
4. lose, threw
5. personnel
6. principal, it's, than
7. where, were
8. quite, your
9. whether, moral
10. Their, they're

□EXERCISE 2

1. It's, than
2. passed
3. past
4. there
5. threw, through
6. woman, lead, women's
7. their, than
8. know, principal
9. Who's, your
10. Peace, quiet

□EXERCISE 3

1. lose, piece
2. too, too, to
3. women, quite, their
4. Whose
5. They're, two
6. You're, there, no
7. threw, then
8. Who's, weather
9. morale, principle
10. Loose, our

□EXERCISE 4

1. Your, personal
2. Whose, where
3. You're, quite
4. led, peace
5. know, whether, than
6. two, principles
7. It's, too, quiet
8. principal, its, loose
9. too
10. past

□EXERCISE 5

1. It's, too, know
2. Our, lose
3. quite, weather
4. principal, coarse
5. woman
6. morale, personnel
7. personal
8. They're, their
9. Their, than
10. threw, through

□EXERCISE 6

1. Who's, there
2. whether, you're, your
3. principal
4. past
5. passed, quite
6. woman, to
7. principal, quiet
8. where
9. Whose, were
10. weather, than

□EXERCISE 7

1. whose
2. You're, your, weather
3. new, affect, except
4. too
5. already, clothes, than
6. piece, advice
7. know, whether
8. personal
9. women, through, their
10. lead

□EXERCISE 8

1. you're, your
2. Where, piece
3. Your, its
4. then, their
5. moral, principles
6. loose
7. principal, its, morale
8. knew, lose, our
9. led, lead
10. forth, then

□EXERCISE 9

1. woman, whether
2. through, chose
3. Where, women
4. peace, quiet
5. threw, then
6. There, no
7. woman, where
8. passed
9. chose, course
10. led, except

□EXERCISE 10

1. know, no, it's
2. You're, quite, clothes
3. weather, too
4. principles, accept
5. threw, passed, course
6. Where, were
7. fourth
8. compliment, you're, too
9. Who's, choose
10. It's, break

Rule for Doubling a Final Consonant (p. 21)

□EXERCISE 1

1. putting
2. controlling
3. admitting
4. mopping
5. planning
6. hopping
7. jumping
8. knitting
9. marking
10. creeping

□EXERCISE 2

1. returning
2. swimming
3. singing
4. benefiting
5. loafing
6. nailing
7. omitting
8. occurring
9. shopping
10. interrupting

□EXERCISE 3

1. beginning
2. spelling
3. preferring
4. fishing
5. hunting
6. excelling
7. wrapping
8. stopping
9. wedding
10. screaming

□EXERCISE 4

1. feeling
2. motoring
3. turning
4. adding
5. subtracting
6. streaming
7. expelling
8. missing
9. getting
10. stressing

□EXERCISE 5

1. forgetting
2. misspelling
3. fitting
4. planting
5. pinning
6. trusting
7. sipping
8. flopping
9. reaping
10. carting

□EXERCISE 6

1. attending
2. compelling
3. napping
4. curling
5. amounting
6. obtaining
7. dreaming
8. crawling
9. cropping
10. descending

□EXERCISE 7

1. permitting
2. despairing
3. eating
4. developing
5. quitting

6. exceeding
7. finishing
8. hitting
9. flinching
10. referring

□EXERCISE 8

1. regarding
2. equipping
3. kicking
4. sitting
5. knocking

6. sleeping
7. skipping
8. leaping
9. shipping
10. mentioning

□EXERCISE 9

1. stirring
2. mending
3. shrieking
4. murmuring
5. viewing

6. meeting
7. speaking
8. succeeding
9. pretending
10. deferring

□EXERCISE 10

1. pulling
2. predicting
3. redeeming
4. patrolling
5. slanting

6. steaming
7. ripping
8. spending
9. tipping
10. tripping

Contractions (p. 26)

□EXERCISE 1

1. Everyone's, where's
2. We're, I'm
3. Who's
4. I'm, I'll, you'll
5. couldn't, wouldn't

6. doesn't, it's
7. they're, they'll
8. You're, aren't
9. you'll, I'll
10. don't, I've

□EXERCISE 2

1. She'll, I've
2. we're, let's
3. Won't, don't
4. He's, can't
5.

6. hasn't
7. haven't, I'm
8. I've
9. Can't, isn't
10. Doesn't

□EXERCISE 3

1. haven't
2. Where's
3. Who's
4. I'd, they'd
5. It's, I've

6. He's, he's
7. There's, we're
8. Aren't, haven't
9. We've
10. I'm, there'll

□EXERCISE 4

1. I'm, you're
2. There's
3. It's, can't
4. I've, I've
5. didn't

6. It's, isn't
7. Can't, don't
8. We've
9. they're
10. It's, that's

□EXERCISE 5

1. It's
2. I'm, I've
3. There's
4. I'd
5. you've, it's

6. It's, it's
7. Don't, you'll
8. We've, we've
9. It's, I'm
10. We've

□EXERCISE 6

1. It's, you're
2. you'll, you'll
3. Don't
4. It's, you're
5. you've

6. They're, you'll
7. you'll
8. It's, you've
9. it's
10. it's

□EXERCISE 7

1. It's, you're
2. you'll, you'll
3. You'll, you'll
4. You'll
5. It's

6. We've
7. I've, there's, I'd
8. haven't, we'll
9. It's
10. I've, I'm

□EXERCISE 8

1. It's, you're
2. I'm
3. There's
4. I'm
5. He's, hasn't

6. She's, won't
7. I'm, I'm
8. hasn't, he'll
9. isn't
10. They'd, they're

□EXERCISE 9

1. Where's, who's
2. who's, It's
3. Where's, Who's
4. She's, isn't, it's
5. It's, he's

6. It's
7. They've
8. Isn't
9. I'm, it's
10. I'm, I've

□EXERCISE 10

1. We're, haven't
2. We've, it's
3. I've, I'm
4. It's
5. we've

6. We've, we're
7. He's, hasn't
8. Isn't, he's
9. I've, he's
10. Nobody's

Possessives (p. 32)

□EXERCISE 1

1. Aileen's
2. girl's, boy's
3. morning's
4. Jim's
5.
6.
7. Andy's
8. week's
9.
10. Jeff's

□EXERCISE 2

1. Browns'
2.
3. James'
4. Norman's
5.
6. Janet's, Wednesday's
7. women's
8. men's, boys'
9. coach's
10.

□EXERCISE 3

1. Cathy's
2. day's
3. Susan's
4. son's
5. Lisa's
6. anybody's
7. Women's
8. mayor's
9. day's
10. morning's

□EXERCISE 4

1.
2. Michael's
3. Pat's, Trudy's
4. twins', Bonnie's
5.
6. dad's, grandfather's
7. Roy's
8. child's
9. Philip's
10. salesman's

□EXERCISE 5

1. pioneers'
2. father's
3.
4. else's
5. Ray's, Scott's
6. students'
7. children's
8. everybody's
9. person's, person's
10. Dickens'

□EXERCISE 6

1. Margaret's
2. women's, girls'
3. mother's
4.
5. Ralph's, Allen's
6. anyone's
7. women's
8. brother-in-law's
9. lecturer's
10.

□EXERCISE 7

1. Beth's
2. president's
3. Ivan's
4. Saturday's
5. night's, today's
6. Dad's
7. uncle's
8. else's
9. sister's
10. world's

□EXERCISE 8

1. Janice's, Charles'
2. dad's
3.
4.
5. Jones'
6.
7. Sandburg's
8. Honolulu's
9. Judy's
10. Richard's

□EXERCISE 9

1.
2.
3. Paul's
4. Someone's
5. day's
6. Tchaikovsky's
7.
8. president's
9. Hardings'
10. Cindy's

□EXERCISE 10

1.
2. parents'
3. Today's, dad's
4. club's
5. Roger's, Guy's
6. children's
7. child's, Carpenters'
8. anybody's
9. instructor's
10. Derrick's

Review of Contractions and Possessives (p. 35)

□EXERCISE 1

1. I'd, person's
2. They're, other's
3. He's, doctor's
4. didn't, Gail's
5.

6. Hasn't, president's
7. He's, men's, boys'
8. I'm, women's
9. women's, girls', men's, boys'
10. We're, Smiths', can't

□EXERCISE 2

1. Jones', yesterday's
2. Shouldn't, Francis'
3. I've
4. Who's
5. Won't

6. There'll, they've
7. It's, there's
8. can't
9. couldn't, they're
10. I'm, I've

□EXERCISE 3

1. There'll, I'm
2. Loren's, doesn't, he's
3. He'd, he'll
4. I'd, haven't
5. Gwen's, Diane's

6. Jennifer's, Becky's
7. Isn't, tutor's
8. We're, Robin's
9. I'm, we're
10. Isn't, she's, Jean's

□EXERCISE 4

1. Browns'
2. It's, Brown's
3. Brown's
4. It's, I'm
5. men's, women's

6. I'm, Ruth's
7. One's
8. I'm, you're
9. don't
10. It's, hasn't

□EXERCISE 5

There's a little lake with steep rocky sides and crystal clear water that you can see down into forever. Some say it's bottomless, but everyone agrees it's deep.

There's one spot where a big tree grows over the lake, and someone's tied a rope to one of its branches to swing on. It's a great sensation, I discovered, to swing out over the water and then let go. I think everyone gets an urge to yell as loud as possible to enhance his awkward dive. It's a great feeling to cast off from the high rocks holding onto the rope as it swings out over the water. Just before the farthest point of the rope's travel is the best place to let go and drop into the water. Those with initiative try flips and twists as they dive, but however it's done, it's a great sensation. Some say it's for kids, but I hope I never grow too old to have fun at it.

Finding Subjects and Verbs (p. 40)

□EXERCISE 1

1. rains came
2. I planted
3. trip was
4. Diet is
5. tree was

6. Schubert earned
7. Change is
8. writing depends
9. (You) stop
10. Mounties get

□EXERCISE 2

1. spruce was
2. He traveled
3. *The Time Machine* is
4. She has
5. briefcase lay

6. (You) say
7. Mr. Stepp understands
8. Mr. Puette is
9. We had
10. conditions improve

□EXERCISE 3

1. pony stood
2. cheetah is
3. I saw
4. I watched
5. (You) sign

6. Captain Cook brought
7. They are
8. palm bears
9. nut weighs
10. fruit requires

□EXERCISE 4

1. Children pick
2. Anxiety is
3. Self-confidence dispels
4. (You) fasten
5. He's

6. What is
7. neophyte is
8. cheerleaders were
9. (You) keep
10. chance is

□EXERCISE 5

1. (You) write
2. harp echoed
3. group turned
4. man is
5. *The Sirens of Titan* is

6. shaft was
7. house was
8. pine was
9. end was
10. Brown called

□EXERCISE 6

1. She drove
2. He was
3. He influenced
4. he encouraged
5. I visited

6. I wrote
7. I had
8. I enjoyed
9. class liked
10. I like

□EXERCISE 7

1. vocabulary is
2. He kept
3. He used
4. He sat
5. I admired

6. He was
7. We watched
8. we heard
9. coat contrasted
10. panels are

□EXERCISE 8

1. mother made
2. She iced
3. brother appeared
4. drifts were
5. We tunneled

6. (You) turn
7. (You) save
8. we went
9. It was
10. I enjoyed

□EXERCISE 9

1. tern travels
2. *Queen Elizabeth II* is
3. I learned
4. It means
5. person talks

6. *sol* means
7. soliloquy is
8. races are
9. It takes
10. participants compete

□EXERCISE 10

1. sun is
2. "black holes" were
3. "black hole" is
4. gravity crushed
5. gravity crushed

6. it "disappeared"
7. It became
8. universe has
9. It is
10. galaxies are

Subjects Not in Prepositional Phrases (p. 45)

□EXERCISE 1

1. One was
2. We followed
3. Clumps bordered
4. stream flowed
5. fish were
6. lanterns were
7. waterfall was
8. steps led
9. atmosphere enveloped
10. Some are

□EXERCISE 2

1. row is
2. spruces are
3. dozens nest
4. jays are
5. birds visit
6. magpies are
7. squirrel hops
8. I hear
9. One is
10. I remember

□EXERCISE 3

1. posters hang
2. he does
3. Both like
4. Most are
5. Three have
6. Each works
7. Most are
8. couple write
9. percent are
10. All welcome

□EXERCISE 4

1. Most practice
2. majority go
3. they give
4. One is
5. people are
6. counselor helped
7. I work
8. I catch
9. letters have
10. I feel

□EXERCISE 5

1. One is
2. painting was
3. One went
4. Most prefer
5. One is
6. Ice made
7. patches appeared
8. sight reminded
9. line broke
10. webs were

□EXERCISE 6

1. we left
2. Neither wanted
3. I found
4. children ran
5. All were
6. she took
7. Most were
8. she passed
9. One gave
10. All were

□EXERCISE 7

1. One is
2. most live
3. Most have
4. None have
5. People speak
6. All write
7. Half lives
8. Saudi Arabia sits
9. Genetics is
10. noise was

□EXERCISE 8

1. age was
2. atoms are
3. star is
4. he had
5. he found
6. I boarded
7. pictures hung
8. I prefer
9. Writing is
10. statement gives

□EXERCISE 9

1. tones rose
2. cymbals crashed
3. sound died
4. Much results
5. call came
6. She juggled
7. One was
8. lovers flock
9. Most are
10. results are

□EXERCISE 10

1. linking was
2. cosmonauts worked
3. environmentalists worry
4. majority give
5. One voted
6. Much bogged
7. changes affected
8. each contributes
9. network is
10. Symbiosis is

More About Verbs and Subjects (p. 49)

☐EXERCISE 1

1. I should have learned
2. I am learning
3. I could concentrate
4. I am improving
5. I have been going
6. I should have been studying
7. I should have started
8. I may finish
9. I must hand
10. I will start

☐EXERCISE 2

1. wind tore, scattered
2. sleet, snow obliterated
3. I shoveled, did tackle
4. woodpecker was hammering
5. Hugh went, cut
6. He sawed, put
7. children unpacked, put
8. decorations had been used
9. Some had been made
10. Everyone was, had

☐EXERCISE 3

1. themes are
2. records are made
3. all are "mixed"
4. results can be
5. business has become
6. It makes
7. companies take
8. I have been wondering
9. you will be giving
10. I am coming

☐EXERCISE 4

1. Americans must decide
2. saying has been
3. saying must be changed
4. exhausts, factories are spewing
5. lead is picked
6. elms were
7. disease struck, has spread
8. elms are
9. government is spending
10. Americans are becoming

☐EXERCISE 5

1. distinction is
2. Nonhumans use
3. use does progress
4. species stores
5. It is passed
6. using has progressed
7. maturity is
8. one needs
9. question is
10. question is, What's

☐EXERCISE 6

1. affair is blossoming
2. spurt is climbing
3. moped is gaining
4. program has selected
5. project will be
6. spacecraft has flown
7. you can find
8. he is putting
9. He has matured
10. He should do

□EXERCISE 7

1. He had worked, deserved
2. Cougars, Hornets played
3. appreciation has progressed
4. she made
5. I have been learning

6. tongue may be
7. Badgers can run
8. *Gulliver's Travels* is considered
9. It was written
10. we can see

□EXERCISE 8

1. attempt is being made
2. criminals commit
3. attack has begun
4. program has been funded
5. it is taking

6. program has put
7. program was
8. justice has proved
9. Criminals fear
10. officials are planning

□EXERCISE 9

1. Americans have won
2. awards are forcing
3. disputes should be settled
4. procedures must be streamlined
5. they walked

6. They had seen
7. He broke, dropped
8. view was blocked
9. you have read
10. Redford, Hoffman gave

□EXERCISE 10

1. Anxiety is, is felt
2. Growing, adapting are
3. people are going, starting
4. Many choose, transfer
5. students are, are

6. education is becoming
7. lights, imagery have entranced
8. some went, saw
9. roots hang, become
10. tree may have

Getting Rid of Run-together Sentences (p. 55)

□EXERCISE 1

1. I have been learning, knowledge helps
2. I've learned, it means
3. disease is, gossip is
4. *Malinger* is, it means
5. brother malingers, I malinger
6. I've learned, it means
7. *Asymmetrical* means, *atypical* means
8. I'm, I am going
9. Writing is, it's
10. It's, it's

□EXERCISE 2

1. I've started, am getting
2. I am learning, I'm learning
3. I do need, I do need
4. I must know, I will understand
5. knowledge is, I will punctuate
6. I recognize, I am avoiding
7. I've worked, it's beginning
8. I must forget, I may catch
9. I will read, I will go
10. I will read, reading will catch

□EXERCISE 3

1. me. She
2. busy,
3. listen;
4. career;
5. time,
6. years;
7. on.
8.
9. circumstances,
10. sending. Reading is receiving;

□EXERCISE 4

1. hospital.
2. suit;
3. application.
4. appointment,
5.
6. time.
7. work. Work
8. indicated. You
9. stories. Their
10. robots. It

□EXERCISE 5

1. country. The
2. stage,
3. students. Attempts
4. semester;
5. far,
6. sink. It
7. provoking;
8. criticize,
9. difficult,
10. all,

□EXERCISE 6

1. acquiring. Making
2. cartons. The . . . white,
3. cupboard,
4. varnish. Then . . . turpentine,
5. antique. It
6.
7. fish. They
8. earth. Some
9. baby. She
10. duck. Keep . . . surface,

☐EXERCISE 7

1. election;
2. 1978. The
3. politics,
4. U.S. The
5. forces. That
6. stores,
7. Louvre. It
8. Confucius.
9. favor.
10. career. None

☐EXERCISE 8

1. days.
2. either. Their
3.
4. year. Their
5. growth. The
6. year-round. They
7. brambles,
8. summer,
9. experiences;
10. money. That . . . advice. Don't
   . . . nickel. Invest . . . yourself.

☐EXERCISE 9

1. man,
2. Korea;
3. holes,
4. it,
5. waterfowl,
6. roam;
7. herbicides. Thus
8.
9. cranes, . . . remain. Three
10.

☐EXERCISE 10

1. Uemura. He
2. world. Everywhere
3. huskies. It
4. Fahrenheit,
5. underwear,
6. dogs,
7.
8. supply. Then
9. bag,
10. returned,

Getting Rid of Fragments (p. 63)

□EXERCISE 1

1. F	6. F
2. S	7. F
3. S	8. F
4. F	9. F
5. F	10. S

□EXERCISE 2

1. F	6. F
2. F	7. F
3. S	8. S
4. F	9. F
5. F	10. S

□EXERCISE 3

1. F	6. S
2. F	7. F
3. F	8. F
4. F	9. S
5. F	10. F

□EXERCISE 4

1. S	6. S
2. F	7. S
3. S	8. F
4. F	9. F
5. F	10. S

□EXERCISE 5

1. You have to practice until using the rules of writing becomes automatic.

2. If you use this book correctly, it will help you to write better.

3. The only difference between an independent and a dependent clause is that the dependent clause begins with a dependent word.

4. If you know the dependent words, you'll have no trouble.

5. If you don't know them, you probably will not punctuate your sentences correctly.

6. A comma is required when a dependent clause comes first in a sentence.

7. No comma is required when the dependent clause comes last.

8. When you have done a few sentences, the rule becomes easy.

9. It will help you when you are punctuating your papers.

10. When you punctuate correctly, your reader can read your writing with ease.

□EXERCISE 6

1. The trouble with most children's television programs is that they do everything for the child.

2. I believe that a child should have time for spontaneous play.

3. "Mr. Roger's Neighborhood" is a good program for children who get too much negative criticism.

4. His neighborhood is a special place where everyone is an important person.

5. Mr. Roger's central message is that each person is acceptable and unique.

6. This is a psychiatric theory that is good for adults too.

7. It's also a major tenet of the Judeo-Christian ethic.

8. I don't know what *tenet* means.

9. I've just looked it up in the dictionary and find that it means "belief."

10. I'm looking up more words than I used to.

□EXERCISE 7

1. that I don't know
2. When I look them up immediately and learn them in their context
3. who were 25 to 34 years of age, who were over 35 years of age
4. which they are preparing themselves for
5. who has always been blind
6. what it would be
7. when they take the elevator instead of the stairs
8. that pervades the universe
9. when the onlookers clapped theirs
10. When they stopped

□EXERCISE 8

1. Since I started to keep a journal
2. that I'll write something in my journal every day now
3. When I write my own sentences
4. if he sets his mind to it
5. When you write a paper
6. what you "ought to say"
7. unless you have conviction
8. who remembers a lady's birthday but forgets her age
9. if you work at it
10. as we need to run a lawn

□EXERCISE 9

1. that really matters
2. Since he couldn't find love
3. because he cares
4. As far as my family is concerned
5. When I wanted to get away
6. Even though it's now gone
7. that one teaspoonful of it would weigh as much as 200 million elephants
8. when dinosaurs were on earth
9. When you love your work
10. When I have written a good paper

□EXERCISE 10

1. that had hung in her college room
2. When she looked at them
3. As she reminisced
4. where she wanted them
5. what she had always wanted to do
6. as we face a growing shortage of energy
7. even though mechanization makes farming more efficient
8. that too many jobs will be lost
9. that are difficult for people to do
10. even though some jobs are lost

More About Fragments (p. 69)

□**EXERCISE 1**

1. F	6. F
2. F	7. F
3. F	8. F
4. S	9. S
5. F	10. F

□**EXERCISE 2**

1. F	6. F
2. F	7. F
3. F	8. F
4. S	9. F
5. F	10. S

□**EXERCISE 3**

1. S	6. F
2. F	7. F
3. F	8. F
4. F	9. S
5. F	10. S

□**EXERCISE 4**

1. F	6. F
2. S	7. F
3. S	8. S
4. F	9. F
5. F	10. F

□**EXERCISE 5**

1. F	6. F
2. F	7. F
3. F	8. F
4. S	9. F
5. F	10. F

□**EXERCISE 6**

1. F	6. F
2. F	7. F
3. F	8. F
4. F	9. F
5. S	10. F

□EXERCISE 7

1. F	6. F
2. S	7. S
3. F	8. S
4. F	9. F
5. S	10. F

□EXERCISE 8

1. Some of the new compact, automatic cameras seem very easy to use until . . . .
2. . . . . We're looking for tough customers who'll ask a lot of hard questions because . . . .
3. I went back home to . . . .
4. Discover a new Horizon, a breakthrough in American automobiles. Plymouth Horizon comes alive with new comforts, new confidence, room for four big people, and . . . .

□EXERCISE 9

1. . . . . He ought to be in your office, your plant, on your farm, learning . . . .
2. . . . . Federal and state laws will determine what your estate is worth, how much of it will go for taxes and many other claims against it, and . . . .
3. We invite you to claim your inheritance: the village where your father was born, the marketplace where your great grandmother shopped, the streets . . . .
4. In fact, 1978 promises to be the most colorful year in *Time*'s history because . . . .

□EXERCISE 10

1. Inside this GE set is advanced computer-like circuitry that uses this VIR signal to . . . .
2. Outward Bound is a shot of high adventure in the wilderness and a lot more. . . . We have special managers' courses, courses for women, courses for your sons and daughters, all . . . .
3. Delta is an airline run by professionals like . . . . He's earned a degree in meteorology, spent four years with the Air Force weather service, and . . . .
4. At Americana, we think getting well is a beautiful thing which . . . . For example: we believe in fine health care at a reasonable cost for . . . .

Review Exercises for Run-together Sentences and Fragments (p. 75)

1. Robert Frost is undoubtedly the most beloved American poet. People who are indifferent to most poetry can often quote "Birches" or "Stopping by Woods on a Snowy Evening." He . . . .

2. There's a place set deep in the woods of northern Minnesota which is very special to me. Every time I go there I'm surrounded with feelings of serenity. The quietness of the area is something that I don't find anywhere else. There's an occasional cry of a hawk circling up above, and sometimes I hear chipmunks scurrying around in the leaves on the ground. These noises always make me feel closer to nature. I . . . .

3. I began wrestling seriously my freshman year. The head wrestling coach was walking around and talking to the kids playing football. He was looking for recruits for the upcoming wrestling season. Several of my friends had decided that they would go out for the team. I decided wrestling would be a good way to keep busy through the winter. Looking back over my wrestling years, I feel it was good for me. I learned that through hard work I could accomplish my goals. My . . . .

4. I know what the chances of survival from cancer are, but I can't give up. I learned as a child during the Depression that it isn't what you've lost but what you've got left that counts. The important thing in any setback is whether you can pick yourself up. One . . . .

5.

"I Have A Dream . . ."

Martin Luther King, Jr.

Five score years ago, a great American, in whose symbolic shadow we stand, signed the Emancipation Proclamation. This momentous decree came as a great beacon light of hope to millions of Negro slaves who had been seared in the flames of withering injustice. It came as a joyous daybreak to end the long night of captivity.

But one hundred years later, we must face the tragic fact that the Negro is still not free. One hundred years later, the life of the Negro is still sadly crippled by the manacles of segregation and the chains of discrimination. One hundred years later, the Negro lives on a lonely island of poverty in the midst of a vast ocean of material prosperity. One hundred years later, the Negro is still languished in the corners of American society and finds himself an exile in his own land. So we have come here today to dramatize an appalling condition.

In a sense we have come to our nation's Capital to cash a check. When the architects of our republic wrote the magnificent words of the Constitution and the Declaration of Independence, they were signing a promissory note to which every American was to fall heir. This note was a promise that all men would be guaranteed the unalienable rights of life, liberty, and the pusuit of happiness.

It is obvious today that America has defaulted on this promissory note insofar as her citizens of color are concerned. Instead of honoring this sacred obligation, America has given the Negro people a bad check, a check which has come back marked "insufficient funds." But we refuse to believe that the bank of justice is bankrupt. We refuse to believe that there are insufficient funds in the great vaults of opportunity of this nation. So we have come to cash this check—a check that will give us upon demand the riches of freedom and the security of justice. We have also come to this hallowed spot to remind America of the fierce urgency of *now*. This is no time to engage in the luxury of cooling off or to take the tranquilizing drug of gradualism. *Now* is the time to make real the promises of Democracy. *Now* is the time to rise from the dark and desolate valley of segregation to the sunlit path of racial justice. *Now* is the time to open the doors of opportunity to all of God's children. *Now* is the time to lift our nation from the quicksands of racial injustice to the solid rock of brotherhood.

Using Standard English Verbs (p.79)

□EXERCISE 1

1. walked, happened
2. doesn't, wants
3. dropped, returned
4. does
5. asked
6. helped
7. finished, talked
8. discussed, helped
9. enjoyed
10. worked, works

□EXERCISE 2

1. asked
2. pleased, asked
3. walked, ordered
4. likes, ordered
5. were
6. had, needed
7. do
8. have, want
9. suggest
10. interest, don't

□EXERCISE 3

1. were
2. were, weren't
3. were
4. observed
5. started
6. are, is
7. asked
8. do, want, does, wants
9. did, watched
10. was, is

□EXERCISE 4

1. does, pleases
2. loaned, asked
3. takes, take
4. jogged
5. like
6. wanted, was
7. is, hope
8. had, invited
9. does
10. wants

□EXERCISE 5

1. contains, contain
2. hope
3. enjoy, dropped
4. wonder, did
5. talked
6. stopped, cooked
7. have, agree
8. used, were
9. played, was, play
10. perform

□EXERCISE 6

1. dozed
2. scared
3. finished, decided
4. discovered
5. appears
6. sealed
7. discussed
8. handed
9. did, answered
10. benefited

□EXERCISE 7

1. walked, asked
2. happened
3. supposed
4. learned
5. asked

6. walked
7. complained
8. has
9. helps
10. does

□EXERCISE 8

1. occurs
2. contains, need
3. do
4. do
5. listened, have

6. don't
7. manage
8. are, are
9. bothers
10. are

□EXERCISE 9

1. performed
2. perform
3. influences
4. insists
5. endeavor, want

6. hope, have
7. celebrated
8. surprised
9. worked, don't
10. volunteered

□EXERCISE 10

1. attended
2. play, played
3. expect
4. worked, learned
5. is

6. plan, want
7. change, have
8. bores, enjoy
9. impressed
10. contained, were

Standard English Verbs (compound forms) (p. 87)

□EXERCISE 1

1. walked
2. walked
3. walked
4. walking
5. walk

6. walk
7. walk
8. walk
9. walked
10. walked

□EXERCISE 2

1. finished
2. finish
3. finish
4. finished
5. finished

6. finish
7. finish
8. finish
9. finish
10. finished

□EXERCISE 3

1. invited
2. danced
3. gone
4. opened
5. started

6. supposed
7. done
8. confused
9. depressed
10. surprised

□EXERCISE 4

1. prepared
2. eaten
3. supposed
4. come
5. disappointed

6. finished
7. begun
8. fallen
9. caught
10. happened

□EXERCISE 5

1. gone
2. needed
3. done
4. enjoyed
5. decided

6. sings
7. sing
8. sung
9. recommended
10. sing

□EXERCISE 6

1. told
2. thought
3. surprised
4. broke
5. broken

6. shattered
7. drove
8. eaten
9. had
10. wanted

□EXERCISE 7

1. liked
2. met
3. met
4. built
5. supposed

6. taught
7. devoted
8. enjoyed
9. gives
10. given

□EXERCISE 8

1. designs
2. concerned
3. caught
4. supposed
5. surprised

6. surprised
7. overwhelmed
8. trained
9. embarrassed
10. frightened

□EXERCISE 9

1. opened
2. fallen
3. begun
4. catching
5. discouraged

6. started
7. gone
8. asked
9. supposed
10. decided

□EXERCISE 10

1. learning
2. learned
3. spoke
4. spoken
5. speak

6. wore
7. worn
8. liked
9. has
10. determined

Making Subjects, Verbs, and Pronouns Agree (p. 95)

□**EXERCISE 1**

1. is
2. were
3. are
4. were
5. have

6. has
7. goes
8. were
9. were
10. were

□**EXERCISE 2**

1. presents
2. help
3. is, his
4. he
5. doesn't

6. has, his
7. is
8. has
9. is
10. stand

□**EXERCISE 3**

1. are
2. are
3. he
4. were
5. doesn't

6. were
7. knows
8. were
9. were, weren't
10. were

□**EXERCISE 4**

1. is
2. has, his, his
3. are
4. seem
5. needs, his

6. were, weren't
7. were
8. were
8. hope
10. has

□**EXERCISE 5**

1. is
2. wants
3. performs
4. is, her
5. Weren't

6. are
7. is, its
8. doesn't
9. claims
10. has

□**EXERCISE 6**

1. intends
2. plans
3. doesn't
4. attend
5. has

6. Doesn't
7. owns, his
8. plan
9. are
10. is

□EXERCISE 7

1. doesn't
2. were
3. were
4. Doesn't
5. are
6. is
7. comes
8. himself
9. are, are
10. remain

□EXERCISE 8

1. has
2. doesn't
3. were
4. were
5. doesn't, doesn't
6. are
7. intend
8. doesn't
9. has, his
10. stresses

□EXERCISE 9

1. were
2. were
3. were
4. were
5. doesn't
6. Were
7. are
8. intend
9. have
10. were

□EXERCISE 10

1. gets
2. is, he misses
3. writes, hands
4. are
5. he gets
6. doesn't
7. like
8. his, he, passes
9. doesn't, gives
10. comes, he, misses

Choosing the Right Pronoun (p. 101)

□EXERCISE 1

1. me
2. him
3. He
4. me
5. me

6. I
7. us
8. me
9. I
10. I

□EXERCISE 2

1. me
2. I
3. him
4. me
5. him

6. they
7. him
8. us
9. me
10. I

□EXERCISE 3

1. I
2. her
3. I
4. me
5. I

6. me
7. me
8. me
9. Bruce and I
10. he and I

□EXERCISE 4

1. My brother and I
2. I
3. him and me
4. I
5. I

6. me
7. I
8. us
9. me
10. him

□EXERCISE 5

1. us
2. me
3. I, him, me
4. me
5. I

6. her
7. her
8. me
9. they
10. they

Making the Pronoun Refer to the Right Word (p. 104)

□EXERCISE 1

1. When Irwin showed the dented fender to his father, his father was upset.
2. His father said, "You will have to get it repaired."
3. The instructor showed us a conch shell and explained how the mollusk lives in it.
4. The parents take turns supervising the park playground, where the children have free use of the swings and slides.
5. He said to his instructor, "I don't think you really understand the novel."
6. His instructor said, "Maybe I haven't read it carefully enough."
7. The salesman said to his boss, "I am too old for this job."
8. When the professor talked with Roland, Roland was really worried.
9. She said to her girlfriend, "Your record collection needs reorganizing."
10. She said to the job applicant, "Come back after you have given more thought to the question."

□EXERCISE 2

1. His motorcycle hit a parked car, but the car wasn't damaged.
2. As I went up to the baby's carriage, the baby began to cry.
3. Anita said to her mother, "My wardrobe is completely out of date."
4. As soon as the carburetor of my car was adjusted, I drove the car home.
5. I couldn't find the catsup bottle, and I don't like a hamburger without catsup.
6. Ignoring his advice turned out to be a good thing.
7. Margo said to Edna, "I failed the exam."
8. Her shyness kept her from moving ahead in her profession.
9.
10. In our physics course, I was happy that we had to do only three experiments.

□EXERCISE 3

1. When the dentist pulled his tooth, the child screamed.
2. I finished my paper, put down my pen, and handed my paper in.
3.
4. She said to her mother, "I need a new car."
5. When I opened the dog's carrying case at the airport, the dog ran away.
6. The cars streamed by, but no one paid any attention to the stalled motorist.
7. Oliver said to Max, "Your parakeet is loose in your room."
8. She likes ballet dancing and would like to study to be a ballet dancer.
9. When Gilbert phoned, his father was quite ill.
10. He said to the salesman, "Come back when I'm not so rushed."

□EXERCISE 4

1. He said, "Dad, your car is in need of a tune-up."
2. After I read about Tom Dooley's career in medicine, I decided that I want to be a doctor.
3.
4. He loves to wrestle and spends most of his time wrestling.
5. The park commission established a hockey rink where people can play free.
6. The doctor said to the orderly, "You have made a mistake."
7. She said to her sister, "Why don't you take my car?"
8. Because I refused the waitress job, my father was displeased.
9. She said, "Mother, you are working too hard."
10. I have always enjoyed helping teach preschoolers, and now I'm actually going to be a preschool teacher.

□EXERCISE 5

1. She said to her daughter, "I was always too shy."
2. Her mother said to Elizabeth, "You may wear my mink coat to the party."
3. The instructor was annoyed because no one had finished his paper.
4.
5. She said to her sister, "My alarm did not go off."
6. The president said to the chief accountant, "I made an error in reporting my income."
7. He said to the cashier, "I've made a mistake."
8. The offer of a job boosted my ego.
9. He said to his father, "You should go back to college for a year."
10. His father said, "I don't have enough money."

Getting Rid of Misplaced or Dangling Modifiers (p. 108)

□EXERCISE 1

1. He watched her walk along the beach garbed . . . .
2. After I had finished . . . .
3. We watched hundreds of fireflies glowing . . . .
4. In years to come, you'll . . . .
5. After I had cleaned the cage and put . . . .
6. I discovered my boyfriend sound . . . .
7.
8. When I was six, my mother . . . .
9. I gave to a charity that blue suit I didn't . . . .
10. While I was answering . . . .

□EXERCISE 2

1. Cruising in the glass-bottomed boat, we could see hundreds . . . .
2. While the baby was playing on the floor, I noticed that it . . . .
3. After I was wheeled . . .
4. While Mark was watching the football game, his bike was stolen.
5. The bank will make loans of any size to . . . .
6. Rounding a bend in the road, I was confronted by . . . .
7. Flying at an altitude of 5,000 feet, I could see . . . .
8. After I had finished mowing . . . .
9.
10. Because I had broken . . . .

□EXERCISE 3

1. After I had done . . . .
2. I spotted a monarch butterfly flitting . . . .
3. After I drank . . . .
4. We thought the cows looked contented standing . . . .
5. The Museum of Science and Industry is the most interesting museum that I have visited in the city.
6. She was going to dinner with a man named Harold who . . . .
7. We gave all the meat we didn't want to the cat.
8.
9. Determined to learn to write, I slowly mastered the textbook.
10. After we had a quick . . . .

□EXERCISE 4

1. The little town where I was born is . . . .
2.
3.
4. She put the clothes she had not worn back . . . .
5. Although it is almost ten years old, he . . . .

6. I saw that my little car was smashed beyond repair.
7. I went out to see what was the matter with my puppy who was barking . . . .
8. Sitting there looking out over the water, she finally made . . . .
9. Because the child was crying pitifully, I tried to find his mother.
10. Because he is a . . . .

□EXERCISE 5

1. A man sold me a secondhand car with generator trouble.
2. I read in the evening paper that . . . .
3. We gave the Boy Scouts all the newspapers that have been lying around for months.
4. She left on the table the meat . . . .
5. The police made a report about . . . .
6. I watched the wren building its nest and twittering . . . .
7. Because he was a conceited . . . .
8. After my dog had smelled up the whole house, I finally gave . . . .
9. While I was . . . .
10. Because I was unsure . . . .

Using Parallel Construction (p. 113)

□EXERCISE 1

1. or skiing without driving very far.
2. and good plays and concerts.
3. and even fly a plane.
4. and clear thinking.
5. or law.
6. and especially camping out overnight.
7. but how you do it.
8.
9. to get our instruments tuned immediately . . . .
10. I admire her, I love her, I need her.

□EXERCISE 2

1. how to think up a good title.
2. and lack of parallelism.
3. and having people come to him for advice.
4. how to organize my time, and how to concentrate.
5. A good salary, pleasant working conditions, and good . . . .
6.
7. and to go to fewer parties.
8. and to get our papers in on time.
9. and am expecting a good grade.
10. than to have money, so they say.

□EXERCISE 3

1. and often goes home to Minnesota for weekends.
2. and inspiring.
3. and raising their children responsibly.
4. and a Methodist.
5. and too expensive.
6.
7. and to get up early . . . .
8. and going to work instead.
9. and really scared of everybody.
10.

□EXERCISE 4

1. and then help his younger brother and sister.
2. to help with the dishes . . . .
3. and to stick to it . . . .
4. but to comprehend more of what I read.
5. as well as understand himself better.
6. and indulgently handed the car keys to her.
7. and a cool breeze coming down from the mountain.

8. than in San Bernardino.
9.
10. and teach him to live with a group of his peers.

□EXERCISE 5

1. to live simply . . . .
2. and with a view.
3. three hundred feet long.
4. and too expensive.
5. and to move at the end of the month.
6. and wash the windows inside and out.
7. and finding work . . . .
8. and how to recognize the various kinds of period furniture.
9. and a message.
10. and maybe also a bit of luck.

□EXERCISE 6

1. and headaches.
2. is usually booked far ahead.
3. and to get more exercise.
4. and also drives . . . .
5.
6. and an old cabinet . . . .
7. and easy to take care of.
8. and act as hostess for one meeting.
9. and standing guard at the front door.
10. and my friends.

□EXERCISE 7

1. and punctual.
2. and promote the firm.
3. and a summary of your experience.
4. and get a better understanding . . . .
5. and of course the balmy weather

□EXERCISE 8

1. and the threat of more government regulation.
2. and developed the ability to speak.
3. or even deliver a baby . . . .
4. and goldfinches with their winter plumage of pale yellow.
5.

□EXERCISE 9

1. and yet eventually got to the top . . . .
2. nor her separation from all her family.
3. and taught eight grades in one room.

4. and always played ball . . . .
5. and encouraging.

□EXERCISE 10

1. Recycling cans and bottles has been worthwhile because
    1.
    2. it has prevented littering.
    3.
2. Inflatable seat bags should be standard equipment on new cars because
    1.
    2.
    3. they are worth the cost.
3. My summer job on the playground for the handicapped was valuable because
    1.
    2.
    3. it gave me an opportunity to do something for society.
4. A camping trip in Estes Park gave me some new insights.
    1.
    2. I have a new interest in nature.
    3. I learned something about ecology.
5. Improving one's vocabulary is important because
    1.
    2. it will lead to a more successful career.
    3. it will give one personal satisfaction.

Avoiding Shift in Time (p. 120)

□EXERCISE 1

1. walked
2. said
3. began
4. gave
5. decided
6. registered
7. came
8. see
9. gets
10. came

□EXERCISE 2

1. were
2. gave
3. washed
4. was
5. doesn't
6. discovered we were
7. comes
8. tells
9. came
10. realized I had

□EXERCISE 3

1. placed
2. added
3. learned
4. overcomes
5. described
6. hadn't
7. solves
8. finished
9. realize
10. try

□EXERCISE 4

1. couldn't
2. said
3. drove, could
4.
5. saw
6. needed
7. pulled
8. had
9. couldn't
10. found I was, got

□EXERCISE 5

1. explains
2. were lying
3. is told
4. says that it must be

□EXERCISE 6

... reached for my bear skin blanket .... I reached but couldn't find it. I checked the floor to see if it had .... My mind woke .... I paused and tried .... I couldn't see ....

I got up, groped for the light switch, and saw that my desk drawers were .... And there was ....

Now my mind raced as I scanned .... my TV was OK, and I hadn't .... someone had been .... someone had been looking ....

.... gave up ...

☐**EXERCISE 7**

. . . . so I grabbed . . . .

. . . . as we moved higher and saw . . . .

. . . . It seemed so easy . . . . and I nervously tried . . . . we weren't going to suddenly fall . . . .

I learned . . . . I learned . . . . Then I was reminded . . . . my instructor asked me if I knew where we were. It had been . . . . I had no idea . . . .

Avoiding Shift in Person (p. 127)
□EXERCISE 1

1. I feel so good when I
2. anyone more than
3. makes me
4. as I grow older, I
5. I have to do a lot of memorizing if I
6. we have
7. he is willing to take what he
8. until he has
9. you really need
10. their gowns

□EXERCISE 2

1. he doesn't really care whether he has
2.
3. Iraq and also many other
4. we could see
5. we got tired
6. we could do
7. we could see
8. they could see
9.
10. I can talk

□EXERCISE 3

1. My room was in a mess.
2. I was terrified.
3. Swimming is the best exercise.
4. Nonmembers can attend the Kiwanis Club breakfast.
5. Specific details always make a paper more interesting.
6. Her paper was excellent; obviously she had spent time on it.
7. A good vocabulary is necessary for success in college.
8. Wide reading will improve one's vocabularly.
9. I felt foolish after saying that.
10. I looked forward to the weekend.

□EXERCISE 4

1. Watching television for an evening will show how much violence is on the programs.
2. One's a different person after taking that psychology course.
3. My two days in Williamsburg were not enough for me to see everything.
4. To keep fit, exercise every day.
5. Call this number for more information.

6. To prevent air pollution, have a tune-up twice a year.
7. The above facts show that many companies still discriminate in their hiring.
8. I was frustrated because I couldn't get there on time.
9. She wore an elegant costume to the masquerade.
10. After such an escape, I felt lucky to be alive.

□EXERCISE 5

. . . . I could see the black mark or "whisker" on each side of the head and the black collar below the light throat. On a few of them I could even see . . . .

Getting Rid of Wordiness (p. 131)

□EXERCISE 1

1. An experienced player would have known what to do.
2. My college roommate was coming to see me.
3. Electronics is a good field to go into.
4. We have two May birthdays in our family.
5. My grandfather told me this story.
6. The government should speed up the judicial process.
7. Justice should be swift and sure.
8. I grew up in a small town.
9. I was too busy to accept their invitation.
10. I didn't know she was leaving.

□EXERCISE 2

1. History interests me.
2. The professor makes his subject interesting.
3. No doubt he spends a great deal of time preparing each lecture.
4. He was arrested for drunken driving.
5. A friend of mine has a unique invention.
6. Ten people were stranded by that avalanche.
7. That's all the work you'll get out of her.
8. She's not interested in her job.
9. Those suits are equally good on you.
10. My barber has been away for almost a week.

□EXERCISE 3

1. The purple martin circled the martin house for half an hour and then disappeared.
2. By the time I arrived, not much was left to do.
3. Modern medicine has practically wiped out polio.
4. A number of spectators couldn't get seats.
5. The grandstand should be larger.
6. A fly has suction cups on its feet, enabling it to walk on the ceiling.
7. My hardest exam last semester was psychology.
8. The exam included things I had forgotten.
9. The magpie is a large bird with a black head, a long greenish tail, and white wing patches.
10. She will always do what she promises.

□EXERCISE 4

1. There is more crime today than in our grandparents' day.
2. But we should remember the many good aspects of life today.
3. Miracle drugs have given us a longer life span.

4. Also labor saving devices have taken the drudgery out of everyday tasks.
5. Consider the pros and cons before you finally decide.
6. The taxpayers objected.
7. They found three kinds of shells new to them.
8. We started at 5:00 A.M. and got there at 6:00 P.M.
9. She thought the administration was trying to correct the salary inequity of the two employees.
10. The administration had to consider the employees' past as well as present performance.

□EXERCISE 5

1. The library book I've been reading is *Brave New World*.
2. Students should be given more help in finding jobs.
3. Her crude remarks annoyed him.
4. In this course we are learning the basics of writing.
5. If you don't know what punctuation to use, refer to the punctuation chapters.
6. Our instructor asks that we keep a list of our misspelled words in the back of our books.
7. We are to list all misspelled words from our papers.
8. I think the professor made a mistake giving me such a low grade.
9. She was wearing an oblong blue pendant.
10. Should we shovel the walks now or wait until it stops snowing?

□EXERCISE 6

1. Because I don't like bridge, I didn't accept her invitation.
2. Her dilapidated coat made her look years older.
3. I think she could make herself more presentable.
4. He didn't know anything about history, but he was a genius in science.
5. She is planning to major in astronomy.
6. Because of her friendliness, she gets invited to lots of parties.
7. There is more freedom of expression today than in the past.
8. The lecturer was speaking about the new suburban zoning laws.
9. I've been too busy to think about zoning.
10. We'll have to face the question sooner or later.

□EXERCISE 7

1. Narrow your subject.
2. She said she would teach me some office skills.
3. That was one of the most interesting Saturdays of my life.
4. I saw your ad in *The Kansas City Star* for a football coach for your summer camp.
5. Our system of justice is not effective.
6. No one told me the speaker had arrived.

7. I think you will find this story pertinent.
8. In August most of our employees take a vacation.
9. I have not had time to prepare an agenda for this afternoon's meeting.
10. I want to repeat my conclusion.

□ EXERCISE 8

1. The governor was there to open the assembly as usual.
2. We found three unique kinds of coral.
3. She had done much to improve her community.
4. Each student has four minutes to tell about his strengths.
5. At the end of the four minutes, the student thanks his listeners.
6. I would have gone except for a previous engagement.
7. Some objected to the new library hours.
8. Most students on this campus prefer the semester to the quarter system.
9. "Renascence" is one of the best-known poems of Edna St. Vincent Millay, a poet of the early part of the century.
10. The article you requested is no longer available. Do you want a substitute?

□ EXERCISES 9 and 10

1. What has been accomplished is a result of the cooperation of the administration, faculty, students, and library staff.
2. So that they will always be available, periodicals do not circulate. Many divisions have facilities for copying articles.
3. The Information Center gives assistance in using the card catalog and basic reference works. A library orientation program explains library procedures and the interlibrary loan service.
4. The Reserve Reading Room contains required reading for current courses.
5. The Music Division has ten listening stations, six of which are equipped with cassette recorders.
6. Much material essential to a new library is no longer available in printed form, but the library contains over one million items on microfilm, microcards, and microfiche, as well as microprint machines for making copies.

Review of Sentence Structure and Agreement (p. 138)

1. A	6. B	11. B	16. B	21. B
2. B	7. A	12. B	17. A	22. B
3. B	8. A	13. A	18. B	23. A
4. A	9. B	14. A	19. B	24. A
5. A	10. A	15. B	20. B	25. B

Punctuation (p. 143)

□EXERCISE 1

1. Are you sure we're on the right road?
2. We agreed to meet that evening;
3. I try to make my long distance calls after 11:00 P.M. or before 8:00 A.M.
4. I took the following items to the exam:
5.
6. I have decided now to be independent;
7. Three things are necessary for winning in any competition:
8. Stop!
9. You changed my mind;
10. Did you know that right and left shoes were thought up only a little more than a century ago?

□EXERCISE 2

1. Today various textile finishes are used:
2. I don't study at night; I get up at 5 A.M.
3. Amazing! How do you do it?
4. Is it more wrong to steal from a little old man on a pension than to steal from a big corporation with Inc. or Ltd. after its name?
5. Wait!
6.
7. Do you know what an odometer is?
8.
9. I learned the difference between two words today:
10. An atheist is sure there is no God;

□EXERCISE 3

1. Did you know there are more than half a million snowflakes in each cubic foot of snow?
2. And did you know that glaciers are formed by snowflakes being compressed for thousands of years into hard ice?
3. Snow delights children;
4. Snow has often influenced the course of history;
5. People think of snow as sterile;
6. There are various kinds of snow;
7. The sign on his door read Noel Thatcher, B.A., M.A., Ph.D.
8. Help! I'm sinking!
9.
10. Out of my wallet fell the following:

□EXERCISE 4

1. If you take this action, where will it lead?
2. How will it affect others? What will it do to you?

3. Will you think well of yourself afterward?
4. There are two kinds of education:
5.
6. Hurry!
7. Money giving, says Karl Menninger, is a good criterion, in a way, of a person's mental health;
8. I've enrolled in a class in oil painting;
9. Great!
10. I'm not very good at it;

□EXERCISE 5

1. I took the following courses last semester:
2.
3. Most of my time was spent on chemistry;
4. Each evening I was tired;
5. I would study until 2:00 A.M.;
6. The design course was not demanding;
7. The other courses were harder;
8. My brother received his B.A.; then he began work on his M.A.
9. But he has other interests besides his academic field;
10. Also he loves to cook;

□EXERCISE 6

1. By what are you remembered? How do people describe you?
2. Your dog's leg is still not strong;
3. Take him home;
4.
5. My indoor interests are these:
6. Checkers is not an overly difficult game;
7. We have bought a place in the country;
8. It's a run-down farmhouse;
9. We enjoy remodeling;
10. Sure, it will take work;

□EXERCISE 7

1. He has become well adjusted;
2. Little things no longer upset him;
3. He used to rant when the boy didn't come early to shovel his walks; now he says, "What difference?"
4. He saves his time and energy for real problems;
5. Is there anything you'd give your life for?
6. I wasn't asking for help;
7. I didn't ignore her intentionally;
8. Was she really hurt?
9.
10. She also treasured the following items:

□EXERCISE 8

1. The track meet was supposed to start at 2:00 P.M.; it began at 2:45 P.M.
2 I won the first race;
3. The next race was the mile;
4. Muhammad Ali refused induction into the army;
5. He was convicted of draft evasion and given a five-year prison sentence;
6. But he could no longer get fights in the U.S.;
7. They're going to the theater tonight, aren't they?
8.
9. There are only two lasting things we can give our children:
10. A child is egocentric;

□EXERCISE 9

1. Will you meet me at 4:00 P.M. tomorrow?
2.
3. The following poets of the early half of the century also were widely read in their day:
4. Our library has an exchange table;
5. It was the first time I had ever received an A on a paper;
6.
7 She owned an Egyptian scarab that was dated 900 B.C.
8. How about going out with me for a coke?
9. Wow! What an absolutely fantastic idea!
10. Well, what would you like to do then?

□EXERCISE 10

1. There are two kinds of pain:
2. We started on our 600-mile trip;
3. He didn't come;
4. They discussed colors, fabrics, styles, etc.
5. Her ideas are antiquated; she seems not to know that we're living in 1979 A.D.
6. The program was dull;
7.
8. My table is set with the following:
9. It's amazing how he looks so young year after year;
10. The Scots-born veterinarian James Herriot has named his best sellers after the lines in an old hymn:

Commas (p. 149)

□**EXERCISE 1**

1. Our language changes slowly,
2. Not only are words added,
3. If you have studied,
4. When a dependent clause comes first in a sentence,
5. I never studied much in high school,
6. When I was in high school,
7. If it had been,
8. By looking up every single word that I'm not sure of,
9. I wasn't upset by the spelling quiz,
10. Having done all the exercises and finished all the writing for the course,

□**EXERCISE 2**

1. Outward Bound gives students experience in rafting, mountaineering, canoeing, sailing,
2. I sent my application for admission to Indiana Vocational Technical College, Indianapolis,
3. Because the lecture had not been well advertised,
4. The speaker said that applause before a speech is faith, during a speech is hope,
5. After the lecture,
6. When everyone had left,
7. She was born on November 2, 1960, in Charleston, Illinois, but her family moved the next year to Spokane,
8.
9. Since he hadn't cared for his records properly,
10. Scientists dream of discovering an easy, efficient,

□**EXERCISE 3**

1. Carl Sandburg was born in Galesburg, Illinois, on January 6,
2. Between the ages of 13 and 17 he was successively a driver of a milk wagon, porter in a barbershop, scene shifter in a theater,
3. Then he went west where he pitched wheat in the Kansas wheat fields, washed dishes at hotels in Kansas City, Omaha, and Denver,
4. After he returned, he went to college, became a newspaper reporter,
5. Because we didn't set our clocks ahead,
6.
7. Well, I promised her I'd pick her up,
8. Her job involves giving travel information, planning trips for people,
9. The wettest place on earth is Mt. Waialeale, Kauai, Hawaii, where there is rain 350 days a year,
10. On the shelf were a tea set from Japan, a vase from China,

☐EXERCISE 4

1. For every ton of newspaper recycled,
2. No, I would never vote for a man who says that when you've seen one redwood,
3. The Nature Conservancy, the Wilderness Society, the Sierra Club,
4. The lowest temperature ever recorded was −126.9 degrees Fahrenheit in Vostok, Antarctica, on August 24,
5. Yes,
6. Oswego, New York,
7. The first power-driven air flight occurred at Kitty Hawk, North Carolina, on December 17,1903,
8. The official air speed record now is 2070 m.p.h. made over Edwards Air Force Base, California, on May 1,
9. Since the era of manned space flight,
10. Jupiter is the largest planet,

☐EXERCISE 5

1. The most important thing in life, he felt, was to leave something for future generations: a child, a law, an invention, a book,
2. As he worked away in his garden, he felt that it would be there forever, that someone after him would enjoy it,
3. He was liked for his honesty, morality, and intelligence,
4. The number of people who are poorly nourished or undernourished can only be roughly estimated,
5. She got the breakfast, got the children off to school,
6. We get along well,
7. When it comes to eating,
8. Her fiancé is handsome, personable,
9. I'm considering various career possibilities: nursing, secretarial work,
10. He is attending George Brown College, Casa Loma Campus, Toronto, Ontario,

☐EXERCISE 6

1. The tallest inhabited building in the world is the Sears Tower on Wacker Drive, Chicago,
2.
3. The earliest parking meters ever installed were those put in the business district of Oklahoma City, Oklahoma, on July 19,
4. Working most of the night,
5. When oxygen, water, and iron come together,
6. For recreation you can go to the Student Union, where you can bowl, play billiards,
7. By pruning the roses drastically,
8. America needs to add order to liberty,
9. The Gesell Institute is located at 310 Prospect Street, New Haven,

10. People who died in 1929—just 50 years ago—had never heard of jet airplanes, Polaroid cameras, food freezers, frozen vegetables, radar, V-8 engines, electric razors, electric typewriters, drive-in movie theaters, color television, the United Nations, the atomic bomb,

□EXERCISE 7

1. We heard a carillon recital from the Bok Singing Tower at Lake Wales,
2. The carillon was designed, built,
3. It is composed of 53 tuned bronze bells ranging in size from the largest weighing 22,300 pounds to the smallest weighing 17 pounds,
4. While the history of carillons in Europe dates back more than 300 years,
5. A Chinese proverb says that when the moon is fullest, it begins to wane, and when it is darkest,
6. The only way to reach him is through American Express, Paris,
7. As you probably know,
8. The accountant's address is 410 Main Street, and he will see you at 10 A.M. on Monday,
9. If you didn't do it right the first time,
10. The highest temperature ever recorded in the shade was 136.4 degrees Fahrenheit in Azizia, Libya, on September 13,

□EXERCISE 8

1. I used to think great writers just sat down and wrote without errors,
2. In preparation for each class hour, we write either a complete thesis statement, a rough draft,
3. A few rough drafts are read aloud,
4. We turn our final drafts in on Friday,
5. I like getting my paper back promptly,
6. A few papers are read aloud to the class,
7. Sometimes my paper sounds better than I thought it was,
8. One thing is sure,
9. I now no longer fear writing a paper,
10. If I work out a good thesis statement,

□EXERCISE 9

1. No one is fool enough to choose war instead of peace, for in peace sons bury fathers,
2. I spoke to the professor about my absence,
3. The boring, wordy,
4.
5. We love old china, old silver, old furniture, and old prints,
6. As of September 1, 1979, their address will be changed to 2936 Capitol Avenue, Sacramento,

7. I went shopping for a cheap little cotton shirt,
8. Beyond a doubt,
9. The U.S. is rather presumptuous in calling itself America. A big chunk of America is Canada, and a big chunk is Mexico,
10. History is what man has done, philosophy is what man has thought, art is what man has created, science is what man has discovered,

☐ **EXERCISE 10**

1. In the issue of *Saturday Review* that came on the newsstands the week before Robert Kennedy was killed, Richard L. Tobin gave the following report of an eight-hour monitoring of three networks and half a dozen local outlets: "We marked down ninety-three specific incidents involving sadistic brutality, murder, cold-blooded killing, sexual cruelty, and related sadism. . . . We encountered seven different kinds of pistols and revolvers, three varieties of rifle, three distinct brands of shotgun, half a dozen assorted daggers and stilettos, two types of machete, one butcher's cleaver, a broadaxe, rapiers galore, a posse of sabers, an electric prodder, and a guillotine. Men (and women and even children) were shot by gunpowder, burned at the stake, tortured over live coals, trussed and beaten in relays, dropped into molten sugar, cut to ribbons (in color), repeatedly kneed in the groin, beaten while being held defenseless by other hoodlums, forcibly drowned, whipped with a leather belt. . . . By the end of the stint we were quite insensitive, almost immune to the shock of seeing a human being in pain."

Commas (continued) (p. 156)

□EXERCISE 1

1. The person I admired most, of course,
2.
3. The lecture was, on the whole,
4. The audience, though,
5. Those who did hear the lecture, however,
6. I wish I could help you;
7. I'll help you next time, however,
8.
9. This time, though,
10. You need help immediately;

□EXERCISE 2

1. Yes, Gregg,
2. I'm too busy this evening, however,
3. It will have to wait, therefore,
4.
5. I can't do it now;
6. I wish, Gregg,
7. Surfing, however, won't get you a college degree,
8. Neither will watching television,
9. OK, OK, I'll turn it off;
10. I do too;

□EXERCISE 3

1. I tell you, Jackie,
2. The boss has cut our coffeebreaks to half an hour, and he's asking, moreover,
3. I don't want to, but I've decided, nevertheless,
4. Hey, Kristin,
5. Most students, I think,
6. A few students, on the other hand,
7. I decided, by the way,
8. He will, I'm sure,
9. I've just heard, however,
10.

□EXERCISE 4

1. Maturity, the lecturer explained,
2. The immature person is egocentric, as a rule,
3. The mature person, on the other hand,
4. The great difference in people, therefore,
5. Also, the speaker continued,

6. I'm afraid, Andrea,
7. But we followed the signs,
8. I know, Andrea,
9. I shouldn't have come, she thought,
10. There comes a time, however,

□EXERCISE 5

1.
2. This car, which I bought three years ago,
3. We're going to our cottage,
4.
5. Frederick Stock, the great conductor of the Chicago Symphony,
6. *The Door into Summer*, a novel by Robert A. Heinlein,
7. Carl Sandburg's best prose work is *The Prairie Years*,
8. "Chicago," which first brought Sandburg recognition,
9. "Fog," however,
10. The early winter months are good for viewing the Milky Way,

□EXERCISE 6

1. Most of the class, I think,
2.
3. The trick is, I've found,
4. After I left Simpkins Hall, the English building, I went to Sherman Hall,
5.
6. The back stroke, which I am just learning,
7. My instructor, who has had lots of experience,
8. He tries, moreover,
9. I have worked hard;
10. I have decided, nevertheless,

□EXERCISE 7

1. The reason students can't write, some people say,
2. They should, some think,
3. Authorities tell us, however,
4. Too much drill on grammar can, in fact,
5.
6. But more important than a lot of grammar drill, we are told,
7. The standardized test, which can be graded by a computer,
8. Students do not, therefore,
9. What is necessary, it seems clear,
10.

□EXERCISE 8

1. It is improtant, therefore,
2. When a student writes about a subject, he learns more, undoubtedly,

3.
4. Martin Fisher, who studies two hours a night for each subject,
5.
6.
7. Lars Larson, who isn't concerned about popularity with students,
8. Dedicated teachers, not fancy equipment,
9. That book, I assure you,
10.

□EXERCISE 9

1. Cherry cobbler, which is really easy to make,
2. Cherry pie, on the other hand,
3. Foods that take a long time to prepare, I have found,
4. Spending a lot of time in the kitchen, as you can see,
5. Most American homes, it seems to me,
6. We could take a lesson, I think, from the Japanese,
7. The traditional Japanese room is decorated with only one picture,
8. One picture and one vase of flowers are, as a rule,
9. Western ways, however,
10. Before long, I fear,

□EXERCISE 10

1. Anthropologist Mary Leakey, wife of famed Louis Leaky,
2. Forty years ago she and Louis worked for a time in Laetolil, a remote area of northern Tanzania,
3. They moved on to Olduvai Gorge, 25 miles to the north,
4. Now, however,
5.
6. The footprint, according to radioactive dating,
7. It is wider than the footprints of Neanderthal man,
8.
9.
10. The whooping crane, one of the first species of birds to be recognized
    as endangered,

Review of the Comma (p. 161)

1. Initiative, hard work,
2. My father, who hasn't had a vacation for three years,
3. My little sister searched for my love letters,
4. While I was watching a pretty face at the curb, the light turned green,
5. Yes, I'd like to go along, Luella,
6. After mending Peggy's mitten, finding lunch money for Tim, and locating a lost workbook,
7. Much of my time, moreover,
8. If you don't like your work,
9.
10.
11.
12. A chimpanzee can aim a ball at a target almost as well as a man can,
13. If the first few shots are unsuccessful,
14. The chimpanzee, however, rapidly loses patience,
15. If the aiming tests are made too difficult,

Quotation Marks (p. 163)

1. "A college education is one of the few things a person is willing to pay for and not get," said William Lowe Bryan, former president of Indiana University.
2. "Honest writing helps a person discover himself," the psychologist said.
3. "Americans have more timesaving devices and less time than any other group of people in the world," wrote Duncan Caldwell.
4. "When you write," our instructor said, "you produce something new, something that didn't exist before."
5. "You'll get satisfaction out of writing," he continued.
6.
7. "Just understanding a rule of writing isn't enough," he said. "You must practice it."
8. "You must practice it," he continued, "until using it becomes automatic."
9. "Education," said Robert Frost, "is the ability to listen to almost anything without losing your temper or your self-confidence."
10. Marcus Aurelius wrote, "No matter what happens, you can control the situation by your attitude."

1. "What's the most important thing you've learned in this class?" Brenda said.
2. "Learning to write a complete thesis statement," Alex said, "because it's going to help me in my writing for other courses."
3. "I know that's important," she replied, "but I think my biggest improvement has been learning to write concisely. My papers used to be so wordy."
4. "That never was my problem," he said. "My biggest achievement besides learning about thesis statements is that I finally decided to learn to spell."
5. "And have you improved?"
6. "Tremendously," he said. "Now I just spell every other word wrong. I used to spell every word wrong."
7. "Come on! You're not that bad. I read one of your papers, and there wasn't a single misspelled word."
8. "I'll admit I have improved," he said. "Now when I'm not sure of a word, I look it up."
9. "What dictionary do you use?"
10. "*American Heritage*," he said, "It's fun to use because of the illustrations."

□EXERCISE 3

1. "I had three chairs in my house: one for solitude, two for friendship, and three for society," wrote Henry David Thoreau in his book *Walden*.
2. "If a man does not keep pace with his companion, perhaps it is because he hears a different drummer," he continued.
3. "The mass of men lead lives of quiet desperation," Thoreau said.
4. "Sometimes," wrote Thoreau, "as I drift idly on Walden Pond, I cease to live and begin to be."
5. "Our sense of humor," wrote Harvey Mindess, "is one of our most valuable faculties."
6. "It can help us contend with adversity, derive greater joy out of living, and maintain our sanity," he continued.
7. In an art gallery a man said to his wife, "I know what that artist is trying to say. He's trying to say he can't paint worth a damn!"
8. "By working faithfully eight hours a day, you may eventually get to be a boss and work twelve hours a day," said Robert Frost.
9. "Golf is a good walk spoiled," said Mark Twain.
10. "Marriage," said the toastmaster, "is oceans of emotions surrounded by expanses of expenses."

□EXERCISE 4

1. "Do commas and periods go inside the quotation marks?" he asked.
2. "Of course," she replied. "They'd look lost on the outside."
3. "What do you do if yon want to quote a whole paragraph from a book?" he asked.
4. "If the quotation is more than five lines long, then you punctuate it differently from ordinary quotations," she said.
5. "What do you do?" he asked.
6. "You indent the whole quotation five spaces, single-space it, and forget about the quotation marks," she said.
7. "I suppose that makes it stand out clearly as quoted material."
8. "Exactly," she said.
9. Victor Hugo wrote, "The greatest happiness of life is the conviction that we are loved, loved for ourselves, or rather loved in spite of ourselves."
10. "The important thing in life is not the person one loves. It is the fact that one loves," said Marcel Proust in his novel *Remembrance of Things Past*.

□EXERCISE 5

1. "No one can make you feel inferior without your consent," said Eleanor Roosevelt.
2. "It isn't that I have so much energy," continued Mrs. Roosevelt. "It's just that I never waste any of it on indecision or regret."
3. "A man who uses a great many words to express his meaning is like a bad marksman who instead of aiming a single stone at an object takes

up a handful and throws at it in hopes he may hit," said Samuel Johnson.

4.

5. "We're just now beginning to discover some of the causes of birth defects," the speaker said.

6. Ralph Lapp wrote, "We are aboard a train which is gathering speed, racing down a track on which there are an unknown number of switches leading to unknown destinations. . . . Most of society is in the caboose looking backward."

7. "No one can make me do something I don't want to do," my father said.

8. "Happiness," wrote William H. Sheldon, "is essentially a state of going somewhere wholeheartedly, one-directionally, without regret or reservation."

9. "Genius," wrote Carlyle, "is the art of taking infinite pains."

10. "We have made a good start on turning the gobbledygook of federal regulations into plain English that people can understand," said President Carter.

□EXERCISE 6

1. "How about going out for coffee?" Lee asked.

2. "Sure, why not? When shall we go?" Jill replied.

3. "Oh, in a few minutes," Lee said.

4. My mother used to say, "Whatever is worth doing is worth doing well."

5. She also used to say, "What isn't in your head must be in your heels."

6. In describing the Taj Mahal, Rufus Jones said, "Only a few times in one's earthly life is one given to see absolute perfection."

7. Oliver Wendell Holmes wrote, "Many people die with their music still in them."

8. "If fifty million people say a foolish thing," said Anatole France, "it is still foolish thing."

9. "Flight Number 485 is now ready for boarding at Gate 60," the airport loudspeaker announced.

10. "More coffee?" asked the flight attendant.

□EXERCISE 7

1. "And what have you been doing with yourself?" Kevin wanted to know.

2. "Oh, I've been doing a lot of reading for one thing," Natalie said.

3. "Still learning new words?" Kevin asked.

4. "Sure, I'm always learning new words," Natalie said. "Yesterday I learned what *energize* means."

5. "And what does it mean?"

6. "Well, the root *erg* means a unit of energy or work, and *energize*

means to give energy to. For example, some people find cold showers energizing," Natalie said.

7. "I prefer to get my energy some other way," Kevin said. "I suppose that same root *erg* is in *energy* and *energetic*."

8. "Right. And it's also in *metallurgy*, which means working with metals. Another interesting word is *George*. *Geo* means earth, and *erg* means work. Therefore *George* is an earth worker or farmer."

9. "I never knew that before," Kevin said. "It really helps to know word roots, doesn't it?"

10. "It helps me," Natalie replied.

□EXERCISE 8

1. "You can't undo history. All you can do is be just in your own time," wrote John F. Kennedy.

2. I have been reading an essay entitled "Gobbledygook" from the book *The Power of Words* by Stuart Chase.

3. "If all misfortunes were laid in a common heap," said Socrates, "whence every one must take an equal portion, most people would be content to take their own and depart."

4. "Habits are first cobwebs, then cables," says a Spanish proverb.

5. "I have been brought up to believe that how I see myself is more important than how others see me," said Anwar Sadat.

6. "People always get what they ask for. The only trouble is that they never know, until they get it, what it actually is that they have asked for," wrote Aldous Huxley.

7. "An excellent plumber is infinitely more admirable than an incompetent philosopher," says John Gardner.

8.

9. "The weather and my mood, " said Blaise Pascal, "have little connection."

10. "The secret of happiness is not in doing what one likes," said James M. Barrie, "but in liking what one has to do."

□EXERCISE 9

The table was a large one, but the three were all crowded together at one corner of it.

"No room! No room!" they cried out when they saw Alice coming.

"There's *plenty* of room!" said Alice indignantly, and she sat down in a large arm-chair at one end of the table.

"Have some wine," the March Hare said in an encouraging tone.

Alice looked all round the table, but there was nothing on it but tea. "I don't see any wine," she remarked.

"There isn't any," said the March Hare.

"Then it was't very civil of you to offer it," said Alice angrily.

"It wasn't very civil of you to sit down without being invited," said the March Hare.

"I didn't know it was *your* table," said Alice, "It's laid for a great many more than three." —Lewis Carroll, *Alice in Wonderland*

□EXERCISE 10

"Are we nearly there?" Alice managed to pant out at last.

"Nearly there!" the Queen repeated. "Why, we passed it ten minutes ago! Faster!" And they ran on for a time in silence, with the wind whistling in Alice's ears, and almost blowing her hair off her head, she fancied.

"Now! Now!" cried the Queen. "Faster! Faster!" And they went so fast that at last they seemed to skim through the air, hardly touching the ground with their feet, till suddenly, just as Alice was getting quite exhausted, they stopped, and she found herself sitting on the ground, breathless and giddy.

The Queen propped her up against a tree, and said kindly, "You may rest a little now."

Alice looked round her in great surprise. "Why, I do believe we've been under this tree the whole time! Everything's just as it was!"

"Of course it is," said the Queen. "What would you have it?"

"Well, in *our* country," said Alice, still panting a little, "you'd generally get to somewhere else—if you ran very fast for a long time as we've been doing."

"A slow sort of country!" said the Queen. "Now, *here*, you see, it takes all the running you can do to keep in the same place. If you want to get somewhere else, you must run at least twice as fast as that."

—Lewis Carroll, *Through the Looking-Glass*

Capital Letters (p. 170)

□EXERCISE 1

1. *Time, Newsweek*
2. Community College
3. Eastern Illinois University
4.
5. European, English

6. English, Social Science, Hall
7. Near East, Professor
8. English, Professor
9.
10. Captain

□EXERCISE 2

1. Labor Day, River
2.
3. Lake Bemidji
4. Fourth
5.

6. Community College
7. Western Kentucky University
8. Dean, Club
9. Dr.
10. *Gift from the Sea*

□EXERCISE 3

1.
2. University
3. Senator, Elks Hall
4.
5. Mom

6. "My Candle Burns at Both Ends"
7.
8. School Board, Lions Club
9.
10. Fifth Avenue

□EXERCISE 4

1. Mr.
2. Cousin Tina
3. South
4. Second Avenue
5.

6.
7. School
8. *Civilisation*
9. History
10. English

□EXERCISE 5

1. Mom
2.
3. *A Doll's House*
4. Community College
5.

6.
7. Mom's
8. Lake Ontario
9. Dad
10. Son

□EXERCISE 6

1. *Age of Fable*
2. Professor
3. English
4. English, University
5. Uncle

6. Dr.
7. Rocky Mountain National Park
8. Rockies
9.
10. Dad

□EXERCISE 7

1. Main, Second Avenue
2. Building
3. English, German, Spanish
4.
5. Lake
6. Memorial Day
7.
8. West Coast, Northwest
9. Rand McNally Atlas
10. Central Y.M.C.A. College

□EXERCISE 8

1. Deep South
2.
3. Valentine's Day
4. Preamble to the Constitution
5. This
6. President's
7.
8. East
9.
10. Midwest, West Coast

□EXERCISE 9

1. Professor
2. Professor
3. Professor, Greek
4.
5. Dad
6. Mom
7. Saturday
8. Saturday, Grocery, Main Street
9. Arctic, Church
10. Art Institute, Avenue

□EXERCISE 10

1. Bay, Lake Superior
2. Mr.
3. Don't
4. *The Sea Around Us*
5. Grandfather
6. Grandmother, County
7.
8. English, French
9. New Year's Day
10. Professor

Review of Punctuation and Capital Letters (p. 174)

□EXERCISE 1

1.
2. When an independent clause comes first,
3. In other words, if the dependent clause comes first, use a comma; if the independent clause comes first,
4. Stop! I'll go with you. Can you wait until 5:00 P.M.?
5. "Yes, Phyllis, you can do it that way, but it will take longer,"
6. "I think, as a rule, it's better to begin at the beginning,"
7. He memorized William Butler Yeats' poem "The Lake Isle of Innisfree."
8. Eric Heiden, a sophomore at the University of Wisconsin in Madison,
9. Heiden, an 18-year-old,
10. While they have a high current income, the Arabs have almost none of the real assets found in any prosperous nation: the schools, hospitals, roads, banks, factories,
11. U.S.
12. Commas are like pounds. You either have too many or too few,

□EXERCISE 2

1. A study has shown that children whose TV viewing was cut back to no more than one hour a day improved their grades in school and seemed happier. They played more with other kids and increased their concentration in school. One child changed from a passive loner into a friendly playmate. Then when the study was concluded,
2. A hundred years ago when Edison was working on his first tin horn phonograph, he wasn't even thinking about music. He just wanted to make a dictating machine. In fact it took almost a whole generation for musicians to get interested in recordings. Fortunately

□EXERCISE 3

1. An Assyrian stone tablet of about 2800 B.C. makes the following statements: our earth is degenerate in these latter days; bribery and corruption are common; children no longer obey their parents;
2. Russia is building a railway across northern Siberia to bring out the riches of that remote region: petroleum, coal, iron ore, gold, diamonds, salt, asbestos, copper, tin, and bauxite. The route covers mountainous regions, areas of permafrost, and many bogs where the ground heaves during the short summer thaw. Some 3,700 bridges and culverts must be built across rivers and streams, and tunnels must be drilled through mountain ranges. Much of the time the temperature is 50 degrees below zero F. By

☐**EXERCISE 4**

1. Yesterday I had my first solo flight at the Flying Club. It's an amazing feeling when your instructor tells you to go flying alone. Then after you take off, you look around and find you really are alone. At that point it's too late to change your mind. You've got to land by yourself sooner or later. It's a great sensation. It's

2. The federal budget speaks in terms of billions, but how much *is* a billion dollars? If a man stood over a big hole in the ground and dropped in a $20 bill every minute day and night,

☐**EXERCISE 5**

Most furniture is expensive, clumsy to carry, costly to move, and uninteresting. Now there is a move to make your own. Cheap furniture does not necessarily mean orange crates and constructions of boards on bricks.

Recently many Americans have discovered that they can assemble stylish, comfortable, totable furnishings with paper, cardboard, plywood, Masonite, rough lumber, foam rubber, epoxy glue, a staple gun, and unlimited imagination. Almost any piece of furniture can be constructed inexpensively and almost instantly.

Spiros Zakas, who teaches in Manhattan's Parsons School of Design, has written *Furniture in 24 Hours* with diagrams and photographs to help the beginner.

Probably the biggest single element in the new trend is the development of urethane foam, which has done away with the necessity for springs. The new supergrip glues are also a boon. They will hold wood joints together durably. One of the most important technical innovations is the staple gun, which can be used for upholstery by tacking the material over foam and onto the frame.

Very simple but attractive furniture can be put together to sit on, eat at, or store in.

Comprehensive Test on Entire Text (p. 177)

1. We girls made the ~~deserts~~ *desserts* for the party; everyone ~~like~~ *liked* them.

2. She ~~ask~~ *asked* my brother and me to wash the dishes; we ~~was~~ *were* glad to help.

3. We ~~lose~~ *lost* that game; nevertheless we still had hopes for the championship.

4. When we got to the end of the detour, we ~~turn~~ *turned* south and then ~~W~~ *w*est.

5. ~~Which~~ *That* turned out to be the wrong thing to do.

6. Each of her trophies ~~are~~ *is* displayed in ~~it's~~ *its* proper place on the shelf.

7. Working hard that semester, ~~my grades improved.~~ *I improved my grades.*

8. I enjoy math, social studies, and gym, but I find chemistry and ~~e~~*E*nglish difficult.

9. Making the most of every opportunity that came her way, *she succeeded.*

10. He spends most of his time, however, reading comic books, and ~~you cant~~ *one can't* do that and get satisfactory grades.

11. I ~~cant~~ *can't* decide whether to get a job, take a trip, or ~~whether I should~~ just loaf this summer.

12. Yes, ~~personally~~ I think ~~Jeanettes~~ *Jeanette's* costume is more striking than ~~Robertas.~~ *Roberta's.*

13. She took ~~to~~ *too* many ~~cloths~~ *clothes* along on her trip: party dresses, beach wear, and half a dozen other outfits.

14. Her mother and father send her to ~~a~~ *an* exclusive school, but she ~~dont~~ *doesn't* appreciate it.

15. Kurt ~~told~~ *said to* his father, ~~he was~~ *"I am* embarrassed by ~~his~~ *your* old car.

16. ~~Their quiet~~ *They're quite* pleased with ~~there~~ *their* new car, but I think it was ~~to~~ *too* expensive.

17. Jerry, you ~~was~~ *were* driving ~~to~~ *too* fast when we ~~past~~ *passed* that cop.

18. We ~~didnt~~ *didn't* know what she was talking about; we had never heard of

    the proposal.

19. ~~Huberts~~ *Hubert's* invitation to my girlfriend and me came as a surprise.

20. Each of the leaves ~~are~~ *is* quite unique in ~~their~~ *its* vein patterns.

21. ~~Ive~~ *I've* been wondering about you and hoping for a letter.

22. She memorized Masefield's poem "Sea Fever" from his book <u>Salt Water</u>

    <u>Ballads.</u>

23. John Masefield, who became Poet Laureate of England, was born on

    June 1, 1878, in Ledbury, Herefordshire, England.

24. "Life's always a struggle. ~~if~~ *If* anything's easy, it's not likely to be worth-

    while," said Hubert Humphrey.

25. "When you get to the end of your rope," said Franklin D. Roosevelt,

    "tie a knot and hang on."

Proofreading Exercise (p. 179)

THE BIG GRIN ON MY FACE

One afternoon I was driving my car when I ~~notice~~ *noticed* a pinging noise in my engine. In a few days the pinging grew to a thumping and then to a loud clunking that couldn't be ignored.

My knowledgeable friends broke the news to me that it was undoubtedly my main engine bearings,and in the same breath they mentioned sums like four or five hundred dollars. Being a poor student, I had only two alternatives—walk or fix it myself.

Necessity ~~force~~ *forced* me to ~~chose~~ *choose* the latter alternative,and I found myself up to my elbows in grease and grime for the next few days. With the help of a lot of free advice from friends, who claimed to be undiscovered mechanical geniuses, and from a good library book on engines, I removed and disassembled the whole thing.

An engine is something I take for granted as long as it goes, and only when it fails, do I really appreciate how intricate and complicated it is. ~~Their~~ *There* are all kinds of odd-shaped, highly polished parts, each one for some function. My taking the engine apart was like a little boy fixing an alarm clock;each new piece was so interesting and so completely unfathomable.

Then when it was all in pieces,the reassembly with new parts began, along with the job of trying to remember where each nut and bolt belonged. This work was a lot slower and required more help,but it was encouraging to watch the motor grow with each new piece.

Finally it was all connected in the car and ready to be tested. It had taken weeks of late evenings of work,but now it was ready at last. My friends stood around offering final advice and checking to make sure I had remembered everything. I held my breath and turned the key—the engine started and turned, a little rough at first, but soon it ran smoothly.

"Eureka! I've done it" I shouted.

overwhelmed

I was ~~overwhelm~~ with a great feeling of accomplishment, and I couldn't hide the big grin on my face.

There's an indescribable feeling of pride in having rebuilt your own engine yourself. It was worth it, not just for saving money but for the experience.

Summary of THE JEANING OF AMERICA— AND THE WORLD (p. 191)

An American symbol of equality now spreading throughout the world is a simple pair of pants called blue jeans. In 1850 Levi Strauss, a Bavarian-born Jew, made the first pair for a miner in San Francisco. Their popularity grew, but one miner complained that the pockets tore. As a joke, his pockets were riveted by a blacksmith, and jeans have had rivets ever since. They can be purchased preshrunk and prefaded for the proletarian look and are sold not only to working people but to all classes. Levi Strauss & Co., now in 35 countries, sells 83,000,000 jeans a year.

Summary of DEATH OR TAXES (p. 195)

With statistics indicating that smoking is a major factor in heart disease and cancer, various organizations are trying to get America to kick the habit. Insurance companies are offering incentives to nonsmokers, and more and more companies are paying their workers to stop smoking. The government, through HEW, has launched a campaign to combat smoking but is undercutting it by subsidizing tobacco growers. Also perhaps the reason the campaign is halfhearted is that while smoking causes deaths, smoking also brings in more than $7 billion yearly in taxes. The government will eventually have to face the problem—death or taxes.

Summary of I AM SOMEBODY (p. 197)

Project EXCEL, a tough self-help program under the direction of civil rights leader Jesse Jackson, has shown that inner-city school students can achieve. He has them repeat, "I am somebody. I may be poor but I am somebody. Nobody can help us but us," and tells them to work hard, aim high, and not depend on help from the outside. Twenty-one EXCEL schools in Chicago, Los Angeles, and Kansas City have less absenteeism, fewer fights, and more students choosing advanced courses. National attention has been drawn to EXCEL, and HEW has awarded it $400,000 to expand into four more cities.

Your Spelling List